CLIMBING
the LITERACY
LADDER

CLIMBING

the LITERACY

INDEPENDENT

FLUENT

TRANSITIONAL

FLEDGLING

LADDER

Small-Group Instruction
to Support All Readers
and Writers, PreK–5

EMERGENT

BEGINNING

BEVERLY TYNER

ASCD
Alexandria, Virginia USA

INTERNATIONAL
LITERACY
ASSOCIATION
Newark, Delaware USA

1703 N. Beauregard St. • Alexandria, VA 22311-1714 USA
Phone: 800-933-2723 or 703-578-9600 • Fax: 703-575-5400
Website: www.ascd.org • E-mail: member@ascd.org
Author guidelines: www.ascd.org/write

INTERNATIONAL LITERACY ASSOCIATION

PO Box 8139 • Newark, DE 19714
Phone: 800-336-7323 • Fax: 302-731-1057
Website: www.literacyworldwide.org
E-mail: customerservice@reading.org

Ronn Nozoe, *Interim CEO and Executive Director;* Stefani Roth, *Publisher;* Genny Ostertag, *Director, Content Acquisitions;* Julie Houtz, *Director, Book Editing & Production;* Jamie Greene, *Associate Editor;* Judi Connelly, *Associate Art Director;* Thomas Lytle, *Senior Graphic Designer;* Valerie Younkin, *Senior Production Designer;* Kelly Marshall, *Interim Manager, Production Services;* Shajuan Martin, *E-Publishing Specialist*

All web links in this book are correct as of the publication date below but may have become inactive or otherwise modified since that time. If you notice a deactivated or changed link, please e-mail books@ascd.org with the words "Link Update" in the subject line. In your message, please specify the web link, the book title, and the page number on which the link appears.

PAPERBACK ISBN: 978-1-4166-2748-7   ASCD product #118012   n8/19
PDF E-BOOK ISBN: 978-1-4166-2842-2; see Books in Print for other formats.

Quantity discounts: 10–49, 10%; 50+, 15%; 1,000+, special discounts (e-mail programteam@ascd.org or call 800-933-2723, ext. 5773, or 703-575-5773). For desk copies, go to www.ascd.org/deskcopy.

Library of Congress Cataloging-in-Publication Data
Names: Tyner, Beverly, author.
Title: Climbing the literacy ladder : small-group instruction to support all readers and writers, preK-5 / Beverly Tyner.
Description: Alexandria, VA : ASCD ; Newark, DW : ILA, [2019] | Includes bibliographical references and index. | Summary: "Literacy educator Beverly Tyner helps teachers plan for small-group instruction that addresses students' six developmental stages of reading and writing, from prekindergarten through 5th grade"—Provided by publisher.
Identifiers: LCCN 2019009817 | ISBN 9781416627487 (paperback)
Subjects: LCSH: Language arts (Preschool) | Language arts (Elementary) | Group work in education.
Classification: LCC LB1576 .T95 2019 | DDC 372.6–dc23
LC record available at https://lccn.loc.gov/2019009817

26 25 24 23 22 21 20 19   1 2 3 4 5 6 7 8 9 10 11 12

I am sure you can identify when I say that I had a professional soul mate—someone who shared my teaching philosophy, dogged determinedness, and a burning desire to help both teachers and students strive for excellence. Martha Temple Todd loved teaching and children. She was the lead teacher for the academic intervention team with the Santa Rosa School District in Milton, Florida, when I first met her. As a consultant to the district for eight years, Martha and I developed both a professional and a personal friendship. Martha was truly a teacher's teacher. She began her teaching career as a 5th grade teacher at Rhodes Elementary School. When Martha was faced with breast cancer and chemotherapy, she refused to leave her class to a substitute but instead taught from her rocking chair in the classroom. Martha affected countless teachers and students. Her steadfast faith, booming laughter, and knowledge of how to teach reading were gifts she never stopped sharing. She is greatly missed by all who knew and loved her. In the depths of her illness, Martha left us the following message: Every day may not be good, but there is something good in every day! This is for you, Martha.

Additional content and downloadable materials

are available on www.beverlytyner.net

CLIMBING *the* LITERACY LADDER

Chapter 1

Small-Group Differentiated Reading and Writing

Introduction

After I finished writing this book, I asked myself, "How much of this information is truly necessary to give teachers the tools they need to be effective literacy teachers for all students?" With that guideline in mind, I proceeded to reexamine each chapter and take out all of the "fluff"—the material that's nice to know but not necessary for busy teachers to wade through. And here we are.

But more important, here you are, starting another book about literacy instruction. What knowledge do you hope to gain from this book? What are you looking to learn? Let me be frank. If you're looking for a book that reviews research in painstaking detail, this may not be the book for you. Research is important, but there are many high-quality resources already available that support the strategies presented in this book. If you're looking for theory or pedagogy that you must translate into practical classroom practice, then I suggest you choose a book written by "experts" who have never darkened the door of the classroom (or haven't in a very long time).

This book is intended to be a "one-stop shop" for teachers in need of a plan, rationale, and materials to differentiate literacy instruction for all students in prekindergarten through 5th grade. You will gain knowledge of the six stages of reading and writing development along with the research that supports the models. You will also find lesson plans,

1

strategies, and activities that support each stage of development, and you will be given access to all of the materials through my website (www.beverlytyner.net) so you can save time and energy. First and foremost, though, my hope is that this book will continue to grow you as a competent and empowered literacy teacher.

Over the past two decades, there has been a growing emphasis on elementary literacy instruction focused on struggling readers and writers. I think it's safe to say that educators have made some accomplishments with our ability to target and teach to our most struggling readers and writers, and that's certainly a fantastic achievement. All too often, however, on- and above-level students have often been sidelined or neglected in the process. Unfortunately, the gap between low-income students and their more affluent peers has continued to be stubbornly wide and stagnant over the last 10 years (NAEP, 2017). It's clear there is still much to be accomplished for all of our students.

So many books have been written about struggling readers that I want to make it clear that this is a book about *all* students and their growth in literacy. Today's standards and assessments hold teachers accountable for growth in every student: students with special needs, English language learners, "gifted" students who are above grade level, and every child in between. Most teachers work hard because they are passionate and want to focus intentionally on instructional practices that support below-, on-, and above-level readers and writers. In my many years of experience in schools across the country, I have found that there is generally a four- to six-year range in proficiency levels among readers and writers in any given elementary classroom. So many teachers walk into their classrooms every day faced with the daunting task of meeting the needs of this incredibly diverse range of students—while also teaching grade-level standards. No wonder teachers are burning out!

Literacy skills are the cornerstone upon which knowledge, self-esteem, and future educational opportunities are built. In my opinion, the biggest obstacle teachers face in advancing literacy skills is addressing this range of readers and writers without the time, materials, or specialized knowledge required to address all students' needs. Research tells us that if students cannot read with comprehension by 3rd grade, then the instructional road in front of them is cast in doubt (Hernandez, 2011). Beginning in 3rd grade, the content standards become so dense that teachers have little time to address literacy deficits or challenge students who already meet the standards. Literacy skills are truly an "open sesame" for acquiring knowledge to read and write about almost anything!

If you've ever been an intermediate grade teacher, you know exactly what I'm talking about. No matter what content is covered on high-stakes assessments, students who can read and comprehend will score higher than struggling readers. As teachers, we often spend countless hours on test prep in hopes that it will benefit our students. I am often asked, "What is the best way to prepare my students for the state assessments?" Although I do believe that some moderate test prep is appropriate, especially as it relates to test formats, a majority of classroom time must be spent advancing reading and writing skills in a variety of subject areas that support grade-level standards. In other words, differentiating reading and writing instruction while still addressing grade-level standards is essential.

Many grade-level skills can be easily taught at a variety of text levels. Teachers can be confident that while their students are expanding their reading and writing abilities, they're also addressing grade-level standards. With this in mind, teachers need a strong voice in making recommendations concerning school purchases, including leveled texts that address those standards. In short, students won't get better at reading unless they read a lot! Our students' futures are all but determined by how well they learn to read and write.

Although teachers know a great deal about reading and writing processes, they often still have many questions about the most effective methods to use when addressing various students' needs. I have encountered far too many teachers who are frustrated and feel they have been led astray by basal textbook programs and boxed materials that claim to differentiate instruction for all students—but fail to meet those promises. Moreover, many teachers often claim they were poorly prepared to meet the needs of a wide range of readers and writers.

The truth is, if teachers have the correct training—along with a wide variety of leveled texts—they truly have all they need to be effective literacy teachers. Too often, I feel we make things too complicated. In this book, I want to strip down the process and look at the basic knowledge upon which teachers can continually build throughout their careers. A teacher who was trained in and used the models in this book once said to me, "Why didn't someone tell me how it worked before?" My goal is to share this information with you.

Let's be honest: I do not have all the answers. Instead, what I offer in this book are two things. First, I want to show you how a reader and writer develops from a nonreader to a late 5th grade level so you understand the "why" behind the lesson plan models I present. Second, I want to provide you with all the strategies and materials you will need to implement the models effectively. As busy teachers, we want to be confident about the instructional models we are using and have the required materials at our fingertips.

My interest in developing these models was a result of my work with Dr. Darrell Morris, professor of reading at Appalachian State University. Using a one-on-one intervention model with 1st graders (known as Early Steps: Learning from a Reader), research in both rural and urban settings showed great success (Morris, Tyner, & Perney, 2000; Santa & Hoien, 1999). My thought was that if this model showed success in intervention, then why wouldn't it also work for small groups in the classroom? I have since published five books centered on small-group differentiated reading for students from kindergarten through middle school, but I wanted to create one book for elementary teachers that addresses not only reading but also writing as it relates to reading comprehension (see Tyner, 2004, 2009; Tyner & Green, 2009). My apologies for not including middle school teachers, but if we can meet the literacy needs of all elementary students and help them reach their highest capabilities in reading and writing, then I count that as a success for both elementary and middle school teachers.

Allow me to share how this book is different from my previous books. This book encompasses PreK through 5th grade. In retrospect, I think it was a mistake to split the prior books as K–2 and 3–8. Elementary teachers need all the materials in one book so they can accommodate all levels of literacy they will encounter with their students. You will also notice that I have created a writing component in this book as it relates to reading comprehension. Writing is a natural extension of reading because, developmentally, the two are very similar. We can't expect students to write about things they can't read. Additionally, the lesson plans are more detailed and include suggested activities for students to complete during independent practice. Finally, all the support materials discussed in this book are easily downloadable from my website (www.beverlytyner.net) for free!

Differentiating Reading and Writing Instruction

As many schools continue to adapt to an increasingly broad range of learners, it has become more important than ever to develop instruction that responds to these academically diverse students. Differentiating reading and writing instruction for elementary students is a critical step to appropriately address the academic diversity that exists in virtually every classroom. In other words, we need to modify our instruction based on our students' readiness. Whole-group instruction is not enough to meet the needs of this wide range of readers and writers; differentiated small-group instruction enables teachers to plan strategically and meet the needs of students at both ends of the spectrum (and everyone in between). Think of differentiated instruction as the individual steps necessary to reach successively higher levels of literacy development. With this in mind, differentiated reading and writing instruction in small groups gives every student the opportunity for literacy growth.

The research-based Small-Group Differentiated Reading and Writing Models presented in this book were created with students' individual developmental literacy needs in mind. Teachers are presented with easy-to-implement lesson plan models that support any student in any given elementary classroom—including special education students and English language learners (ELLs).

Differentiated instruction begins when children first enter school, whether that's in a prekindergarten or kindergarten program. Beginning this journey requires teachers to assess each student's literacy knowledge and provide instruction that will appropriately advance the child's literacy learning. Students enter a typical prekindergarten or kindergarten classroom with very different levels of printed-language knowledge, and instruction must be adapted for these differences. Some educators feel that small-group reading and writing instruction is inappropriate for young children. On the contrary, I firmly believe that young children deserve the same literacy opportunities as older children.

For example, students entering school with solid alphabet and letter-sound knowledge should progress to the next logical instructional step—which would typically target standards addressed in late kindergarten or 1st grade. On the other hand, numerous young children are often left behind when they fail to acquire foundational skills and knowledge critical to literacy development, such as alphabet knowledge, phonemic awareness, and the ability to track print. We need to simultaneously meet the needs of these two very different groups of students. This is the essence of differentiated instruction.

Low- and high-performing students in the upper elementary grades face an even greater gap. Many teachers are frustrated by the conflict of teaching specific skills to small groups versus grade-level standards in whole-group instruction. This is not an either-or scenario. Standards can be taught in whole groups using modeled and shared reading and writing strategies and then applied in small groups with leveled materials that students are capable of reading and understanding. Small-group differentiated literacy instruction builds foundational skills students may be lacking, or it may accelerate growth for students who already meet grade-level standards.

This book, then, provides concrete examples that address grade-level standards with materials that are appropriate for below-, on-, and above-level students, including special needs students and ELLs.

The Development of Small-Group Differentiated Reading and Writing Models

So now we come to the nuts and bolts of the models. Teachers are often told to do specific things in the classroom, but they typically aren't given the *why* behind those directives. I'm probably not going to buy into something unless it makes sense to me, and I'm sure many of you are the same way. So follow along while I try to show you why these models work.

At their core, the models presented in this book use research-based components and strategies embedded in developmental frameworks that recognize the stages through which readers and writers naturally progress. Reading and writing are not all-or-nothing skills; alphabet knowledge, phonemic awareness, phonics, print-related knowledge, word recognition, fluency, and comprehension are all integral parts. This, then, is the basis for the small-group differentiated reading and writing models presented in this book. As students are assessed to determine their literacy strengths and weaknesses, teachers will group students strategically and deliver instructional strategies to accommodate for these differences. As a result, all students will move forward in their literacy journeys.

The models include a variety of reading and writing strategies and activities that are based on the developmental needs of individual readers and writers—not on students' age or grade level. Although accommodating for differences might be difficult at times, they must be recognized and addressed. If we are sincere about having students achieve at their highest literacy potential, and if we have our students' best interests at heart, then we must differentiate literacy instruction. Students have different starting points, and we must provide the most appropriate level of challenge to increase their literacy learning.

Few educators would argue that effective reading and writing instruction includes a combination of strategies to teach all children to become proficient readers and writers. A differentiated approach that includes the best research practices will more likely meet a much wider range of learners (National Institute of Child Health and Human Development [NICHD], 2000). The models in this book attempt to capture the best instructional practices for elementary readers and writers through the integration of carefully differentiated instructional strategies at each stage of development. Rather than relying on one approach or another, each strategy has been carefully weighed in relation to research and its importance to the reading and writing processes.

Most literacy researchers and practitioners acknowledge that the teaching of reading and writing is multifaceted; there are no quick or easy fixes. There is, however, a recognized set of components that is imperative to reading and writing instruction. The most current and comprehensive examination of these was completed by the National Reading Panel (NICHD, 2000). The panel reviewed the reading research for the foundational years of kindergarten through 8th grade to identify the components that consistently relate to reading and writing success. These five components were identified as (1) phonemic awareness, (2) phonics, (3) fluency, (4) vocabulary, and (5) comprehension. These components are, therefore, included in the lesson plan models.

The small-group differentiated literacy models presented in this book are differentiated in two important ways. First, through the six stages of developmental reading and writing: Emergent, Beginning, Fledgling, Transitional, Fluent, and Independent levels are clearly differentiated as students progress toward increased independence. Second, the research-based instructional components—fluency, word study (including phonemic awareness and phonics), vocabulary, and comprehension (expressed through both speaking and writing)—are differentiated according to each student's stage of development. In the following section, we look at each of these components and their place in small-group instruction.

Research-Based Lesson Plan Components

Each of the instructional components is discussed below, along with the rationale for including it in the small-group models.

Fluency

Fluency is the ability to read quickly, accurately, and with enough expression to understand the text's message. In other words, it means reading comfortably and without struggle. In my opinion, accuracy is the most critical part of reading fluency. The ultimate purpose of reading is to understand a text. If students truly understand what a text means, it must be read at a high degree of accuracy. So it makes sense that speed would follow when students can accurately recognize the words.

I have begged teachers to put the stopwatches down and stop grading the speed part of fluency! Unfortunately, the response is usually "We are required to." I have also come to believe that expression is not necessary to understand text. Think about those 4th grade students who read like robots and have the highest comprehension scores in the class. Perhaps expression belongs more in the realm of "drama"! Without question, fluency is an important gateway to reading comprehension; when students struggle to read words correctly, it is difficult for them to focus on comprehension.

The differentiated models in this book will ensure that all students practice fluency at levels that appropriately support growth in this essential process. Knowing that fluency must be supported by appropriately leveled text, it is therefore best developed during small-group time or independent practice. By design, texts read in small groups should be at an appropriate instructional level—neither too easy nor too hard. With teacher support, students can read and comprehend the text successfully. As students reread, it should be at an independent level that builds fluency. As students enter the independent stage, fluency is generally discontinued in small groups because these students are fluent readers and can maintain this skill in independent practice.

Word Study

The study of words included in this book includes phonemic awareness, alphabet knowledge, phonics, word features, prefixes and suffixes, syllabication, multisyllabic words, and Greek and Latin roots. Students learn that spelling patterns are recognizable and help them decode unfamiliar words and unlock meaning. Word study provides students with the opportunity to investigate and understand patterns in words and how word parts affect meaning. Traditionally thought of as spelling, word study is a different concept and does not support the type of drill and practice that leads to random memorization and a weekly spelling assessment.

Word study develops hand in hand with reading and writing, and there are opportunities in both the whole group and small groups to address these important skills. Research supports the idea that the study of words increases comprehension as it supports decoding and increased vocabulary knowledge (Kamil, 2004).

Phonemic awareness is the understanding that the sounds of spoken language work together to make words. I want to emphasize that this is a listening skill—not a writing skill. A student can have phonemic awareness and not be able to read or write words, but to benefit from phonics instruction, a student needs to demonstrate good phonemic awareness. Phonemic awareness is a subset of a larger category called phonological awareness, which includes identifying rhymes, syllables, and manipulating sounds. These are addressed in Stage 1A, the emergent reading and writing stage. A sequence of lessons supports students in developing these important foundational skills and will be fully discussed in Chapter 4.

I have observed students who are reading but still lack basic phonemic awareness. These students often struggle with phonics, which can eventually lead to poor decoding skills that affect their ability to access more difficult text. Explicit instruction and monitoring of phonemic awareness has been primarily taught in whole-group settings. In a small-group setting, teachers can provide support to meet individual students' needs or advance students who have already mastered these skills and need to move forward in phonics instruction.

The ELFS (Early Literacy Foundational Skills) lessons presented in Stage 1A include a specific lesson sequence that gamifies the process of developing phonemic awareness skills and also includes recognizing and producing alphabet sounds, hearing initial consonant sounds, blending sounds to make words, segmenting sounds, and discriminating rhyming words. The Beginning and Fledgling stages also include activities that support the development of phonemic awareness while also focusing on recognizing beginning consonant sounds and distinguishing short vowel sounds in one-syllable words. For many students, the supported small-group setting allows them to focus on and build these important skills.

There are distinct stages in word study development that are addressed in the small-group lesson plans. Students at different stages of proficiency attend to and represent different patterns and features in their reading, writing, and spelling—from simple to complex. These skills also build on the foundational knowledge in previous word study lessons to progress to more complex patterns. Word study is guided by simple spelling/meaning assessments that help the teacher place each student at an appropriate instructional level. Instruction is deliberately sequenced so students can build word knowledge that propels them in their reading and writing development. The activities that support word study require students to become word detectives who are engaged in ongoing attempts to make sense of word patterns and their relationships to one another. Spelling "rules" are not dictated by the teacher for students to memorize. Rather, students discover spelling patterns and generalizations on their own.

If word study is only addressed in the whole group, struggling readers will very likely miss foundational pieces of the sequence, especially phonics. At the other end of the spectrum, students who have already mastered the grade-level skills need to be presented with an appropriate level of challenge. These small-group differentiated lessons embrace the notion that differentiating word study heavily supports the advancement of reading and writing in general.

Vocabulary

Many students come to school with a limited oral vocabulary and need a language-rich classroom filled with words: in stories, in conversations with adults and other students, in rhymes, and in the environment around them. Since a lack of vocabulary knowledge is a contributing factor to poor comprehension, it must be front and center in all small-group instruction (Glende, 2013). Early readers first master basic high-frequency words (as their initial focus on vocabulary). After students have mastered these words, the focus then moves to words that support understanding of the text. Vocabulary development should be naturally differentiated according to words selected from the leveled texts read in the small groups.

Comprehension

It is an understatement to say that we all read to comprehend. It is the only reason we read. Teaching reading comprehension is a fine art, and a deliberate, well-thought-out lesson plan developed prior to instruction is essential to successfully guide students' comprehension as the lesson unfolds.

Traditionally, basal reading instruction focused on one comprehension strategy each week. I often hear teachers tell students that they are reading the text to find, for example, cause-and-effect relationships. This statement is somewhat troubling and certainly not conducive to a thorough understanding of the text. A more realistic scenario would be to use this strategy in a way that students can personally connect to. This naturally comes in the form of a question such as, "Why did John act that way when he got the test back?" (In other words, what was the cause for the way that he acted?) When we make a strategy more personal, true comprehension can be taught. We must begin to show students that readers adjust strategies based on what they are reading, and multiple strategies work together as meaning is constructed. As good readers, we don't naturally begin reading a story with the intent of looking for cause-and-effect relationships.

Teachers routinely tell me that their students' biggest reading issue is comprehension. Comprehension does not stand alone but is intertwined with fluency, vocabulary, and decoding. Students who can't read at an appropriate speed will certainly struggle to understand the text. Students who don't understand what words mean will also struggle. Poor decoding skills can affect both vocabulary and understanding. We must be aware of all the pieces that make up comprehension. For that reason, the lesson plan models in this book include the development of fluency, word study, vocabulary, and comprehension simultaneously.

The early stages of reading and writing are heavily focused on the decoding process, and there is a gradual transition toward more intentional comprehension instruction in each subsequent stage. Although texts at the early levels are so simplistic that they require few higher-order skills to comprehend, teachers should still have students make simple predictions, summarize, and ask questions. As students progress to more advanced stages, comprehension becomes the primary focus of small-group instructional models and is explicitly taught before, during, and after reading.

Reading and writing relationships begin when reading and writing start (Graham & Hebert, 2010). Although reading and writing are closely connected, writing that supports comprehension has been often overlooked in the past. However, it is now at the forefront of both standards and assessments. The research is clear that writing instruction can raise reading achievement (Shanahan, 2015). Writing about texts is effective because it requires students to consolidate and review information. This written comprehension, as I call it, requires students to organize and integrate ideas. Translating a text's meaning into one's own words is the ultimate summarizing activity. Additionally, students are gaining knowledge from their own reading and writing. In my observations, writing improves when students can actually read the text they are writing about. Much of the writing discussed in this book is framed and supported in small groups but takes place independently after the teacher carefully discusses the focus of the writing through guided questions.

Many of the components associated with writing—grammar, text conventions, organization, mechanics, topic-centered sentences and paragraphs, word choice, sentence structure, paragraph organization—can be addressed as students respond to texts. As teachers continue to struggle with time limitations, incorporating these skills in authentic writing (rather than with isolated workbook pages) will not only save time but also teach the skills with a specific purpose.

Starting in 3rd grade, most states require students to take standardized writing assessments that are generally based on one or more texts. The scoring rubrics for these assessments include mechanics, structure, and how well students respond to a comprehension prompt. Therefore, writing must be an integral part of reading comprehension in the small-group models—from the very earliest developmental stages—if students are expected to meet these demanding standards.

Developmental Stages of Reading and Writing

Research shows that reading and writing are closely aligned (Shanahan, 2015). In fact, reading and writing depend on some of the same skills and strategies. Please pay close attention to this section; it should clarify the *why* behind the developmental stages of reading and writing instruction and how they relate to the differentiated lesson plan models presented in this book. Understanding brings power and confidence to your literacy instruction. I often have teachers tell me that their school's principal says, "I don't want you to do this or that." I respond by asking, "Do you agree or disagree?" Rather than simply complying, be empowered by knowing *why* you are doing what you do in literacy instruction. Be ready to have a fact-based conversation that demonstrates your depth of knowledge about your instructional decisions.

To guide the reading and writing processes effectively, there must first be an understanding of the associated developmental stages—and of the demands placed on readers and writers at these different stages. The six stages—Emergent (i.e., a nonreader), Beginning, Fledgling, Transitional, Fluent, and Independent—end at a 5th grade level. Students advance through these stages as they build upon their knowledge and move forward at their own pace. Each stage will be thoroughly discussed in Chapters 4–9.

Although appropriate grade-level designations are given to each stage for reference, students will be assessed to determine their actual stages of development. This instruction centers on a text selection that is at an appropriate level for the group—that is, text that students can read with 90–95 percent accuracy and understand with the support of the teacher (Rasinski, 2010).

A lesson plan model has been carefully developed to accommodate the literacy needs of students in each developmental stage, with instructional focuses in fluency, vocabulary, word study, comprehension, and writing. These models can be found in the relevant chapters and are carefully weighted at the appropriate developmental level to address the needs of a specific group of readers and writers.

Differentiating Time Spent in Small-Group Instruction

As discussed earlier, small-group differentiated reading and writing provides an opportunity for all students to grow. In addition, it presents struggling readers with an opportunity to make the gains needed to close achievement gaps. Struggling readers particularly need ample exposure to appropriately leveled text choices to provide those growth opportunities. During small-group differentiated instruction, it is important to address each essential reading component (fluency, word study [including phonemic awareness and phonics], vocabulary, comprehension, and writing that supports text comprehension). Many struggling students might also be a part of the school's intervention program. The additional small-group time in the classroom should be carefully orchestrated to complement and solidify skills taught in intervention.

Those students who successfully read grade-level text are not exempt from small-group instruction. They also need additional text selections and instruction at an appropriate level to hone their literacy skills and continue to flourish. The opportunity to reflect and share in a small-group setting allows students to think more deeply about their reading. Although these grade-level readers may not need to work in small groups daily, a sensible goal would be for them to do so every other day.

Above-level students also require support to navigate more complex text. If these students are limited by the grade-level texts presented in whole-group lessons, it is difficult for them to grow to their full potential. A wide variety of genres—in both literary and informational texts—should be included to address the needs of these more accomplished readers and writers. Many times, teachers continue to present thick chapter books as a way to address the needs of advanced readers, but longer books do not necessarily produce better readers and writers. I am often reminded of a student who was placed in an advanced reading group. She told me in no uncertain terms, "Just because we are good readers does not mean we like thicker books."

Another mistake we often make with above-level students is to leave them on their own for independent reading. If I am honest, I often assumed that above-average students did not need my support. I was dead wrong. I now know that they need support at a differentiated level to support their more advanced literacy levels. Growth requires texts that are challenging enough to require the teacher's support with comprehension strategies. Even students who read at the highest levels need to be guided with in-depth conversations and discussions. Although these independent readers read extensively on their own and will require much less time in a small-group setting, the teacher should still routinely meet with them in small groups.

Differentiating Text Selections for Small-Group Instruction

If students don't have books they can read—and a lot of them—then implementing these developmental strategies will not work effectively. Children only get better at reading when they read texts they can understand with 90–95 percent accuracy. This pertains to books that students can read and comprehend with a teacher's support in small-group instruction. The most essential component in small-group differentiated instruction is a text that best matches a student's developmental reading needs. This is no small task.

Clearly, we have come a long way in leveling books according to difficulty level. I still encounter many schools, however, that have insufficient resources to meet the needs of all readers. Teachers need sufficient leveled texts to address literacy levels and content standards that progress in difficulty levels. It is unrealistic to expect a 4th grade student who reads two grades below level to read and understand a 4th grade level text. Even with strong teacher support and scaffolding, the text would be so challenging that the student would become frustrated—along with the teacher. Although teachers can present these higher-level texts during interactive read-alouds or shared reading, this approach alone is insufficient for assisting these students in literacy growth.

Another concern is the misunderstanding that all leveled texts are created equally—that is, all leveled using the same guidelines. Teachers are the best decision makers in choosing appropriate text selections. Preview the structure, vocabulary, and appropriateness of all texts prior to introducing a new book in small-group settings. Be sure to consider the text complexity as it relates to your readers and the current task.

Although I am a strong proponent of the important place that leveled text plays with struggling readers, I believe that we may need to be more diligent concerning the difficulty levels. In many instances, text selections are too easy for some students, which inhibits their growth. This is especially true with struggling readers. I think we often become so excited that these students are reading well that we linger a little longer than necessary with texts that are too easy. As we begin to address the more demanding standards, we must be vigilant and ensure that the text selections we use represent an appropriate mix of genres and complexity.

Implications for English Language Learners, Special Needs Students, and Intervention

Perhaps the most important reason that small-group differentiated reading and writing models are successful is their ability to meet the needs of a wide range of readers and writers. Teachers continue to be challenged with students who have special needs, including those who are learning to speak English. As these teachers more thoroughly understand the stages of reading and writing development, they feel better equipped to meet the needs of these challenges.

English language learners (ELLs) who have developed a good English listening vocabulary are often easy to place in small groups because the lesson plans already allow for differences among learners. Of course, ELLs generally lack the vocabulary of some of their peers. Teachers need to spend extra time developing the vocabulary necessary for good comprehension. This is easier to do when using a model that places students in appropriate reading, writing, and word study levels. School districts have used these frameworks with ELLs with good success, and some have taken the frameworks and translated then into differentiated instruction for developing Spanish literacy.

ELLs with limited English proficiency may lack the vocabulary needed to support their decoding and comprehension efforts. I have found that selecting books with a strong text-to-picture correlation supports both their vocabulary development and their comprehension. Beginning with relatively simple texts also allows ELLs to develop a sense of predictable sentence structure, which is critical to their success. Small-group differentiated instruction provides the environment and components that ELLs need to be successful readers and writers.

Additional intervention outside the literacy block is also important for students performing below expectations. New federal guidelines in the RTI model suggest that early intervention for struggling students be delivered in an explicit and consistent manner outside the literacy block. A prevalent model for delivery of reading instruction and intervention is called the three-tier model. This three-tier model is an attempt to prevent reading failure through early intervention rather than testing and placing students into special education. It consists of three levels of instruction: Tier I includes the basic reading instruction delivered in both whole-group and small-group settings, Tier II includes additional reading intervention that takes place outside the literacy block, and Tier III includes additional intense instruction for students who continue to struggle and have been tested for learning issues.

The small-group differentiated reading and writing models play a key role in each of these levels. All too often, the case has been that if students were not progressing in Tier I instruction, then they should be thrust into a different program. On the contrary, these students need extra time in small-group instruction to focus more intensely on fluency, word study, vocabulary, and reading and writing comprehension. This provides the true "intensity" these students need and makes it much easier to track progress and provide extra layers of support.

There is also this notion that if we "drill down" to uncover the deficits these students have, then we can simply work with segmented pieces of the reading process. For example, an assessment might suggest that a student is weak in reading comprehension. A cause could be traced back to a lack of fluency or decoding skills, or perhaps the student lacks the vocabulary needed to understand the text. In my numerous years in focused literacy interventions, it was very rare to see a struggling reader who was only struggling in one discrete aspect of reading, such as cause-and-effect relationships. Reading and writing are holistic processes and cannot easily be broken apart.

One of the most enlightening bits of knowledge I have gained over the years is this: most special education students do not learn to read differently than any other students. I have been successful with students with autism, Down syndrome, and lower academic functioning. Look no further than differentiated instruction to address the needs of these students. In my opinion, students with special needs deserve "regular" small-group differentiated instruction in the classroom; a smaller, more focused second small group; and a special education setting with one or two other students who share similar levels of proficiency and functioning. In other words, all three groups would focus on the text, word study, and writing at the appropriate instructional level. This provides the intense instruction that every special education student deserves.

Conclusion

Perhaps the biggest challenges teachers face today is the academic diversity present in most elementary classrooms and how to make critical decisions about the most effective methods to deliver literacy instruction to all these students. Differentiating literacy instruction using the small-group models discussed in this book will provide a framework for addressing a wide range of readers and writers. The small-group differentiated reading and writing models presented in this book provide teachers with concrete models that are both developmental and anchored in research.

The lesson plan components outlined in these models provide focused instruction in the basic literacy components. The strategies and activities that support these research-based components are critical. Unlike other small-group models, each of the components is carefully integrated with differentiated strategies that are included as important parts of the daily lesson plan. The reading and rereading of appropriately leveled texts provides the centerpiece for small-group reading instruction. Additionally, developmental word study is addressed with appropriate strategies and activities, and each lesson is inclusive of a strong vocabulary focus. These components, in turn, support both reading and writing comprehension and function congruently to provide a solid foundation for continuous literacy growth.

A Look Ahead

Now that you have read a bit about the rationale behind how the models were developed, let's take a look at how the rest of this book is structured.

Chapter 2 begins with an in-depth look at each of the reading research–based components and the strategies and activities that support each stage of the small-group differentiated reading and writing models. It also presents literacy extensions that can be completed out of group to support each of the lesson components.

Chapter 3 discusses assessments that can be used in conjunction with the small-group models. Chapters 4–9 are structured similarly and present the six stages of elementary reading and writing development. In each chapter, a brief review of student characteristics associated with each stage is presented along with instructional focuses for that stage. Lesson plan formats that support each stage are also included in each of these chapters. Step-by-step directions are given for implementing the lesson plan, followed by selected teacher and student dialogue that supports the lesson. This dialogue is included to demonstrate the activities in an authentic small-group setting (all student names are pseudonyms). Independent literacy extension activities are interspersed throughout the chapters to provide suggestions for easy-to-implement activities that are appropriate for each lesson plan.

Chapter 2

Research-Based Components, Strategies, and Activities

Introduction

The power of the small-group differentiated reading and writing models lies in the solid research base of the components, strategies, and activities that support them. Let me define each of these terms. *Components* are the research-based pieces embedded in each lesson plan, which include fluency, vocabulary, word study, and comprehension. Remember, I use the term *word study* as an umbrella for phonemic awareness, phonics, and the study of the meaning of words and word parts. Think of a *strategy* as a process that helps readers and writers effectively address one of these research-based components. For example, if the component being addressed in a lesson plan is word study, then relevant strategies might include card sorting. *Activities* for sorting might include an open sort, a closed sort, or a writing sort. On the other hand, if the focus component is fluency, then an appropriate strategy might be rereading, and specific activities to support rereading would include choral or whisper reading.

The lesson plans that support each of the six stages of reading and writing provide both the strategies and the activities to address the research-based components in a supportive and meaningful way. Specific steps for implementing each developmental stage are fully discussed in Chapters 4–9.

Let's begin by examining each of the research-based components and the importance for their inclusion in the lesson plan models. We'll also discuss differentiated strategies and activities supporting each component that can be implemented during small-group lessons.

Fluency

Fluency is the vehicle that takes a child from focusing on individual words to focusing on the meaning of a text. The foundation of fluency is in the ability to identify words quickly and accurately in context, as well as using the correct intonation needed to understand the text's message. What this means is that students ultimately direct their attention toward constructing meaning from the text rather than decoding text. The National Reading Panel report (NICHD, 2000) describes fluency as the ability to read "with speed, accuracy, and proper expression" (p. 11).

To acquire oral reading fluency, students must have enough guided practice in reading for the process to become automatic. There is strong evidence to support that students who spend a lot of time reading become good readers (Farstrup & Samuels, 2002). Rereading is therefore key to building oral reading fluency. With that in mind, each lesson plan in the first five stages of the small-group differentiated reading and writing models begins by having students reread a text or a part of a text they previously read.

Students in the Emergent and Beginning stages begin practicing fluency as they recognize high-frequency words quickly and accurately in simple text. The need for rereading to build fluency in each subsequent stage becomes even more critical since it builds a bridge to reading comprehension. Within the Fledgling, Transitional, and Fluent stages, text becomes more complex, so fluency (especially as it relates to accuracy) becomes even more critical to the comprehension process. Students who have mastered fluency (i.e., generally those at the Independent stage) should continue to practice fluency in independent practice.

Whereas other small-group models do not encourage individual oral reading, the small-group differentiated reading and writing models presented in this book embrace oral reading as an essential activity. The National Reading Panel report points out that guided oral reading with teacher feedback has a significant positive impact on word recognition, reading fluency, and comprehension (NICHD, 2000). In fact, the report further states that guided oral reading benefits all readers (regardless of their proficiency level) through at least 4th grade. When students read aloud, they typically get far more instructional feedback from the teacher than students who are just following along in the text (Kuhn & Stahl, 2003). Furthermore, oral reading gives teachers observable characteristics of an otherwise unobservable process. This provides teachers with a means for checking progress, diagnosing problems, and focusing instruction. Ultimately, oral reading is an opportunity for readers to share their abilities with both peers and teachers. I rarely find a student in small-group instruction who doesn't want a turn at being the lead reader when faced with a text he or she feels successful reading. With text that is too difficult, however, I have seen students put their heads down, act disinterested, and even misbehave. If we want students to love reading, then they must have access to texts that allow them to experience success and joy. We often fail to realize that our daily decisions can either promote or discourage students to be lifelong readers.

Simply stated, fluency rates will only improve when students read and reread text they can read successfully with support or independently. Unfortunately, many students spend very little time each day reading texts they can actually read well enough to understand. This becomes more common as students reach the upper elementary grades—when more rigorous standards in the content areas increase. With the increased curricular demands, teachers are torn between teaching content and finding time for students to practice reading at an appropriate level. Students require multiple opportunities to read during the school day. Time spent reading (and increasing fluency) results in dramatic increases in word recognition, speed, accuracy, and—therefore—comprehension (Grabe & Stoller, 2013; Kuhn, Rasinski, & Zimmerman, 2014).

Small-Group Strategies and Activities That Support Fluency

Rereading is, without a doubt, the most effective strategy to engage students in building oral reading fluency in a small-group setting (Chard, Vaughn, & Tyler, 2002). In most cases, it's the only time we can be assured that students can actually reread text with a high degree of accuracy. The following activities are intended to help provide students with multiple opportunities to reread orally. It is important to note that some activities are more effective during a first read versus a reread because they are more supportive and teacher-led. Therefore, the following activities are in order from most supportive to least supportive. Each of the following fluency activities requires all students to orally read each word of the text. You will notice that round-robin reading is not listed because it requires students to read alone while others follow along. I have found this to be an ineffective activity since many students become less engaged and do not follow along.

Echo Reading: Echo reading is only used in the early Emergent stage. The teacher simply reads a section of text while students point to the words on the page. The students then read in unison the same section of text after the teacher; they "echo" what the teacher just read. This activity helps students access the text when they are nonreaders. As soon as they become familiar with text conventions or are comfortable using picture clues, echo reading is discontinued.

Teacher-Led Reading: As the lead reader, the teacher reads out loud as students point to the text and follow along as they whisper read. It's important to be mindful of your speed; don't read too fast and drag students through the text. If students are unable to keep up at an appropriate speed, you may need to drop down a book level. This activity can be appropriate at all stages.

Choral Reading: Choral reading takes place when the teacher and students read a text (or part of a text) in unison. The teacher may begin this activity by modeling fluent reading of the first part of a text. Choral reading should not take the place of individual reading practice, but it can be used to provide fluency support for students, when necessary. This activity is powerful throughout the stages of reading development and is appropriate to use at any stage.

Stop-and-Go Reading: This is a modified version of choral reading that is more appropriate at the Emergent, Beginning, and early Fledgling stages. As the teacher and students choral read, the teacher stops at various points and allows students to continue. The teacher may rejoin the group, if necessary, to model and assist with fluency, speed, or expression. This activity builds reading stamina and allows students to carry the responsibility of reading a text without complete teacher support.

Student-Led Reading: Student-led reading can easily replace round-robin reading in a much more powerful way. In this activity, one student reads out loud while the other students whisper read along with him or her. This highly engaging activity is helpful in keeping all students on task. It also provides teachers with an opportunity to evaluate individual students as they read aloud. I have heard from teachers in higher grades who say that their students "can't" or "won't" whisper read. I respond with, "Routines, routines!" As routines and expectations are established and monitored, students will respond appropriately. I have never had this problem and fear that some teachers simply give in to their students too easily. The value of student engagement cannot be overstated, and enforcing this activity will pay great dividends.

Whisper Reading: This activity can be used in two different ways and for two different purposes. First, teachers ask all students to reread a text by whisper reading at their own pace—not in unison with other students. This provides an opportunity to listen to students one at a time to assess fluency and offer support, as appropriate. As students grow, this activity can be used another way. While reading a new text, the teacher might ask students to whisper read the next page or section for a specific purpose. This is an excellent way for students to build reading stamina and begin to orchestrate a wide range of comprehension strategies that support individual strengths and weaknesses. Don't make the mistake of assigning too much text at one time. No matter which stage you are working with, there will always be faster and slower readers. This strategy is most effective for students at the Fluent and Independent stages.

Word Study

Word study is the systematic, developmental study of words (Bear, Invernizzi, & Johnston, 2007; Ganske, 2000), which serves several important purposes, including the development of decoding skills and vocabulary understanding. When we consider the practice of word study for elementary readers and writers, systematic phonemic awareness, alphabet knowledge, phonics, word features, syllabication, and a recognition of Greek and Latin roots all play important parts.

Phonemic awareness and phonics skills have historically been taught in whole-group settings (along with spelling), but this approach often lacks an appropriate scope and sequence or the intensity needed to be successful. This usually culminates with a weekly spelling test, and if I am honest, I unfortunately did this on a regular basis. The truth is, however, that words memorized and spelled correctly on a Friday test simply fade by Monday, only to be replaced by another spelling list for the week. Think about this, though. Most classrooms have both students who can already spell the new words every Monday and students who can't even read the words they are given. There's also a group in between that needs focused practice with the words.

With time at a premium, does it really make sense to spend time giving a weekly assessment? Giving up weekly spelling tests is difficult for some teachers. I often hear, "I have to give the spelling tests because the parents expect it" or "I give spelling tests to improve my students' reading grades." It is time for us to stand up for what is right for our students! I hope to make the case that word study should be a part of small-group instruction and based on both what students already know and what comes next in a concrete scope and sequence. The framework presented in this book provides a systematic, developmental scope and sequence for word study that provides students with the opportunity to internalize patterns by comparing and contrasting—not by memorizing words for a weekly test. This, in turn, encourages students to apply their knowledge in meaningful reading and writing situations. Here's the best news: you can give a short word study assessment in small groups when students finish a set of word patterns. Instead of using all the words, choose no more than 10. This saved me so much time, and I really saw growth with my students.

The most effective way to meet the developmental needs of a wide variety of students is to assess each student and identify strengths and weaknesses in word study. By providing teachers with a developmental scope and sequence that is driven by student assessment, teachers can differentiate their instruction and reach every student. In other words, word study is no longer a hit-or-miss prospect but is uniquely structured to meet the needs of all students. To do this, teachers must first assess students and place them in appropriately leveled small groups, according to the scope and sequence. The assessments that support the small-group differentiated reading and writing models are discussed in Chapter 3.

Recently, I have seen an increasing number of teachers implement developmental spelling models for word study that are driven by student data. Research continues to support the connections among a student's ability to spell, read, and write. Invernizzi and Hayes (2004) found that spelling scores for almost 70,000 1st graders correlated with both word recognition in isolation and oral reading accuracy. Word recognition in isolation continues to be the best predictor of a student's reading level. If a student can read words in isolation, then it is likely that he or she can also read the words in context. Being able to decode words accurately allows readers and writers to focus on meaning rather than structure. The processes of spelling, reading, and writing are so intrinsically woven, though, that one cannot be discussed without also considering the others.

Word study for early readers and writers initially focuses on phonemic awareness, alphabet recognition and production, and foundational phonics (Armbruster, Lehr, & Osborn, 2001). Phonemic awareness is specifically addressed in the Emergent stage, typically taught in prekindergarten and kindergarten, and is defined as the student's "ability to hear, identify, and manipulate the individual sounds—phonemes—in spoken words" (Armbruster et al., 2001, p. 3). Phonemic awareness development does not introduce letters as they relate to sounds; this is known as phonics. There is an important difference. Phonemic awareness is an auditory skill, whereas phonics is the ability to make the connection between sounds (phonemes) and written letters (graphemes). The success of systematic phonics instruction delivered in small-group settings is well documented (Morris, Tyner, & Perney, 2000; NICHD, 2000; Santa & Høien, 1999); therefore, it is an important component in the small-group differentiated reading and writing models.

Although most primary (K–2) teachers recognize the need for phonics instruction, they often overlook the importance of word study as it relates to students' continued development and success. This is particularly important for those 3rd,

4th, and 5th grade students who are just beginning to have reading and writing difficulties. Their difficulties might be due, in part, to a sheer lack of decoding skills. They rely on rote memorization and are without the skills needed to decode more complex words. Such students can sometimes make it through 2nd grade, but they run into the proverbial brick wall in 3rd grade when presented with more difficult, multisyllabic words in complex text. Memorization takes a student only so far; students need explicit, sequential word study instruction along with specific decoding skills.

Spelling is generally embedded in vocabulary standards that address the word study element for each grade level. First and foremost, make sure the appropriate grade-level standards are covered. This is understandable. It might be necessary to rearrange some pieces of the scope and sequence in the models provided if those needs are not met. Nevertheless, we can no longer overlook the importance of a word study component in small-group instruction as it relates to elementary readers and writers. Word study is developmental—like reading and writing—and is a consistent element in each of the six stages of reading and writing development.

Small-Group Strategies and Activities That Support Word Study

In a small-group setting, the following activities can be used during the word study part of the lesson. However, for purposes of differentiated instruction, I have noted which activities are more appropriate for each developmental stage. Some of the activities in this section have corresponding reproducibles on the website, and this information is noted after each activity.

A specific scope and sequence that guides lesson pacing is also available in the appendixes and can be downloaded from www.beverlytyner.net for all six stages of word study development. As a rule of thumb, do not stay on a lesson longer than the scope and sequence suggests. You can, however, skip lessons when you feel that your students have already mastered the concepts. There are built-in reviews as the lessons progress, and an assessment at the end of each stage should be used to identify patterns that might need to be reviewed.

Keep in mind that only one of the following activity types should be completed each day. Rotate among them, but regardless of the activity (except an open sort), you should begin with a minilesson that introduces the focus patterns and includes key word cards displayed on a classroom sorting board.

Sorting: Picture and word card sorting can be completed by sorting cards according to initial sounds with picture cards, vowel patterns, or word parts being studied (see Figure 2.1). Writing sorts are also included and involve the teacher calling out the words while students write the word in the correct category according to pattern. Writing sorts require students to actually write the correct sound or word as they sort rather than just sorting cards. Over the years, it became evident to me that students retain much more when they sort and write at the same time. These sorting activities support the in-depth investigation of word structure and allow students to compare and contrast varying patterns—which in turn promotes the application of those patterns in independent practice. Perhaps the most powerful—yet overlooked—activity that supports word study is (generally teacher-led) student discussion about word patterns. Regardless of which sorting activity is used, students should be able to discuss their discoveries about word patterns.

Figure 2.1
Word Sort in a Small Group

Automaticity in recognizing and writing words with the focus patterns is the hallmark of success. In other words, how quickly and automatically can students identify, decode, and sort or write the words correctly? Although sorting word cards based on patterns is appropriate when new patterns are introduced, I generally stop card sorting after the first day and focus on activities that require students to write the words—as in a writing sort. I want to make an important point here: *students must write the words as they sort them if they are to commit the patterns to long-term memory.* I have seen too many teachers get frustrated because their students do not master the patterns, but it's only because they spent most of their time engaged in group sorting cards rather than writing the sorts.

There are two activities that can be used with card sorting. The first is called a closed sort, wherein the teacher clearly establishes the word study focus with key words that contain the target patterns placed on a sorting board (i.e., a tabletop pocket chart). The teacher then discusses the patterns for the week, and students sort the word cards based on the patterns. Teacher-led discussions and questions solidify this activity:

- Tell us why you placed that word in this category?
- What sound or meaning does this pattern represent?
- What letter pattern makes that sound?

At the Fledgling stage, the teacher might start with a minilesson about the word families that are being studied and then put three word cards that exemplify the identified patterns on the class pocket chart. The teacher then asks students to look at their word cards (which were previously distributed) to identify the word families represented and sort those words on the class pocket chart. In later elementary stages, students can sort words according to various features (e.g., plural endings). Closed sorts are less time-consuming than open sorts (discussed in the following section).

The second activity is an open sort. Although open sorts provide students with an opportunity to further explore word patterns on their own, the process is very time-consuming. In a true open sort, the teacher would distribute word cards among pairs of students and let students identify the patterns and decide how to categorize the words. Students would then be asked to explain how they sorted the cards and why. If students fail to identify the appropriate word features or patterns, the teacher can redirect the activity by being more explicit in the sorting directions. For example, the teacher might say, "Look at your cards again, and sort them based on the vowel sound you hear in each word."

Writing Sort: A writing sort is an important activity after students have been introduced to and worked with specific features. This type of sort is critical for solidifying students' ability to recognize and reproduce the patterns being studied. In this activity, the teacher calls out words for students to simultaneously sort and spell on writing sort activity sheets. Writing sorts are appropriate at the Fledgling, Transitional, and Fluent stages (with either three- or four-box writing sort activity sheets, depending on the number of features studied).

Writing sorts are essential for students to transfer knowledge from sorting to writing. In some instances, it will only be by sight that students know how to correctly spell a word. For example, consider the word *sir*. How do we know it is spelled *ir* instead of *er* or *ur*? All three of these patterns can make the same sound. It is only because we have seen the word written correctly numerous times that we know how to spell the word correctly. Figure 2.2 shows a writing sort for the Fledgling reader and writer.

Figure 2.2

Writing Sort: Fledgling Stage

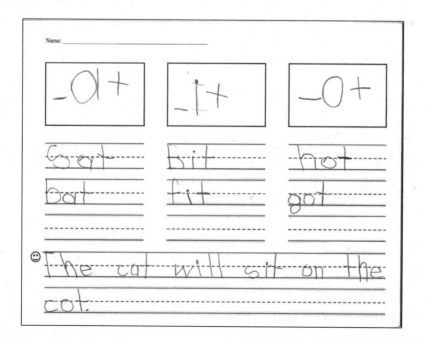

There will generally only be time for students to write two words per pattern during a lesson. After each word is written correctly, the teacher places the word card under the correct pattern on the sorting board and has students read the column of words from top to bottom. A writing sort is not appropriate when students are studying features such as homophones, prefixes, suffixes, compound words, or root words where the focus is more on meaning. Even a kindergarten student could sort all the words with the same prefix without reading the words. A better activity might be to discuss the meaning of each prefix and how it changes the meaning of a word. An in-depth discussion of the appropriate activities that support word study are found in Chapters 4–9.

Sound Boxes: Sound boxes are another word study activity that can be used at the Fledgling, Transitional, and Fluent stages. They serve two purposes: (1) students can determine how many sounds are in a word (i.e., it's an oral language activity that supports phonemic awareness), and (2) students can write a word with the corresponding number of boxes needed for each sound. Keep in mind that more than one letter could represent an individual sound, and there can only be one sound in each box. Sound box templates (with both three and four boxes) can be found in the Appendix and can be downloaded from www.beverlytyner.net (along with "cheat sheets" for teachers who lack solid phonics knowledge). They contain models for each type of pattern written in the sound boxes. I cannot express enough the importance of using sound boxes as students isolate vowel patterns in an explicit way. Figure 2.3 shows some examples of how sound boxes are used.

Figure 2.3

Sound Box Examples

c	a	t	
sh	u	t	
c	r	ow	d

Word Scramble: In this activity, which can be used at the Fledgling, Transitional, and Fluent stages, students are given letter cards or magnetic letters to make (and then write) words. For example, the teacher calls out a word and students use their letters to spell out the word. When finished, students write the word while the teacher monitors. Prewritten word scramble activity directions (available for each stage at www.beverlytyner.net) also incorporate the manipulation of letters as students add and drop letters to make new words. In addition, there is a word scramble template on the website that can be used for this activity. It provides a place for students to line up letters at the top, a space for students to create the words, and a line for students to write the word they made. Figure 2.4 is an example word scramble activity for use at the Fluent stage.

Figure 2.4
Word Scramble Example

Available letters: *a, b, c, f, l, p, s, t*
1. Make the word *bat.*
2. Change one letter to spell *fat.*
3. Change one letter to spell *cat.*
4. Change one letter to spell *cap.*
5. Change one letter to spell *lap.*
6. Add one letter to spell *flap.*
7. Change one letter to spell *slap.*
8. Change one letter to spell *clap.*

Meaning Discussion: Meaning discussions are appropriate at all stages and are crucial to understanding, especially at the Independent stage. These are simple discussions about the words and word parts that help define the words. For example, after sorting some word cards with simple prefixes, the teacher chooses one from each category for further discussion. Another example would be a discussion of homophones, the meaning of each word, and sentences with the different words. Students would then write the correct spelling for the words they hear in context. For instance, the teacher might say, "All of the toys in the store are on sale. Write the word *sale.*"

Small-group environments provide rich opportunities for students to discuss word meanings with classmates. Teachers can easily assess students' knowledge when these discussions take place. Most lessons are supported by a plethora of words, so teachers must be intentional about the number of words that can realistically be discussed in the lesson each day. This dialogue among students and the teacher is critical at all reading and writing stages. It is also important for teachers to have a full understanding of the words students are studying; thus, it is worth the time for teachers to purposely plan their discussions.

Cut-Up Sentences: At the Emergent stage, use sentences that are short with repetitive, early high-frequency words. Using a sentence strip, tell students the sentence for the day and have students repeat the sentence several times while counting each word on their fingers. Then use student input to write the sentence on the sentence strip (so students can watch as the sentence is constructed). Do not make the mistake of prewriting the sentence or writing it so students see it upside down. If you can't write upside down, post it on the wall behind you. Focus on the letter names, capital letters, punctuation, and spacing between words. When the sentence is complete, cut the words apart and randomly give each student a word or punctuation mark. Students should then work together to put the sentence back together. Cut-up sentences are used at the Emergent and Beginning stages only. The Emergent sentences contain many repetitive sight words, and Beginning stage sentences contain words that have some of the same beginning sounds that are the focus of word study. For your convenience, I have created sentences that support this activity. Students can use these sentences to cut up and put back together. I will discuss this as an independent activity in Chapters 4 and 5. All sentences can be downloaded from www.beverlytyner.net, but Figure 2.5 includes a few examples.

Figure 2.5

Example of Cut-Up Sentences (Beginning Stage)

The	sheep	are	in	the	grass	.
The	wheel	is	on	the	floor	.
The	cherries	are	in	the	glass	.
Do	sharks	eat	cheese	?		
The	sheep	was	thirsty	.		

Dictated Sentences: This activity can be used at the Fledgling, Transitional, and Fluent stages. Here, I have prewritten sentences that can be dictated for students to write each day. Each sentence contains a word (or words) that is representative of the word study focus for the week. Although sorting is at the crux of word study instruction, this activity cannot be the only one that students complete with these words. Students need to be involved with daily writing activities (e.g., spelling sorts, sound boxes, word scrambles, writing sentences) and oral discussions for the features to transfer to their everyday reading and writing skills. If time is short, students can create their own sentences with specified words and write them independently. Figure 2.6 shows a set of dictated sentences created for the Transitional reader and writer.

Figure 2.6
Dictated Sentences: Transitional Reader

1. Dad made a trap for the shark.
2. We will play a card game.
3. It is hard to chase a snake.
4. I have the same hat as my mom.
5. Turn the page in the big book.
6. Park your car beside the barn.
7. They will chase the cat in the dark.
8. We play at the park near the lake.
9. We put the jam in a jar.
10. We will name our new cat Max.

Vocabulary

Vocabulary development is widely considered to be the cornerstone of reading achievement (Blachowicz & Fisher, 2000; Hennings, 2000). As students transition from learning to read to reading to learn, vocabulary instruction becomes essential. This is increasingly important as students encounter more content-specific vocabulary. Thus, vocabulary development is embedded in the small-group models through explicit word study discussions and with targeted vocabulary and comprehension instruction. Word study includes the study of word parts and how they relate to the meaning of a word, and comprehension requires an understanding of how words are used in a text. Vocabulary, therefore, is arguably the most important piece of reading comprehension, and it must be addressed in a powerful way. Teachers must commit to teaching vocabulary in a way that explicitly supports comprehension—from the primary grades through the upper elementary grades.

Small-Group Strategies and Activities That Support Vocabulary

High-Frequency Words: Vocabulary development is grounded in the automatic recognition of the first 100 high-frequency words seen in Beginning readers (Figure 2.7). Word cards for these high-frequency words can be downloaded from www. beverlytyner.net. The study of these words (which should be done at the Emergent, Beginning, and Fledgling stages) is generally completed by the middle of the Fledgling stage. Some kindergartners may know 100 words by the end of the year, whereas others may struggle with 20. These lesson plans can accommodate both struggling and above-level students.

I have found that mastery of high-frequency words is highly correlated to the book level students are capable of reading (see Figure 2.8). Keep in mind that these are just general guidelines; most students will not fit neatly into boxes. Other means of assessment, such as a running record, can often give false information when determining early reading levels. I would suggest assessing high-frequency word knowledge and then finding the corresponding book level. Try this level for a few weeks. The most common mistake I see is when teachers keep students in Levels A and B for far too long. After students recognize 15 new high-frequency words and can track print with a return sweep, they should move on to the next level (Level C) where the text structure is not so repetitive. The wrong instructional decision here can keep students from progressing.

Fish Pond: This game is appropriate for students at the Emergent and Beginning stages—when they know fewer than 20 high-frequency words. Before the game, the teacher reviews the high-frequency words that are currently the focus and then places word cards face up in the middle of the table (i.e., the fish pond). Each student gets a turn to "fish" for a word from the pond. If a student needs more support, the teacher might say, "Can you fish for the word *is*?" If the student needs even more support, the teacher should hold up the word *is* from an identical set of cards and say, "This is the word *is*. Can you find another word *is*?" The game continues until all cards have been fished out of the "pond."

Word Wizard: Students love this game, which is appropriate at the Emergent, Beginning, and early Fledgling stages. Prepare for this game by reviewing 20–25 high-frequency words for one or two minutes. Then start the game by showing the

Figure 2.7

First 100 Hi...

1. the
2. a
3. and
4. to
5. I
6. in
7. is
8. on
9. you
10. it
11. of
12. said
13. can
14. for
15. my
16. but
17. all
18. we
19. are
20. up
21. at
22. with
23. me
24. they
25. have
26. he
27. out
28. that
29. one
30. big
31. go
32. was
33. like
34. what

54. there
55. into
56. day
57. look
58. eat
59. make
60. his
61. here
62. your
63. an
64. back
65. mom
66. dog
67. very
68. did

69. her
70. from
71. had
72. got
73. put
74. came
75. just
76. cat
77. them
78. tree
79. where
80. away
81. time
82. as
83. water
84. home
85. made
86. long
87. has
88. help
89. good
90. going
91. by
92. how
93. house
94. dad
95. or
96. two
97. red
98. am
99. over
100. saw

Source: This list was derived from a survey of 1,000 pre-primer, early, and first readers. Copyright 1998 E. Bodrova, D. J. Leong, and D. Semenov.

Figure 2.8

High-Frequency Words/Book-Level Correlation

Lesson Plan	Book Levels	High Frequency Words
Emergent Reader and Writer	Levels 1–2 Level A	0–15 words
Beginning Reader and Writer	Level 3 Level B	15–25 words
Fledgling Reader and Writer	Level 4 Level C	25–35 words
	Level 5 Level D	35–50 words
Fledgling Reader and Writer	Level 6 Level D	50–60 words
	Level 7 Level E	60–70 words
	Level 8 Level E	70–85 words
	Levels 9–10 Level F	85–100 words
Transitional Reader and Writer	Levels 11–16 Level G/H/I	Vocabulary from books
Fluent Reader and Writer	Levels 17–22 Level J/K/L/M	Vocabulary from books
Independent Reader and Writer		Vocabulary from texts

first student a word. He or she has three seconds to recognize the word before it goes to the next player. If the student recognizes the word in three seconds, then he or she gets to keep the word card. If two students in a row miss the same word, then it goes in the "fish pond." When all word cards have been played, students have a chance to go back to the fish pond to pick up extra words. It's a good idea to regularly substitute words in the word bank. In other words, drop five words that most students recognize and add five new words. Never have more than 20–25 total words, however, since time will not allow for more. As an alternative way to play that adds more excitement and engagement among students, you can add in word cards that say *Pass* (pass your cards to the next player), *Reverse* (play reverses order), and *Zap* (you lose all your words). The student who has the most words at the end of the game is the Word Wizard of the day!

Vocabulary from Text: After the first 100 high-frequency words have been mastered, the teacher should then select focus vocabulary words from the text being read. Choose no more than seven or eight words that are important to the meaning of the text and write them on index cards. Prior to reading, quickly introduce the words and discuss the meaning of the words. Students should then look for these vocabulary words as they read the text and identify context clues that help determine the words' meanings. A balance of direct teaching and letting students "uncover" the meanings of the words is beneficial. When applicable, teach words that are necessary for understanding, such as unfamiliar academic vocabulary (Ebbers & Denton, 2008). It is also important to teach multiple-meaning words, as these words may be particularly confusing for students. Vocabulary is fundamental to comprehending text; as students encounter new words without knowing their meanings, their ability to comprehend the whole text is compromised. Indeed, Nagy and Scott (2000) report that children must be able to comprehend the meaning of 90–95 percent of the words in a piece of text for it to be fully understood.

Summarize with Vocabulary: This activity is completed after a text has been completely read. Use the focus vocabulary words on index cards that were introduced prior to reading and redistribute the cards to students. Students choose or are assigned a word and must use that word in a sentence about the text or that demonstrates something they learned from the text. This activity is a great way to summarize text and practice important vocabulary. When students can "hang" a new vocabulary word on a story or piece of text, then it is more likely they will remember it. You could also ask students to write these sentences as extension practice.

Comprehension

When my principal asked me to leave kindergarten and move to 3rd grade, my biggest fear was that I had no idea how to teach reading comprehension! I now know that learning how to teach comprehension was a complicated and complex set of skills. Knowing that a student's ability to comprehend text affects every aspect of his or her educational endeavors made it feel overwhelming. It still feels overwhelming, but I have learned a lot and want to share that with you—knowing that you will be building on your own background of knowledge and experiences. Teachers know that the desired result of reading and writing comprehension is for students to fully understand text and demonstrate that understanding through discussions and writing. In the early stages of reading and writing development, students are primarily operating in the decoding phase. As they begin to master basic decoding skills, fluency plays a more important role as students begin to develop speed, accuracy, and expression.

Early readers and writers spend time mastering phonemic awareness and simple phonics patterns in simple text. Independent readers and writers continue to develop important word study knowledge, but the primary focus shifts to comprehension. Good readers comprehend text with little effort. Others, for whom it becomes a laborious process, require a skilled teacher. Comprehension should be taught through systematic instruction across the content areas. Different comprehension strategies are needed for different kinds of text.

The teaching of comprehension must begin in prekindergarten. Just as phonemic awareness is a precursor to phonics, listening comprehension is a precursor to reading comprehension. For example, the strategies associated with story structure, sequencing, and summarizing begin in prekindergarten or kindergarten with interactive read-alouds. These strategies are essentially the same ones employed by older elementary students as they read and write independently.

The ability to teach comprehension is a skill that must be studied and practiced by teachers as they learn how to effectively teach students to think about reading. Expert teachers guide comprehension by threading meaningful discussion as the text is read. This process leads students to a deeper understanding of the text. Comprehension is a continual thought process that requires students to adapt and apply a wide variety of strategies. Teachers must consistently model these strategies, and students need to practice applying the strategies while reading at an appropriate level of text difficulty (Duke & Pearson, 2002). The teacher (or another more experienced guide) should explicitly model an explanation and demonstration of how to perform a skill.

The most powerful way to teach reading comprehension is through a small-group model. This setting allows teachers to support students as they read and practice comprehension strategies at an appropriate reading level and apply appropriate comprehension strategies as they navigate the text. Gradually, the teacher provides less and less guidance until students can perform the comprehension strategies on their own. The zone of proximal development, also an element of Vygotskian theory, suggests that a teacher should provide scaffolded learning opportunities for students while slowly withdrawing support as it becomes less needed (Vygotsky, 1978). Learning and applying new comprehension strategies is most successful in a supportive environment and when associated with a text appropriate for the learner. As readers progress through the developmental stages of reading and writing, comprehension becomes more important; therefore, the lesson plans have been adjusted to support more advanced comprehension skills.

One of the most critical aspects of comprehension development is simply overlooked. It is the dialogue that occurs between the teacher and the students—as well as the dialogue that occurs among students. These conversations—a natural exchange of ideas, knowledge, and perceptions—are worth their weight in gold when it comes to student understanding. In many classrooms across the country, teachers still cling to a basal scope and sequence or pacing guide to determine the comprehension strategy on which they should focus during a given week. Although I am not opposed to a special focus on one strategy or another, this should be tempered with the knowledge that readers do not use just one comprehension strategy in isolation as they read. Duke and Pearson (2002) also recommend teaching comprehension skills and strategies to support achievement but with an important caveat. Neither the teacher nor the students should lose sight of the need to coordinate or orchestrate comprehension strategies. Strategies are not to be used singularly—good readers do not read a book and only make predictions; rather, good readers use multiple strategies constantly.

Small-Group Strategies and Activities That Support Comprehension

Many times, as teachers, we fail to recognize the power of teacher-led discussions as one of the best strategies to increase comprehension. For many years, blackline worksheets were the go-to activity to support comprehension. As teachers, we felt that we somehow needed concrete evidence to prove that our students were making progress. Teaching comprehension involves interactive conversations before, during, and after a text is read. I cannot stress enough the importance of meaningful teacher-led discussions and questioning that needs to occur during small-group instruction. In most cases, small-group time is the only time during the school day when students can engage in meaningful, instructional conversations that deepen true comprehension.

Before Reading

Building Background Knowledge: This activity must be addressed cautiously! The teacher should already know if additional background knowledge is necessary for students to read and understand the text. If the relevant information is explained in the text, do not use valuable classroom time to build background knowledge prior to reading. I can remember times when I gave everything away before students read the first page! The point of reading is for students to read to find out this information. On the other hand, if students have limited background knowledge and need certain knowledge to understand the text, then you should quickly give students the appropriate information. For example, if students are reading about something about which they have no background knowledge, such as a piano recital, an earthquake, or a tsunami, then it is appropriate to explain the pertinent information prior to reading.

Picture Walk: A complete picture walk is appropriate only at the Emergent and Beginning stages. After this, only a few pages will be used in this type of activity, and it should be completely discontinued by the Fledgling stage (or when students can recognize most of the first 100 high-frequency words). Prior to distributing a book, the teacher completes a picture walk by pointing out vocabulary that is supported by illustrations in the book. This process also allows teachers to introduce the storyline and preview characters so students will be better prepared to read the story.

Previewing Vocabulary: After students have mastered the first 100 high-frequency words, teachers will preselect vocabulary words that are essential to understanding a given text. As a rule of thumb in the early stages, select vocabulary words you would expect to hear if students retold the story. In the later reading and writing stages, consideration should also be given to words with multiple meanings, words used in an unfamiliar way, words that will be seen across genres, and content-specific words. A lack of vocabulary is a major contributor to a lack of comprehension, so we cannot assume that students know words that we might view as familiar. English language learners (and other students) may lack basic vocabulary knowledge that cannot be ignored. Therefore, teachers should revisit these vocabulary words throughout the teaching of the text—and after.

Setting the Purpose: This is perhaps one of the strongest activities that can be completed before reading. Without a purpose, students can easily lose their train of thought and get to the end of a text without knowing what they read. Avoid setting up comprehension purposes such as, "Let's read this book to work on making inferences" or "Let's read to work on our fix-it-up strategies." Would that make you excited to read a book? Certainly not, and the same applies to children. In the earlier stages of reading and writing development, a comprehension focus could be as simple as "Let's read this book to find out the problem that Bobby had when he went to school and how his problem was solved." Although this addresses the text structure, the purpose is far more engaging than asking students to read a book to find a problem and solution. By establishing a clear purpose, we're allowing students to specifically focus on a particular structure (i.e., problem and solution) but in a more personal and meaningful way. Students have to read the text to answer the purpose for reading.

An example at the Independent stage could be "Let's read this fable to determine the lesson the author wants us to learn and how he showed us the lesson in the story." Research demonstrates that having a clear purpose for reading and writing affects students' ability to read and write (Duke & Roberts, 2010), helps readers use different patterns of strategies for different purposes (Zhang & Duke, 2008), and affects the kinds of inferences readers generate (Narvaez, van den Broek, & Ruiz, 1999).

Setting the purpose can be easier said than done. Knowing this, I have created some examples for setting the purpose for reading that can be found in the Appendix and on the website. The purpose for reading should culminate in a focus for discussion after reading, which ultimately becomes a focus for independent writing. Students should walk away from a comprehension-focused discussion with the information needed to complete a well-constructed reading response.

During Reading

Text-Dependent Questioning: Text-dependent questions are an incredibly powerful component to the comprehension process and add a sense of urgency to a teacher's questions as a text is explored. Text-dependent questions can only be answered with evidence provided in the text. Learning how to construct text-dependent questions and knowing when to use them can be a formidable task, however. With that in mind, I developed a list of text-dependent question stems so teachers can reference them as they plan for instruction (see Appendix).

Tagging the Evidence: As the teacher poses questions about a text, each student is given a small sticky note. After the evidence is tagged, students share with their partners and justify their choices. For example, the teacher might ask students to find evidence that shows Bobby was disappointed. Each student would take a sticky note and place it in the text where Bobby's actions showed he was disappointed. Students then share their responses with a partner and justify their answers.

Predicting: Predicting should be considered a part of questioning. There are special circumstances for when or when not to use predicting as an effective strategy. Predicting before reading can sometimes lead to wild guessing (i.e., when the predicting can't be supported by clues given in the text). For example, it would be fruitless to ask students to predict what a book is going to be about when they haven't yet opened it. By contrast, good predictions are steeped in information provided in the text that lead to some logical thoughts. Ask yourself this question before asking students to predict: "Will these predictions help my students better understand the text's message?"

I once observed a situation where a teacher had students predict before the text was read. Twenty minutes later, the lesson was over, and the students were still making predictions that were useless in understanding what they were going to read. Be very stingy with your time. How you spend each minute in small group is important!

After Reading

Summarizing with Vocabulary: This simple activity can be powerful at all stages because the complexity of the vocabulary grows as the stages progress. Review the preselected vocabulary you previewed before reading and ask students to use each word in a sentence that tells something about the story or information they learned from the text. Be sure that students use the words in complete sentences that are about the text and not about themselves.

Revisiting the Purpose: At the conclusion of every lesson, the comprehension focus will be discussed in detail. Do not overlook the power of a comprehension conversation. These conversations should always begin by returning to the original purpose given prior to reading the text and should be strongly supported by evidence from the text. Finally, it should be followed up with a written assignment centered on the comprehension focus.

Writing About Reading

The teaching and practice of reading and writing should go hand in hand. In the frameworks presented in this book, students write about a text they read in small groups. Here is what you must know and understand. Writing has a strong effect on reading comprehension. Graham and Hebert (2010) carried out a review of more than 100 studies that documented students' writing about texts and found without question that the students who responded to text with writing improved their comprehension. Additionally, they did better than students who only read and reread or only read and discussed. That is impressive!

But if you think about it, the skills and strategies you use for reading are very similar to the skills needed when writing. As you explore the rest of this book, you will see that at each developmental stage, the writing assignments closely correlate to reading levels. In fact, the Common Core State Standards often call for teachers to combine reading and writing. How can we expect students who read at a 2nd grade level to meet 3rd grade writing standards? Although writing is not taught directly in small groups, you will teach writing in whole-group instruction. The beauty of small-group instruction is that students can apply their writing knowledge as they respond to text they can actually read. The comprehension discussions during small groups will clearly support the writing extension so students are more confident. It may sound obvious, but I find that my students perform much better in writing when they can read and understand the text they are writing about.

There is a plethora of writing extensions that can be completed independently as a follow-up to small-group differentiated reading and writing. In small groups, the teacher can introduce writing responses with the expectation that students will complete them independently. Although most of the writing about reading will take place in independent practice, you will still want to demonstrate how to construct written responses in small groups. This is particularly important when students are asked to write in a new format. With more advanced students, the teacher may also model the use of a graphic organizer or another activity so students are confident using them when they write independently.

Independent Literacy Activities: Extensions That Support Small-Group Differentiated Reading and Writing

One of the most common questions teachers ask is "What are the other students doing while I am teaching small groups?" Teachers often work harder than their students when they create activities to keep students busy. The management of small-group differentiated instruction is often the most difficult part of its implementation. This requires appropriate texts and meaningful extension activities that support students' learning outside the small-group environment. As the teacher is providing small-group instruction, the other students should be engaged in meaningful extension activities, which extend from the work completed in small groups and are designed to keep students occupied in learning activities that will continue to develop them as readers and writers—rather than simply keep them busy. Why didn't I think of this 30 years ago?

What are the most effective activities for students to engage in independently? The answer is quite simple. Look to the research-based components of small groups that should be practiced and reinforced independently: fluency, word study, vocabulary, and comprehension. The bottom line is this: Students need to be doing more reading, writing, and word study at their respective independent developmental levels. The next step, therefore, is to identify practical, easy-to-implement activities that provide independent practice for these critical components.

Fluency is the easiest to implement and appropriate for everyone. For example, the extension might be "reread your book with your small-group partner." All students use a book from small group so you just differentiated the activity for your whole class. Even better, you know they can actually read the book! Older students might enjoy choosing a poem to practice during the week and then present to the rest of the class.

Just as students perform at differing reading levels, they also differ in their word study and writing levels. By following the word study scope and sequence described in this book and administering the spelling assessments, teachers will be knowledgeable about individual students' levels. Apply the same philosophy for Independent word study activities. For example, if students in the small groups have completed work on common vowel patterns for *i* and are now working on patterns for *o*, an appropriate Independent activity would be to practice with both the vowel patterns previously taught and the patterns currently being studied.

Word hunts where students search for words in books that follow the same patterns they are studying are also a hit. One of my favorite easy activities is to ask students to be "word detectives." Students have a list of the words being studied, and they are asked, for example, to see how many words they can make plural. How many could be a homophone? Use two words as nouns in a sentence. Find words with multiple meanings. The possibilities are endless! This is a sneaky way to include those pesky grammar skills without wasting valuable whole-group time!

Vocabulary in independent practice can be two-fold. Younger students can work on sight words or write sentences with text vocabulary to summarize, and older students can search for words with a specific Latin root. Differentiating activities never looked so appealing!

Writing in response to reading can be trickier. What about students who aren't yet writing? Drawing and scribbling are precursors to writing, so allow students who can't write to draw their responses to text. The writing that students complete should be centered on books they have read in small groups or that you have read to them. Writing that encourages the comprehension of text is important. Gradually introduce and model written responses in your whole-group instruction. Model this for students as you complete a shared writing activity in response to a read-aloud or shared reading. As students reach the later Fledgling stage, they should be producing most of their own writing.

Let me again emphasize that for students to be successful with independent activities, teachers should model and discuss the expectations for each activity. This can be easily accomplished in both the whole group and small groups. It is essential that teachers model for and practice with students before asking them to complete any of these activities on their own. Chapters 4–9 provide additional extension activities appropriate for each developmental stage.

The activities discussed in this chapter provide additional practice with materials and activities that spin out of small-group instruction. Thus, students in every small group could complete the same extension activity—but with material that is on their respective levels. Please keep in mind that students need uninterrupted time to write, and most of that writing is completed outside small-group instruction. The extension activities allow for meaningful learning while you are working with other small groups.

Conclusion

Without question, we must look to the strong research base in reading and writing to guide our literacy instruction. Perhaps the most frustrating part of this process is when we take this research and incorporate it into everyday literacy instruction. It has been my mission to provide this information to teachers so they have more time to plan and teach. This chapter reviewed the research base upon which the small-group differentiated reading and writing models were created. Unlike a basal or boxed program (which requires teachers to conform to a rigid format), teachers are encouraged to make instructional decisions based on the students in their classrooms. With a firm grasp on the developmental stages of reading, word study, and writing, teachers will be able to make informed instructional decisions that will promote literacy success for all students. As teachers plan with these research-based components in mind, students' learning will intensify.

Chapter 3

Assessments

Introduction

Perhaps the most frustrating part of teaching today is an overabundance of assessments. Are you part of the club that feels like you spend most of your instructional time testing? You are not alone. Across the nation, teachers assess for a multitude of purposes stemming from federal, state, and district mandates. However, far too many of these assessments provide far too little valuable information to help teachers plan for appropriate instruction. In fact, many states do not receive scores from end-of-year testing until the fall. Teaching without vital information concerning students' strengths and weaknesses is like driving at night without headlights. The glare from the confused and misinterpreted use of assessments often confuses our insights about children and their learning. Unfortunately, the result can be a blinding glare from countless headlights pointing in different directions, and most assessments do not provide teachers with the information they need for day-to-day instructional decisions. Hang with me. The assessments presented in this chapter will be easy to administer and make you far more comfortable in making solid day-to-day instructional decisions.

The assessments that support the models presented in this book are simple and take very little time away from instruction. Additionally, the information from these assessments gives you the information needed to immediately guide instruction for that particular group of students. Unfortunately, we have no choice concerning the assessments that are mandated. We do, however, have an opportunity to use easy-to-administer assessments that can guide our everyday decisions about small-group literacy instruction. It takes time to decide which assessment might be the most effective and appropriate in a situation. My goal is to help teachers so they have more time to teach passionately, with boundless energy and patience. The assessment tools in this book will increase your confidence in recognizing each student's literacy strengths and weaknesses and how to effectively address them in small-group instruction.

Formative Assessment

The small-group instructional model is grounded in formative assessment used to guide the instructional process. Formative assessment is an ongoing process, not necessarily the end result of instruction that is reflected by a grade or score. The data provides feedback that is used to adjust teaching throughout the instructional sequence. The responsive nature of any formative assessment creates a cycle that transforms instruction as well as the learner. In other words, formative assessment revolves around how students learn and is embedded in the instructional process.

Formative assessment is critical in guiding the small-group differentiated reading and writing models presented in this book. Using these models, teachers use formative assessment to guide decisions about instructional reading levels, word study sequence, writing, high-frequency words, and vocabulary. Formative assessment qualifies as "assessment *for* learning" rather than "assessment *of* learning," and it can turn the classroom assessment process and its results into an instructional intervention that increases—not merely monitors—student learning (Stiggins, 2005).

Fluency Assessments

Assessing fluency goes hand in hand with assessing the text level appropriate for small-group instruction. This is important! The most effective text to use in small groups is the one that most closely resembles a student's instructional reading level. There are three reading levels used to describe a reader: independent level, instructional level, and frustration level. Independent text levels, where students read at 96–100 percent accuracy, should be used when students are reading without teacher support, including center work or take-home assignments. Instructional level texts (90–95 percent accuracy) are ideal for small-group instruction as teachers guide readers through slightly more difficult text than a student can read independently. Finally, the frustration level (below 90 percent accuracy) should be avoided at all costs. Students will likely be crying or misbehaving when presented with text they cannot read or understand, even with teacher support. Additionally, asking students to read text at this level will most certainly cause you to pull your hair out! Nevertheless, these harder texts are great for teacher read-alouds!

So how can we assess this as painlessly as possible? Remember, fluency is defined as the speed, accuracy, and expression students need to read and understand a given text. That said, I am convinced that the accuracy piece is the most important. Chances are, your district may already require you to use one assessment or another to gather this information. Go with what you already have to do. Look at the accuracy score closely and give it more weight than speed or expression if you have that leeway. In the following sections, I discuss ways to evaluate fluency and appropriate instructional text levels for small-group instruction. Don't do more than is necessary to get the information you need to make good decisions.

Running Records

The crux of a running record, in terms of small-group instruction, is to establish a student's appropriate instructional text level. Running records may also be used to identify patterns in errors that can be helpful for guiding instruction. They are also the most commonly used tools when assessing fluency and can be used to assess speed, accuracy, and expression (Clay, 2000). This type of formative assessment documents teachers' observations of reading behaviors to collect and analyze students' reading abilities. In essence, the teacher acts as a camera writing down the significant behaviors and interactions as they happen.

Begin with a text that is approximated to the student's instructional level (i.e., a book read between 90 and 94 percent accuracy). If you are unsure, start with a grade-level text and adjust up or down to the correct level as you record findings. For example, if a student only makes one accuracy mistake in a passage, choose the next text up in difficulty for assessment. Fluency is monitored more frequently at the Fledgling, Transitional, and Fluent stages because text level moves more quickly at those stages. In my opinion, you can observe individual students in small groups and glean much of this same information and save yourself a lot of time.

One of the most important insights I have gained is the fact that completing a running record at the Emergent, Beginning, and early Fledgling stages often gives misleading information and may track students into a book level that is too low. Why? Students are penalized for accuracy in reading proper nouns and are expected to use picture clues to understand non-decodable words. Many times, students don't even know the names of the pictures! Too many students have been left in repetitive text when they have the sight word knowledge necessary to move forward. When teaching young students to read, the focus is on concept of print, tracking print, and a return sweep to the next line. When students are held responsible for words that are not common sight words, the value of the assessment is questionable.

Please understand that until students can recognize and read 100 high-frequency words, you may be much more accurate in determining appropriate text levels using their high-frequency word knowledge as a guide to instructional book level. I developed a correlation chart over the years that very accurately predicts the number of high-frequency words a student recognizes automatically and the instructional book level appropriate for that student. This has been a big "a-ha" in my continuing professional work. I was struggling to figure out why so many students never left level A or B when I realized that the standard had been set for students to read all these words without support. What we should actually be assessing is the concept of a word, tracking print with a return sweep, and some very simple sight words. Armed with this information, I began to see students make great strides in their instructional book levels.

With that in mind, refer to Figure 2.8 (page 34), which correlates the number of high-frequency words students know with instructional book level. Please trust me—this is tried and true. When we only use a detailed running record with early readers, we could be holding them back for the reasons previously discussed.

A running record is real-time observational evidence that supports the teacher's instructional decisions using the most valuable tool for learning: the student. There are, however, some drawbacks with running records. Teachers must be highly trained in this process, and they can be very time-consuming to administer. Don't let this scare you off! Use the running records, or the parts you like, and move on. Do you have extra time to give each student a running record that could take 30–45 minutes? I sincerely doubt it. Using a true running record with your struggling readers might be another option, and perhaps you could use the Reading Review (discussed in the next section) for the remainder of the class.

Reading Review

For schools that have a standard assessment in place for determining fluency and instructional reading levels, I recommend staying with that assessment. There is no need to reinvent the wheel. Therefore, use that information along with the Reading Review as a tool to monitor student reading progress informally. Although running records are important in diagnosing specific strengths and weaknesses in readers, a complete running record may not be necessary to determine when to move a group to the next reading level. A simplified version of the traditional running record model, the Reading Review (which I developed) serves this purpose and acts as an oral reading fluency measure for accuracy.

The Reading Review is a quick assessment that can be completed with relative ease, allowing you more chances to record students' oral reading accuracy than if you were completing a more time-consuming running record. Again, we are trying to identify the student's appropriate instructional level, which is somewhere between 90 and 95 percent accuracy. This is the highest level a student can read successfully with supervision and support by the teacher. This "zone of proximal development" is the place where students are ripe for instruction (Vygotsky, 1978). Children learn best when they receive help from experts on tasks that would be too difficult for them to accomplish on their own.

Begin by selecting a book that students have never read before as a basis for assessment and mark a 100-word passage. (Do not include words on the cover or title page.) This should be a book at the small group's current instructional level. For early readers, a picture walk of the book might be appropriate; more advanced readers should be given only the title and a brief introduction to the book. As students read, the teacher makes a check whenever the student misses a word. Words that are self-corrected within three seconds are not counted as mistakes. Proper nouns are counted as incorrect the first time only. If a student skips a line, it is counted as one mistake. If a student does not know a word, wait three seconds and then tell him or her the word—then count it as one mistake. When the initial passage is completed, quickly check to determine the percentage of correctly read words, counting one point for each mistake. If the student reads with a 96 percent or greater accuracy rate, then the book is too easy, and a book at the next level up should be attempted. Students reading at 90–95 percent accuracy are at the appropriate instructional level and make good candidates for a cohesive small group. For a student reading below a 90 percent accuracy rate, complete Reading Reviews at subsequently lower levels until the student can read with an accuracy rate of between 90 and 95 percent.

This strategy can also be used for students reading at a lower level. Simply use 50-word passages (instead of 100). The accuracy rate is determined by counting two points for each mistake. Be sure that the test is administered consistently among readers; follow the same procedures for all students for the most reliable information. Keep in mind that Reading Reviews are not appropriate at the earliest reading stages. Students must first be confident in tracking print and have substantial high-frequency word recognition before this assessment is valid.

Although it may not always be possible to group students based on their exact instructional levels, the Reading Review is useful for group placement. Reading groups should remain flexible as students are routinely assessed and rearranged among groups. Reading Reviews allow teachers to collect a significant amount of data on students as they progress through the year.

To complete the Reading Review, a set of benchmarks must be dedicated to the assessment process. Several textbook companies offer sets of these books. Alternatively, each school or group of teachers can meet and assign books for each level. These benchmark books should be used only for Reading Reviews—for ongoing, formative assessment—and for making decisions about when to move individuals or the entire reading group to the next level. If most students in a group do well at the current book level, then the teacher should feel confident about moving them all up to the next level. Conversely, students who do poorly could be shifted to a lower reading group.

Word Study Assessments

Most teachers are aware of the importance of instructional reading levels, and in many instances, they have reading assessments in place. Word study, however, is typically taught as spelling in whole-group instruction and grounded in grade-level standards. Any word study in small-group instruction, if at all, is generally a review of the whole-group skill. This might work well for on-level students, but for students who are significantly below or above level, this routine misses the mark. Struggling students can miss important foundational skills they lack, and advanced students are restricted to instruction they no longer need. As teachers become more aware of their students' word study levels, they will become more skillful in delivering both whole-group and small-group instruction.

Spelling Assessments

These spelling assessments are used to guide word study at the Emergent, Beginning, Fledgling, Transitional, and Fluent (5A) stages. They can also be used at subsequent stages where the focus is solely on the spelling patterns. Other word meaning assessments will become more appropriate for the later stages. With spelling assessments, we are simply assessing how well students have mastered the patterns being taught. These assessments can also be used initially to group students. For example, a 1st grade teacher might administer an assessment for common word families at the beginning of the school year (Stage 3A) to form initial groups. A score of 80 percent and above is considered mastery for all spelling assessments. After this, the teacher could group students and test for the next stage up or down for group placement.

Let's look at an assessment given after a group of six students completed Stage 3A in small groups. The group assessment results show that four of the six students reached mastery at 80 percent or above; however, the other two scored 70 percent and 50 percent. (See Figure 3.1 for an example of one of these spelling assessments.) At this point, the teacher could look for common mistakes and plan for a week of reteaching. Most likely, the student scoring 70 percent will pass the next assessment, but the other student may not reach proficiency. If this is the case, the teacher needs to look for a more appropriate group placement for that student. Alternatively, she will have to provide additional support during intervention time or allow the student to work between two groups, which makes good sense for struggling readers and writers.

Once an initial word study placement is made, the teacher follows a specific scope and sequence as students progress through the word study guidelines provided in this small-group framework. Consider the word study scope and sequences for each stage as pacing guides. Each lesson in the sequence is for one day of instruction. A rule of thumb is to never stay longer on a pattern than the sequence dictates. I have found that it is more useful for students to be exposed to all the patterns since they begin to see relationships among word patterns. On the other hand, if the teacher feels that a group has mastered the patterns earlier than the sequence indicates, it's fine to move to the next pattern sequence. In other words, lessons can be skipped but not added. After students reach Fluent Stage 5B, it is suggested that the patterns be studied for one week. Again, teacher judgment will determine the amount of time spent with each set of patterns.

All word study assessments, word study cards, and supporting materials are located online at www.beverlytyner.net. In Chapters 4–9, the assessments, word study scope and sequences, and activities that support each stage will be thoroughly discussed. When the group finishes the sequence, the word study assessment is given to the group.

Meaning Assessments

As students master basic vowel patterns, the meaning aspect of words and word parts become equally important. For example, in the study of prefixes and suffixes, you would want to know not only if students can spell the words correctly but also if they can write a sentence with the word to demonstrate the correct meaning. These are two different—though equally important—skills. After giving a spelling assessment for prefixes, students could then independently write a sentence with each word. You can make decisions about how you want to assess based on the patterns being studied.

Figure 3.1

Sample Spelling Assessment

Spelling Assessment Sheet

Assessment Stage: _3A_

85%

1. Wet
2. sic
3. duck
4. bac
5. sit
6. jig
7. fen
8. van
9. sot x
10. jop x

11. mob
12. sok x
13. shut
14. plug
15. bell
16. map
17. bat
18. shed
19. when
20. sun

Vocabulary Assessments

The importance of understanding a wide variety of vocabulary words for reading and writing comprehension cannot be overstated. For a variety of reasons, students are at more of a deficit than ever when it comes to vocabulary knowledge.

I suspect that it has a lot to do with a multitude of other distractions, a diminishing number of parents who read to their children, and limited opportunities to engage in authentic conversation. Whatever the reasons, our job is to adjust our instruction to address this need. No, we can't go home with them every night, but we can be intentional in small-group instruction and develop the vocabulary students need to understand the text. Although conversations about the words and pictures in a story are a given, intentional vocabulary instruction begins with an intense focus of the most common sight words seen in beginning text. After these words are mastered, selected vocabulary should be discussed before, during, and after reading to summarize the text.

High-Frequency Words

The mastery of the first 100 high-frequency words is an important milestone in the early reading process. It is one of the critical pieces in determining when to adjust instructional reading levels in the first three stages: Emergent, Beginning, and Fledgling. The High-Frequency Word Assessment (Figure 3.2) can be given initially to make sound instructional decisions and then for monitoring purposes as students master the first 100 words.

As students complete the first 100 high-frequency words, teachers will be focusing on vocabulary selected from the text. Teachers can easily assess vocabulary by asking students to write a sentence using each word that tells something about the text. Not only can vocabulary be assessed in these written sentences, but it can also be done as students give sentences orally after reading the text. Additionally, students could write another sentence of their own with the word in the correct context. Teachers often ask how they can assess students in small groups; this is an example of a quick and easy way to assess not only vocabulary but also comprehension, as students are required to give vocabulary in the context of the text. Figure 3.3 shows a written vocabulary assessment for a 3rd grader after reading *King Midas and the Golden Touch*. This assessment shows that the student has a clear understanding of these vocabulary words, and it was completed in an independent extension. This gives the teacher a clear way of assessing the focus text vocabulary. Remember, the vocabulary from text written in content areas may also be included so you can build vocabulary in all subject areas.

Comprehension Assessments

Without a doubt, comprehension is the most difficult skill to assess. Comprehension is best described as a web of reading and writing skills that must come together in a precise way to create an understanding of text. As you are reading, questioning, and guiding students through text, there are numerous opportunities to informally assess comprehension. Historically, a Friday comprehension test was the baseline for competency. However, many teachers read a story multiple times with students, as well as sending it home to read again. It is unrealistic to think that one assessment of a text is indicative of true independent reading comprehension. For this skill to be correctly assessed, students must read and answer questions independently.

A true gauge of comprehension would be when a "cold read" is given to students, who then answer (either orally or in writing) supporting text-dependent questions. Reading and discussing the text in small groups and then writing about it may be a good comprehension assessment but only if that piece of comprehension was not previously discussed. For example, after reading a text about pollution, you could ask students to choose which type of pollution (water, air, or land) is the most dangerous and why, using text evidence for support. This is opinion writing, but the topic was not discussed in small-group discussions.

Text-Dependent Questions

Please remember that all assessment does not need to be for a grade. When students answer text-dependent questions, they help guide you where to go next in your instruction. A powerful in-group observation can be done when students are asked to tag evidence and answer a question with a sticky note. Which students are delving quickly into the text to find the answer? Which students immediately look to their neighbors for help? Never ridicule a child for looking to another student for help; this simply tells you that they don't know what to do and need your guided support. Many teachers simply write five to eight text-dependent questions for students to respond to in writing when they need a grade.

Writing in Response to Reading

Perhaps one of the most efficient ways to assess comprehension is by having students write in response to a text they have read. Not only does this demonstrate certain aspects of comprehension (e.g., character traits, lessons learned), but it also assesses many grammar standards along with grade-level writing standards. This provides an opportunity to cross curricular lines and assess more efficiently. Remember that everything that is assigned does not need to be assessed. Students need to be given support in mastering new skills without the threat of always being graded.

Figure 3.2
High-Frequency Word Assessment

Name of Student: _____ Number Correct: _____

1–25	Date	Date	Date	Date		26–50	Date	Date	Date	Date		51–75	Date	Date	Date	Date		76–100	Date	Date	Date	Date
1 the						26 he						51 be						76 cat				
2 a						27 out						52 now						77 them				
3 and						28 that						53 when						78 tree				
4 to						29 one						54 there						79 where				
5 I						30 big						55 into						80 away				
6 in						31 go						56 day						81 time				
7 is						32 was						57 look						82 as				
8 on						33 like						58 eat						83 water				
9 you						34 what						59 make						84 home				
10 it						35 not						60 his						85 made				
11 of						36 do						61 here						86 long				
12 said						37 then						62 your						87 has				

#	Word	#	Word	#	Word	#	Word
13	can	38	this	63	an	88	help
14	for	39	no	64	back	89	good
15	my	40	too	65	mom	90	going
16	but	41	she	66	dog	91	by
17	all	42	went	67	very	92	how
18	we	43	see	68	did	93	house
19	are	44	will	69	her	94	dad
20	up	45	so	70	from	95	or
21	at	46	some	71	had	96	two
22	with	47	down	72	got	97	red
23	me	48	little	73	put	98	am
24	they	49	come	74	came	99	over
25	have	50	get	75	just	100	saw

Figure 3.3

Vocabulary Assessment

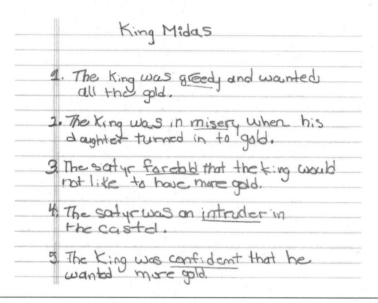

King Midas

1. The King was greedy and wanted all the gold.

2. The King was in misery when his daughter turned in to gold.

3. The satyr foretold that the king would not like to have more gold.

4. The satyr was an intruder in the castel.

5. The King was confident that he wanted more gold.

Writing Rubrics

Writing naturally lends itself to the use of portfolios and rubrics to qualify expectations and judge products objectively. In the small-group differentiated models, writing is addressed as it demonstrates a comprehension of text but can also include elements of grammar and writing structure. This writing can cover narrative text, informational/explanatory text, and opinion writing. Considering the developmental nature of writing, maintain observational checklists to guide individual writing conferences with students. A vital factor in writing assessments is the teacher's ability to prompt students to narrow the focus for the purpose of revisions.

Writing products may be assessed holistically or by specific targeted traits using rubrics. Writing rubrics describe common traits found at various levels of development or skill attainment. An example of a teacher-created writing rubric that assesses an understanding of character traits is shown in Figure 3.4. This rubric clarifies the teacher's expectations for 2nd graders who are identifying a character trait with an example from the text. The student sample in Figure 3.5 shows a 2nd grader's grasp of writing in a focused and well-organized manner at the Transitional stage. Based on the rubric, the teacher gave this student a 4. The character and trait were identified and supported by text evidence. The writing was also well organized and included an appropriate closure.

Figure 3.4

Sample 2nd Grade Writing Rubric

Identifying Character Traits and Supporting with Text Evidence		
Level	Description	Looks Like...
1	Unobservable	• Lacks relevant identification of character trait or example from the text • Lacks closure or organization to response
2	Emerging	• Includes loose ideas with little connection to text evidence • Includes minimal details and development of idea
3	Developing	• Identifies appropriate character trait but gives incorrect example from text evidence • Includes some extraneous details and/or limited organization
4	Proficient	• Identifies appropriate character trait identified with example from text for support • Includes sequential organization and sense of closure to response

---

Figure 3.5

Sample 2nd Grade Writing Response: Character Traits

The Secret Cave

In the book the "Secret Cave," he and his sister got lost. When they hear strange noises, Peter has to be brave and find out what is making the noise. It was dark inside the cave and it was raining, but Peter still tried to be brave. When he went in, he found bats. The bats were scary, but not as scary as a bear! This is how Peter was brave in the story.

Writing Conferences

Let me include a word or two about writing conferences. Understand that writing conferences should not take the place of small-group instruction. As we seek to improve students' writing, nothing replaces a one-on-one writing conference.

These conferences allow teachers to focus on areas of strengths and weaknesses in writing as well as comprehension, and they help establish goals for future written comprehension responses. You are working not only on comprehension but also on grammar and structural issues.

Writing Checklists

Teaching students the art of writing was difficult for me. I and other teachers like me have found writing checklists helpful in providing guidance for students as they compose text. Checklists provide opportunities to focus the writing on specific purposes, and they can be easily used as a rubric. In Figure 3.6, a 5th grade teacher developed a detailed writing checklist after reading *The One-Inch Boy* in small groups. The teacher set the purpose for reading by asking students to look for character traits that made the One-Inch Boy successful. This checklist was used as a guide for students as they wrote independently. The teacher also used the checklist as a scoring rubric, assigning scores to each of the four points. Figure 3.7 shows an example of a student's completed assignment.

The student response was well organized and met the criteria in the first, second, and fourth points. Although there was a final paragraph, it included only three sentences. The teacher expected more information and a more cohesive paragraph. The student scored a 90 percent. This tells the teacher that perhaps she should include more details about the paragraph length in the next assignment.

Figure 3.6
Writing Checklist for The One-Inch Boy

The One-Inch Boy overcame his small size and used it to his advantage to reach his goals. Additionally, he exhibited strong character traits that contributed to his success. Write an essay describing how this was shown in the story.

- 25 points: Include a strong opening paragraph that gives a short summary of this folktale. Make sure you have enough information about the story so that anyone reading it will understand the topic. Make it clear to your audience what you will be writing about.
- 25 points: In the next paragraph, discuss at least three character traits the One-Inch Boy displayed in the story and how they helped him be successful. Give text evidence to support your discussions. Include at least one quote to support this discussion.
- 25 points: Use your final paragraph to tie the main ideas together and show how you've addressed your original topic.
- 25 points: Check your capitalization, punctuation, and spelling carefully.

Figure 3.7

Sample Student Response

You may think that a one-inch boy could not do many things. But in the story, "The One Inch Boy," the boy could do many things. He was found on the doorstep of a man and a woman. He helped them around the house and they loved him. He wanted to leave and seek his fortune and he told his parents he would send for them. After he killed the ogre and married the princess, he sent for his parents. He was able to reach his fortune even though the One-Inch Boy was so small.

The character traits that the boy showed in the story helped the One-Inch Boy reach his fortune. First, he was very brave. When the Ogre took the Noble's daughter, he challenged him not to do that or he would use his sword. The boy said, "Leave this beautiful lady alone, or you shall feel my sword." He had to be really brave to say that to the Ogre, and he would never have reached his fortune. One of the most important traits that helped him reach his fortune was his persistence. He was persistent when his parents did not want him to go and said, "I want to go to Kyoto to seek my fortune if you would allow it." It paid off because they decided to let him go to Kyoto. He was persistent in his journey, like when the boat was getting ready to sink, he did not give up. He also didn't give up when he met the Ogre. Finally, the One Inch Boy was a hard worker. He helped his parents with the chores. When he asked the Noble if he could stay there, he told him, "I will serve you well for food and a place to stay." Because he was willing to work, he eventually married the Noble's daughter.

The One Inch boy was successful and reached his fortune. He was brave, persistent, and hardworking. These traits all helped him reach his goal.

Observational Records

When you routinely spend time with students in small groups, you have ample opportunities to observe students as they participate in activities and discussions. I find these observations extremely valuable to judge students' progress. For example, as students complete a spelling sort in a small group, you can note who may need extra assistance. During a discussion of words with focused homophones, you might observe students who struggle to create oral sentences that demonstrate their knowledge of the word meanings and spend extra time on this during the next lesson. What I am saying here is to trust your eyes, ears, and gut, and stop worrying so much about assessments!

Many skills in the area of literacy can be assessed through observation. Levels of social development and oral language are seldom assessed accurately through other means. Many cues to instructional implications can only be determined through observation of student conversations. Concept awareness, use of sentence structure, and vocabulary functioning are highlighted through informal observations during small-group instruction. Effective teachers are adept at picking up on students' behavioral signals and adapting instruction accordingly. Teachers are able to hear students' conversations to determine their true depth of knowledge.

Portfolio Assessment

Many states are now turning to portfolios as a means of tracking student progress. A portfolio is a collection of purposefully selected artifacts that showcase individual students' successes and achievements. A portfolio broadens the scope of assessment by considering a range of skills or concepts the student has achieved over a period of time according to known criteria.

Small-group differentiated reading and writing provides an excellent opportunity to include portfolios. For example, a chart that tracks reading levels can provide valuable information. Word study assessments can also contain information concerning both decoding and writing. Vocabulary assessments demonstrate growth as students grow as readers and writers. Writing in response to text evidences comprehension and is a valuable addition to a portfolio. To get the most accurate snapshot of literacy development, provide a variety of opportunities for students to write across content areas and in response to literature and expository text. The portfolio and accompanying rubrics become a base upon which you can balance assessment and measure next steps for instruction. Writing samples yield evidence of coordinated skills application and drive enhancement of skills or remediation. Include your own observational and anecdotal records and review the portfolio regularly with the student.

Conclusion

Perhaps no other topic is as frustrating or important than assessments and grading. There are certainly many formal assessments that can be used, but they are often lengthy and time-consuming. Many teachers are already overwhelmed with state- or district-mandated assessments to administer additional "tests." That said, choose any additional assessments carefully and for a specific purpose.

Generally, mandated assessments give teachers very little information in terms of guiding literacy instruction for individual students. These assessments also take major chunks of time away from classroom instruction. For this reason, it is not my intention to saddle teachers with even more assessments that give little data to guide student instruction. The assessments described in this chapter are short and effective in assessing reading levels, word study levels, high-frequency word knowledge, vocabulary awareness, and comprehension—both orally and written.

Without these valuable data, teachers are "shooting in the dark" and will surely miss the mark in terms of delivering developmental literacy instruction that all students need to reach their highest potential.

Now that we have established the basic frameworks and research that support these frameworks, Chapters 4–9 will delve into the specific implementation of each stage. In other words, we have established the "why," and now we're onto the good stuff... the "how"! Each of the following chapters will define the characteristics of students at each stage and include step-by-step lesson directions along with dialogue that allows you to "become an inside observer" in how the lesson unfolds. As you move through each chapter, you will become more aware of the developmental progression of students as readers and writers.

Chapter 4

The Emergent Reader and Writer

Characteristics of Emergent Readers and Writers

Early Emergent readers are usually nonreaders with little alphabet knowledge or are just beginning to exhibit some characteristics of early readers. They are typically prekindergarten to midyear kindergarten students who recognize less than half the alphabet. In some cases, they may not recognize any letters. Another characteristic of Emergent readers and writers is their inability to track print or point to individual words as they read. Emergent readers know few—if any—high-frequency words. Finally, Emergent readers generally lack phonemic awareness; they are unable to attend to individual sounds within spoken words. These students have special needs in the area of written language learning that are difficult to meet in the context of whole-class instruction. It is, therefore, important to address all the critical needs of Emergent readers and writers in a small-group setting.

There are other students who may fall into this Emergent stage who are not in prekindergarten or kindergarten. They could include students with special needs, ELLs, or even capable children who have never been in school before. I was recently in a situation where two boys entered school for the first time (they had supposedly been homeschooled), and they recognized less than half the alphabet. They were placed in 2nd grade and were 9 years old. These were clearly Emergent readers and writers regardless of their age or grade. To become literate, they had to work with someone to fill in huge gaps in a hurry, starting at the

Emergent stage. The school talked about putting these students in kindergarten, which was less than a brilliant idea. These boys needed to be with peers—or at least not 5-year-olds!

On the other end of the spectrum, some kindergarten students may have already passed through the Emergent or even Beginning stage and need to be placed in the Fledgling stage. When we truly engage in differentiated instruction, we must look at what students can and cannot do—not necessarily their age and assigned grade level.

The Emergent stage has two very distinct parts. In the first part (1A), students are introduced to small-group instruction with the Early Literacy Foundational Skills (ELFS) lessons. Because students are not given text to read, the lesson plans are significantly different from the subsequent plans beginning in Emergent 1B and throughout the other stages. These ELFS (26 lessons) are intended for prereaders and focused on building alphabet recognition and production and on basic phonemic awareness (including recognizing beginning consonant sounds, rhyming, and blending and segmenting word parts). The ELFS lessons also focus on oral language development and sentence structure.

The second part of the Emergent stage (1B) moves to a more structured lesson plan that supports fluency, vocabulary (high-frequency words), word study (alphabet recognition and production), and comprehension. This stage supports putting books in the hands of students with more directed instruction in reading and writing. Don't make the mistake of waiting until students know the entire alphabet or numerous high-frequency words before allowing students to "read" books. On the contrary, young children need plenty of experiences with books to learn how the process of reading works. The books can be very short and supported with a repetitive sentence structure. Students are also working on the automatic recognition of the first 15 high-frequency words they will most likely see in these early texts.

Word study for Emergent readers and writers begins with the ELFS lessons in Stage 1A. Students are engaged in activities that support hearing individual sounds in words, as well as blending and segmenting these sounds and identifying rhyming words. Their study of the alphabet includes both recognizing and producing individual letters. As students progress to the 1B stage, they will continue to solidify their alphabet knowledge. The development of reading and writing occurs simultaneously and reflects development in oral language and phonics knowledge (Sulzby, 2000).

The expectations at the Emergent reader and writer stage—including book level, word study, high-frequency words, comprehension, and writing—are shown in Figure 4.1.

Figure 4.1

Stage 1: Emergent Reader and Writer

	Fluency	Vocabulary	Word Study	Reading Comprehension	Writing About Reading
Emergent 1A	• Typically, mid-PreK to mid-K • No books used	Oral language development	Early Literacy Foundational Skills (ELFS): • developing phonemic awareness • rhyming • blending • segmenting beginning, middle, and ending sounds • segmenting word parts • recognizing and writing the alphabet	n/a	Drawing and "writing" about books read aloud by the teacher
Emergent 1B	• Book Levels EI 1/2, F&P A/B • Patterned text • Rereading to develop fluency	Recognizing the first 15 high-frequency words	Alphabet recognition and production	• Using memory and pictures to read • Concepts of print • Tracking print in repetitive text	• Producing some alphabet letters in writing • Drawing and "writing" about reading (scribbling/letter strings) • Dictating appropriate sentence to the teacher about drawing that reflects purpose of response

EI: Early Intervention   F&P: Fountas and Pinnell

As students begin to receive formal instruction in writing, it is important to remember that Emergent writers are still focusing on recognizing and writing individual letters. Both Emergent stages (1A and 1B) support this alphabet focus. Writing (or drawing) about reading focuses on students' responses to the books they read in group. For example, they could draw and color their favorite part of a book. In the beginning, students may begin writing anyplace on the page if not given parameters. As beginning readers experiment with writing, there is generally no sense of the left-to-right progression of text. Their writing usually includes large strokes, random marks, and scribbles. As students "draw" about a story, they should be able to tell the teacher about the picture, but their descriptions are usually very vague. The teacher should serve as a scribe to record student talk about their pictures. Although these early writers are just beginning to write about reading, this process allows them to see the connection between reading a story and drawing and writing about the story. Common prekindergarten and kindergarten standards that could be addressed in the lesson components at the Emergent stage are found in the Appendix.

Emergent Readers and Writers: Stage 1A

The Early Literacy Foundational Skills (ELFS) developed out of a need to provide prekindergarten and early kindergarten students with focused instruction on basic literacy foundational skills. Although I observed most teachers working on these skills in whole-group instruction, many students failed to master these critical pre-reading skills. Additionally, some students had already mastered these skills and were not progressing. With an eye on both the standards and the developmental stages of reading and writing, I set out to develop appropriate materials.

This book offers my first opportunity to share these ELFS lessons with all teachers. Each lesson plan is already written, which is especially helpful for busy teachers. Five lessons focus on specific consonant and vowel sounds (and their representative letters), phonemic awareness (including segmenting and blending words and word parts), hearing rhyming words, and isolating initial consonant sounds. Each of the lesson plan elements is supported by activities that are interactive and engaging for students.

It is not expected that all students will recognize and be able to write all letters at the end of the lesson sequence for ELFS. Emergent Stage 1B accommodates for continued instruction in letter recognition and production. There will also be an opportunity to repeat the ELFS lessons for students who still lack basic foundational skills.

Preassessment for ELFS Lessons

When deciding how to group students for instruction, giving a straightforward alphabet recognition and production assessment is very helpful. You may also use additional information gained through direct observations or other mandated assessments. This information usually gives enough data to place students in small groups of no more than six students. Keep in mind that this is not an assessment of how many sounds students can associate with letters—rather, it's how many letters students recognize and can produce (write). Because these groups are flexible, don't spend a lot of time with preassessment; you can move students flexibly after the groups have started.

I suggest letting all prekindergarten and kindergarten students go through these ELFS lessons using the recommended adjustments for higher or lower students. For example, more advanced students can spend fewer than 5 days on the lesson sets if they show mastery, and slower students might divide a lesson plan and spend 10 days on the prescribed five lessons. Use your judgment, but be careful that you are not holding students back. Prekindergarten teachers may start groups earlier or later in the year, depending on the capability of the students. Even the most inattentive students seem to do better when they are in a small-group setting, engaged in activities at which they are successful. Regardless, it is helpful for all prekindergarten students to have the opportunity to go through these lessons before moving to kindergarten. Even students entering kindergarten may sometimes lack phonemic awareness and letter production skills.

Each of the ELFS lessons is structured similarly with seven activities. Note that each activity should be completed in the lesson each day. Lesson pacing is particularly important to ensure that each activity is addressed on a daily basis. With less focused students, the lesson could be divided into two parts that are taught at two different times during the day. Another option is to identify your most struggling students and place them in an intervention group that will repeat the lessons. Figure 4.2 is an example of an ELFS lesson plan. All lesson plans and other materials that support these lessons can be downloaded from www.beverlytyner.net.

ELFS Lesson Plan Elements

Alphabet Matching: Matching uppercase and lowercase letters helps students recognize and discriminate the shapes of various letters. This is a hands-on activity in which each student has his or her own set of letters. This provides high student engagement and supplies teachers with important observational information. It is also valuable for the teacher to have his or her own set of letters that are placed on a tabletop sorting board for reference after students complete the activity. Figure 4.3 shows the pocket chart used by the teacher as the letters are introduced.

Alphabet Production: This activity supports both alphabet recognition and letter production. Simply recognizing the alphabet is not enough; students must also learn how to produce the letters correctly. Many teachers struggle to find time to

Figure 4.2
ELFS Lesson Plan 1

Focus Letters: **B**   **S**   **M**   **A**   **C**

1. Alphabet Matching (uppercase and lowercase letters and their sounds):
- Using only the teacher's set of letters, go over the name and the sound of each uppercase letter as you place them on the board.
- Present the lowercase letters while placing each under the related uppercase letter. Ask if it matches. The students give thumbs up or thumbs down.
- The name and sound for each letter should be repeated as the uppercase and lowercase letters are matched.

2. Alphabet Production:
- Model the letter formation on a whiteboard; then write it again as students make the letter in the air.
- Students use a whiteboard to form the uppercase *B* and lowercase *b*.
- Make sure students continue to make the /b/ sound every time they write the letter.

3. Guess My Word (segmenting and blending onsets and rimes):
- Begin by saying, "Guess my word."
- Vocally segment the word. Students should then say the word.
- Show the picture of the word and ask a volunteer to use the word in a sentence.

Words: ball, cake, man, saw, map

4. Sound Boxes (phoneme segmentation and blending):
- Each student will need a sound box strip and a magic button.
- Say, "Now we are going to listen for sounds in some words. Our first word is *cab*. Say *cab*. Let's touch the sounds in *cab*." (Hold up your hand and touch one finger for each sound: /k/ /a/ /b/.)
- Say, "Watch me write the sounds." Write the letters in your sound boxes. (The students do not write the letters in the box until they can write them quickly and correctly.)
- Say, "Put your magic button in the starting box. Put one finger on your magic button. Let's say the sounds in *cab* the bumpy way." Demonstrate moving your magic button into each of the boxes on the sound box, sound by sound, moving from left to right (i.e., the bumpy way).
- Say, "Now we will say the word the smooth [or fast] way." With a sweeping motion from left to right, have students choral read with you and say the sounds more connected. Students should move their magic buttons across the words.

Words: cab, Sam, bam, Mac

5. Picture Strips (phoneme matching and initial sound fluency):
- Each student will need a picture strip and a magic button.
- Say, "Cover the picture that starts with _____."

Sounds: /b/, /m/, /a/, /k/, /s/

6. Letter Strips (initial sound fluency and initial sound isolation):
- Each student needs a letter strip and a magic button.
- Say, "Cover the letter sound that begins _____."

Words: sandwich, bird, matches, ant, corn

7. Rhyming Bingo Cards:
- Each student needs a bingo card and tokens.
- Say, "Cover the picture that rhymes with [say the first word of the pair]."

Words: mall/ball, make/cake, draw/saw, cap/map, tank/bank, track/sack, take/lake, trap/cap, pan/fan actually teach students correct letter formation. I have found a strong correlation between learning to recognize letters and simultaneously learning how to write the letters. Since each lesson only focuses on one letter, you have time to model the correct formation of each letter and assist students in the process. It's also important to use lined paper with a top, middle, and bottom line. Students are more successful in letter formation when they use lines for correct proportions.

Figure 4.3
Pocket Chart

Guess My Word: This activity is strictly completed orally as it develops important listening skills. The first two sets of lessons focus on onset and rime, which is a common prekindergarten and kindergarten standard. The next three sets of lessons focus on word parts (i.e., syllables). The teacher segments the syllables and the student blends the sounds together to make a word. Students can also create sentences with the words to develop oral language skills. Figure 4.4 shows an example of picture cards for the Guess My Word Activity for Day 1. All the Guess My Word cards are located at www.beverlytyner.net.

Figure 4.4

Guess My Word Picture Cards

Sound Boxes: Without question, the use of sound boxes is a powerful way to teach students that letters make up words and that each letter has a sound. In the beginning lessons, this is strictly a phonemic awareness activity as students segment and blend sounds orally and move a "magic" stone through blank sound boxes to indicate that each box represents a sound. A magic stone can be anything, really. I use smooth acrylic stones that are commonly found in the floral department of craft stores, but you could just as easily use anything you have on hand. The teacher, however, will write the letters in the boxes so the students have a visual to match the sound with a letter. As students become more adept with letter writing, they should write the letters in the boxes along with the teacher. Figure 4.5 is an example of sound boxes used for the word *cat*, as written by the teacher. The sound box template can be downloaded from www.beverly tyner.net.

Figure 4.5

Sound Box Example for the Word *Cat*

c	a	t

Picture Strips: Picture strips allow students to recognize a picture and isolate the beginning sound of the associated picture. This is a very different skill than recognizing that the sound for *b* is /b/. This activity asks students to say a word (by naming a picture) and isolate and produce its beginning sound orally. It is, therefore, a phonemic awareness activity. More advanced students may place the picture strip on a whiteboard and write the initial letter under each picture. All picture strips are different so students don't rely on their neighbors for support. Figure 4.6 shows an example of one of six picture strips provided that can be downloaded from www.beverlytyner.net.

Figure 4.6
Picture Strips

Letter Strips: Letter strips with both uppercase and lowercase letters are used for this activity. The teacher can either rotate the two sets of strips or choose one or the other. If you think about it, students generally learn the uppercase letters more quickly than the lowercase ones, so I use the lowercase strips more frequently. This activity requires multilevel processes and will need to be heavily supported for struggling students. Each student has an individual letter strip. The teacher says a word and then asks students to find the letter that represents the beginning sound in that word. More advanced students can also identify medial or ending sounds in words. Figure 4.7 shows an example of an uppercase and lowercase letter strip used in the first five lessons.

Figure 4.7
Letter Strips

B	S	M	A	C
b	s	m	a	c

Rhyming Cards: Bingo-like game boards are used for this activity. The teacher simply says a word and asks students to find the picture that rhymes with that word. More advanced students can also come up with their own rhyming words to match the picture. Each picture card varies, and students can get a new card each day. Try numbering the back of each card to help with this process. Figure 4.8 shows an example of a rhyming word card for the first five lessons.

Figure 4.8
Rhyming Cards

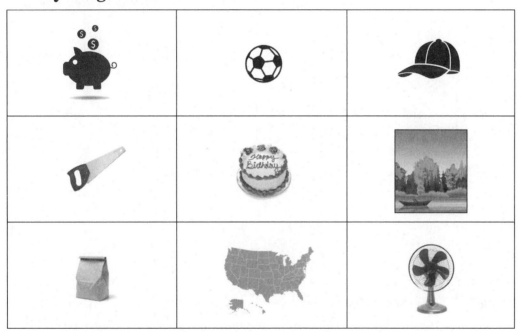

ELFS Detailed Lesson Plan and Vignettes

The following lesson explains each activity in detail with a group of prekindergarten students. Each activity will be discussed in detail, followed with a vignette from the group.

Alphabet Matching: The lesson begins as you give each student a set of the five uppercase and lowercase letters. You also have a set. Hold up a capital letter and say the appropriate name and sound for the letter. After the capital letter is placed on the tabletop pocket, students find the same letter in their personal letter cards, place it on the desk in front of them, and say the letter name and sound. The teacher then presents the lowercase letter and asks students to find the same one in their cards and place it under the matching capital letter. Again, students name the letter and make its sound. This process continues with all the focus letters. As students become more proficient, the teacher can say a letter name and ask students to identify it without visual support. Be vigilant about not giving students too much support.

I have created a template for this activity, which can be downloaded from www.beverlytyner.net, so each student can organize and line up the uppercase and lowercase letters. This will help students keep their letters orderly and not all over the table.

◇◇

Teacher: Let's start today with our alphabet cards. I am going to give each of you a set of five capital and lowercase letters. Please line these letters up in front of you.

(The teacher hands out the capital and lowercase letters Bb, Ss, Mm, Aa, *and* Cc. *The teacher also puts the same letters on the tabletop pocket chart for support, if needed.)*

Teacher: First, I want you to find the capital *B*.

(The teacher observes to see if students need additional support. If they need more support, the teacher could point to the capital B *on the pocket chart so students can locate it more easily.)*

Teacher: I see that most of you found the capital *B*. Now I want you to find the lowercase *b*.

(The teacher places the lowercase b *under the capital* B. *This process continues until five capital and lowercase letters are matched. When each student has his or her own set of letters, the lesson is much more engaging for students and allows the teacher to assess student knowledge of the letters more accurately. This is especially true for students struggling with alphabet recognition. If students already recognize capital and lowercase letters, skip this activity and spend more time in alphabet production.)*

Alphabet Production: Using dry-erase boards with primary writing lines, the teacher demonstrates the formation of the focus letter from the lesson plan. The teacher demonstrates writing the capital letter and then writes the letter again while students practice drawing the letter in the air. Students then practice making the letter on their personal dry-erase boards or on paper. Students should say the appropriate sound as they write. If needed, the teacher may assist struggling students by making a "dotted" letter to trace. The process continues and is repeated with the lowercase letter. As students become more confident in writing the letters, remove the visual cues and ask students to write them from memory. Knowing that there are varying ways to construct the letters, it's a good idea to seek consistency within the school so conflicting methods don't confuse students. Additionally, interchange the terms *uppercase letters* with *capital letters*.

◇◇◇

Teacher: Today we are going to be writing the letter *B*. I am going to make the capital *B* first. Please watch me. I am going to start at the top line and pull straight down to the bottom line. Then I am going to pick my marker up and go back to the top line. I am going to make a half circle that ends at the dotted line in the middle. Now I am going to make another half circle that sits on the bottom line. I want you to write in the air as I write another capital *B*.

(The teacher writes while students pretend to write the letter in the air.)

Teacher: Now you write a capital *B*.

(The teacher monitors and assists where needed. If support is offered to struggling students, the other students are asked to write five more Bs to keep them engaged. The activity continues by writing the lowercase b.*)*

Guess My Word: The teacher vocally segments the first word from the lesson plan and isolates the first sound (the onset). For example: /b/... oat (*boat*). After students have correctly identified the word, the teacher shows students a picture of a boat. Then the teacher asks one student to use the word *boat* in a sentence, modeling a sentence if necessary. If the student fails to give a sentence, the teacher should help the student construct a sentence. This process is repeated for each of the words in the daily lesson. Make sure each student has a chance to make one sentence during the lesson.

Teacher: Now we are ready to play Guess My Word. Listen carefully and see if you can guess my word. Give me a thumbs up if you think you know the word.... /b/ ... all. Maria, what do you think?

Maria: The word is *ball.*

Teacher: Great job with that, Maria.

(The teacher then shows a picture of a ball.)

Teacher: Who can give me a sentence using the word *ball*? What about you, Joshua?

(The teacher gives Joshua the picture card for ball.*)*

Joshua: Ball.

Teacher: Yes, it is a ball. Tell me something about the ball.

Joshua: I can bounce my ball.

Teacher: That is a great sentence. Can you tell us what color the ball is?

Joshua: Red.

Teacher: Now tell us the whole sentence about the red ball.

Joshua: I can bounce my red ball.

Teacher: Now everybody give me ten fingers in the air. Let's touch all the words in that sentence as we repeat it.

La'Toya: There are six words in that sentence.

Teacher: Yes, we counted six words.

Sound Boxes: Sound boxes are a very effective strategy for both struggling readers and above-level students. For struggling students, give each student a sheet made up of three sound boxes along with a "magic button." The teacher says a word (e.g., *cab*), and students touch on their fingers the sounds they hear in the word (/k/, /a/, /b/). Then the teacher writes the letters that represent those sounds in the sound boxes while naming the letters. The magic buttons are then placed in the first box and the student pushes the button into each box that represents the sound, names the sound, and finally says the word. As soon as possible, students need to begin writing in their own boxes, thus beginning the progression from phonemic awareness to phonics. You could start by letting students write just one of the words in a lesson. Be sure that you write each word in your sound boxes every time so students recognize that the sounds are represented by letters and words.

◇◇

Teacher: Now we are going to listen for sounds in some words.

(The teacher distributes a three-sound box sheet and one magic button to each student.)

Teacher: Our first word is *cab*. Say *cab*. Let's touch the sounds in *cab*.

(The teacher holds up his or her hand and touches one finger for each sound: /k/ /a/ /b/.)

Teacher: Watch me write the sounds.

(The teacher writes the letters in sound boxes. Students do not write the letters in the box until they can write them quickly and correctly. This is first and foremost a phonemic awareness activity. Can students hear three sounds in the word?)

Teacher: Put your magic button in the starting box. Put one finger on your magic button. Let's say the sounds in *cab* the bumpy way.

(The teacher demonstrates moving his or her magic button into each of the boxes, sound by sound, moving from left to right [i.e., the bumpy way].)

Teacher: Now we will say the word the smooth way.

(With a sweeping motion from left to right, the teacher and students say the sounds more connected as they move their magic buttons across the word. Continue the same procedure with the remainder of the words for the day. This activity focuses solely on phonemic awareness, or hearing sounds in words.)

Teacher: Let me give you your sound boxes. How many boxes are on your sheet?

Ava: I have three sound boxes.

Teacher: Yes, we all have three sound boxes. The first word we are going to do is *cap*. Say *cap*. Let's touch the sounds in cap [/k/, /a/, /p/]. Now watch me write the letters that make those sounds in my boxes. Now put your magic buttons in your starting boxes. Let's do this the bumpy way first. Watch me while I move my magic button. Make yours move the same way.

(The teacher segments the sounds and moves the button to appropriate boxes.)

Teacher: Good. Now let's do it together. All magic buttons need to go back to the starting box. Slide your buttons as we say the word *cap* the smooth way. Watch me first.

(The teacher smoothly glides through the boxes and connects the sounds.)

Teacher: Now let's do it together.

(The group completes the other words in their sound boxes using the same routine.)

Discontinue teacher modeling as soon as most students can complete this activity without assistance. If there is a child who still struggles, simply lean in and assist as necessary. It is much better to give one child extra support than to over-support the entire class. More advanced students will write letters in the sound boxes.

Picture Strips: On the first day of a new set of letters, the teacher should hold up picture strips one at a time and identify each picture. In subsequent days, it's OK to review any pictures that may be difficult. If students don't know the picture names, then this activity will not be purposeful. The teacher distributes a picture strip to each student. (Students should already have their "magic buttons" from the previous activity.) The teacher then tells students to cover the picture that begins with /b/, for example. Students are prompted to listen for the sound—not the letter name. Students then place their buttons over the picture on their strips that begin with the correct sound. After checking individual responses and assisting when necessary, the activity continues with the rest of the sounds using the same process.

Teacher: Now we are ready for our picture strips.

Jayla: Oh, boy. This is my favorite game!

Teacher: We talked about each picture yesterday. Take a look at your picture strips to make sure you know the name of each picture. Ava, remember that you have the picture of the ambulance. Say *ambulance*.

(From experience the prior day, the teacher knows this is a difficult word for students.)

Teacher: Find the picture that begins with /s/. Put that sound in your mouth.

(The teacher monitors and goes first to two students who have it correct.)

Teacher: Remmy, what did you cover?

Remmy: I have *socks*.

Teacher: Yes, *socks* begins with /s/.

Leo: I covered *sandwich*.

Teacher: Can you tell us why you covered the sandwich?

Leo: Because it sounds like the letter *s* that says /s/.

Teacher: Ava, what picture did you cover?

Ava: *Bat.*

Teacher: /s/. . . bat. Do they make the same sound at the beginning?

(The teacher assists by helping Ava place her button on the picture of the sun.)

Teacher: Ava, now say /s/. . . sun.

Ava: /s/. . . sun.

Teacher: Yes, you can hear the /s/ sound at the beginning of *sun*.

Letter Strips: The teacher distributes a letter strip to each student. (Students already have their magic buttons from the previous activity.) Using the words listed on the lesson plan, the teacher asks students to cover the letter that makes the sound at the beginning of *sandwich*. This is reinforcement for the beginning sound. The remaining target words are used following the same process. In the beginning, the teacher may have to give additional clues, such as "*Sandwich* begins with /s/. Can you find the letter that makes the /s/ sound?" The teacher may have to point to each letter and ask, "Is this /s/?"

◇◇

Teacher: Before I give you a letter strip, let's review the letter cards.

(The teacher hands out strips for both uppercase and lowercase letters. She gives support only if needed. The teacher starts the activity as the directions suggest and then adds layers of support as needed for each student.)

Teacher: I think you are ready for your uppercase letter strips. Listen carefully. I want you to cover the letter that makes the sound you hear at the beginning of the word *bird*. Say *bird*. Cover the letter that makes the sound you hear at the beginning of *bird*.

(The teacher observes that only two students identified the letter B correctly, so she moves to the next layer of support.)

Teacher: I hear the /b/ sound and the beginning of *bird*. Which letter makes the /b/ sound?

(All but one student now identifies the B correctly. The teacher points to the letter B on the pocket chart and leans in to Javon.)

Teacher: Javon, this is the letter *B*. It is the capital *B*. Can you find the *B* on your letter strip?

Javon: Here it is.

Teacher: Yes, that is the capital *B*.

Rhyming Cards: The teacher reviews the names of pictures and then distributes the cards to each student. Using the word pairs given on each day's lesson plan, the teacher says a word and prompts students to identify a word that rhymes with that word. This game can be played like bingo with additional magic buttons.

Teacher: Here is our last game for today. Let me give each of you a rhyming card.

(The teacher reviews each picture on the card from the previous day.)

Teacher: Do you have your magic buttons ready?

All: Yeah!

Teacher: Find a picture that rhymes with *big*. Say *big*.

(The teacher observes and assists as needed. When all the students have their magic buttons on the pig, they say the rhyming word pair aloud.)

When to Move to Emergent Stage 1B

After completing the ELFS lessons, it is important to reassess alphabet recognition and production to determine the next instructional sequence. If students still recognize and produce less than 50 percent of the alphabet, they should repeat the ELFS lessons. When these students have repeated these lessons (intervention counts as the second time), reassess once again. At this point, students who still recognize and produce less than 50 percent of the alphabet should begin at Stage 1B, which continues alphabet recognition and production, along with learning how to track print and recognize some high-frequency words. Students who score better than 80 percent should be given the assessment for Stage 2A, which focuses on initial consonant sounds. Students failing this test will begin in Stage 2A; students passing this test with 80 percent or better should move to Stage 2B.

Emergent Readers and Writers: Stage 1B

Exposing Emergent students to text supports their reading efforts and affirms their belief that they will become readers. Emergent readers begin by reading books with repetitive text and high picture support. Instructional book Levels 1 and 2 and Fountas and Pinnell Levels A and B are appropriate for Emergent readers. The first level generally has only one line of repetitive text (with one word change on each page) and is accompanied by strong picture support. The second level has two sentences of repetitive text (or one sentence over two lines, which requires a return sweep to complete). These two beginning book levels are extremely critical to the success of the Emergent reader. Wordless books are not appropriate for these early readers; books must provide clear, repetitive print with high picture support so students learn how to track text and develop print concepts. All standards that can be addressed at Emergent Stages A and B are located in the Appendix.

Figure 4.9 shows the lesson plan for Emergent Stage 1B, which also suggests component activities that extend from group to independent practice. Use these sections to make notes on specific problems or successes with your students. This will allow you to make decisions regarding the pace of instruction (i.e., whether to move forward or to review).

The following sections explain each lesson plan component, along with appropriate strategies and activities that support it. After the discussion of each component, a classroom vignette will be presented that demonstrates the component. This lesson plan follows a mid-kindergarten group of students.

Fluency

Emergent fluency development includes learning to recognize words quickly, track print, and develop basic word concepts. Begin the lesson by rereading the previous day's text. The teacher reads the first page, and then students read the same page together as they point to each word in the text (echo reading). After several pages of echo reading, students should be encouraged to read chorally with the teacher. Echo reading on the first several pages is important to get students "into the story," as it provides them with character names and repetitive sentence patterns used in the book. Usually, the hardest part of any story for Emergent readers is the first few pages. Therefore, providing this up-front support makes good sense for young readers. Whisper reading (either as a whole group or with one student serving as a "lead reader") is also a good option for rereading at the Emergent stage. This approach adds variety as students begin to refine their beginning fluency skills. It also provides teachers with an opportunity to observe individual students and assess progress.

It is important for students to consistently track print with the dominant hand. Tell students to tuck all their fingers in except for their "magic reading finger." After completing the book, point to a word and let students track up to the word to identify it. Suppose the sentence is *The fish is in the lake*. After reading the sentence together (chorally), point to the word *in*. Then ask, "What's this word?" If there is no response, ask students to whisper read the sentence in a quiet voice until they get to the unknown word. When students reach the word, they should say it in a louder voice. This is referred to as "tracking up to a word" and encourages the development of print concepts.

Figure 4.9

Lesson Plan: Emergent Stage 1B

In Group	
FLUENCY	**FLUENCY EXTENSION**
Reread _____ ☐ Choral Read ☐ Stop-and-Go Reading ☐ Lead Reading ☐ Whisper Reading	☐ Read with a partner. ☐ Buddy read. ☐ Other
WORD STUDY	**WORD STUDY EXTENSION**
Alphabet Focus: _____ ☐ Match Game (uppercase and lowercase letters) ☐ Alphabet Production ☐ Cut-Up Sentence	☐ Cut and paste focus letters in magazines. ☐ Trace the letters. ☐ Cut and paste alphabet letters (uppercase and lowercase). ☐ Work on individual cut-up sentence. ☐ Other
VOCABULARY	**VOCABULARY EXTENSION**
High-Frequency Words (1–15) ☐ Fish Pond	☐ Make and write words (magnetic letters). ☐ Trace words (rainbow words). ☐ Practice with a partner.
COMPREHENSION	**COMPREHENSION EXTENSION**
New Read: _____ Text Level: _____ **Before Reading** ☐ Build background knowledge. ☐ Preview three high-frequency words from text. ☐ Conduct a picture walk. ☐ Set the purpose. **During Reading** ☐ Stopping points. • • • • **After Reading** ☐ Revisit purpose of reading. ☐ Revisit high-frequency words from text. ☐ Discuss independent writing assignment.	Draw and write about reading *(with support if needed).* ☐ My favorite part of the book is… ☐ My favorite character is… ☐ I liked the book because… ☐ I did not like the book because… ☐ Other

As students gain familiarity with a text, reduce support during the rereading. Have students choral read with as little support as necessary. Try "stop-and-go" reading, offering support only when necessary. This strategy allows the teacher to support or discontinue support as students read. In other words, read with them chorally and tell students to continue reading when you stop reading. By contrast, lead reading allows individual students to read pages out loud (the "lead reader") while the rest of the group whisper reads. I often tell students they are "back-up" readers and must whisper along and loud enough for me to hear. This allows all students to practice rereading while offering individual students the opportunity to lead the group. Rotate lead reading with choral reading.

◇◇

(This dialogue focuses on a group of Emergent kindergarten students who are rereading a Level 1 book. The teacher feels that most students can confidently track one line of print.)

Teacher: Yesterday, we read the book *In Our Classroom*. What things did we read about in the classroom?

(Students recall information from the previous day's read.)

Teacher: Let's try reading this book again today. Remember to point to the words, and we can read together. Do you remember how it starts?

Laura: I forgot.

Teacher: I'll read the first page to get us started. Put your pointer finger under the first word and follow along while I read the first page.

(The teacher reads the first sentence while students track the words by pointing to them.)

Teacher: Now let's read the page together.

(The students and teacher read together as the teacher monitors students' tracking of text.)

Teacher: That was great. Now let's turn the page. Take a look at the picture. What is the little girl hanging on the wall?

Alisha: A bookbag.

Teacher: Yes, it is a bookbag, but they just call it a bag.

(The teacher points to the word bag.*)*

Teacher: Put your finger under the first word. Who knows what the first word is?

Jackson: *The.*

Teacher: You're right. Now let's all read this together.

(Students and teacher choral read.)

Teacher: Let's all turn the page. What is the little girl putting on the table?

Meredith: Some pencils.

Teacher: Yes, she is showing the boy that the pencils go there. Meredith, would you be the lead reader on this page? While Meredith reads aloud, we will all whisper read along with her.

(Students and teacher read together. After the page is complete, the teacher points to the word go *in the sentence.)*

Teacher: Do you know what this word is?

(Four of the six students recognize the word.)

Teacher: Let me show you how to figure out what the word is. If we start at the beginning of the sentence and whisper read over to the word, we should be able to figure out what the word is.

(The teacher emphasizes print concepts and automaticity in recognizing some basic high-frequency words. The book is completed using choral reading and lead reading strategies. Note that the teacher might decide to keep the book a third day for rereading based on his or her observations. This would mean that a new read is introduced every other day, which is a good strategy for students who have not mastered tracking print or if the number of leveled books available is limited.)

Teacher: When we finish our group today, you will reread this book with your group partner. Take turns being the lead reader on one page while your partner whisper reads with you. On the next page, switch jobs. Remember, if your partner needs help, give some time to think about it first. When you finish, put the books in your reading folder.

(This daily routine incorporates fluency practice at an appropriate instructional level as students place the texts in their group's reading box.)

! Independent fluency extension activities include the following ideas:

- Keep copies of the books previously read in individual or group boxes so students can reread them for fluency practice.
- Have students buddy read, which gives them choices. Each week, students choose books from the book box to read to a selected buddy. The title of the book is recorded on a Buddy Reading Log, and the buddy signs it after they read the book together.
- Try recording the texts and letting students follow and read along.

Word Study

Begin word study for Emergent readers by reviewing individual alphabet assessments. Based on the assessments, create a systematic plan for "attacking" the alphabet. If students know only a few letters, follow the scope and sequence for Emergent readers that focuses on teaching the alphabet in a five-week sequence (see Appendix). Generally, five letters should be taught each week. However, don't be concerned if whole-group instruction introduces letters in a different sequence. The goal is to recognize and produce all 26 letters. When small-group instruction reflects the objectives of whole-group instruction, differentiated instruction is compromised. Four activities for word study are listed in the lesson plan: match game, alphabet recognition, alphabet production, and cut-up sentences.

The classroom vignettes within this section feature a small group that has limited alphabet knowledge and is on the fifth day of recognition and production of the focus letters *B*, *M*, *F*, *S*, and *A*.

Match Game: This initial activity includes matching uppercase and lowercase focus letters. The teacher and students should have a set of letters for this activity. Using letter cards, students match lowercase letters to their uppercase counterparts. Be sure to have children say the letter names and sounds as many times as possible. If you find that five letters is too challenging, feel free to reduce the number of letters to four.

Teacher: Let's take a look at some letters we have been working on.

(The teacher gives each student a set of uppercase and lowercase letters for the lesson.)

Teacher: Line your letters up in front of you. Find the big *S* and push it down to the line.

(The teacher observes and notices that Ian needs assistance. She points to the S *card.)*

Teacher: This is a capital *S*. Can you find your capital *S*?

Ian: Here it is.

Teacher: Good job. Push it down to the line. Now, let's all find the uppercase *M*. Push the capital *M* to the line. Now find the lowercase *m*.

(The teacher continues until students have identified five uppercase letters. Note that the teacher uses the terms capital, uppercase, *and* big letter *interchangeably. Students will often hear these terms in many situations and should be aware of the names they might hear.)*

Alphabet Recognition and Production: For Emergent readers, this activity is simply the production of the letters being studied. This activity should be completed with dry-erase boards or lined paper placed in a sheet protector, so they can be reused and mistakes can be erased easily. Randomly call out the five focus letters, one at a time. Have students write both the uppercase and lowercase versions. If necessary, leave the letter cards out so students can have as much support as needed. Gradually take the cards away as students become more confident in writing the letters independently. If students struggle with this activity, help them by making dotted lines for the letter and allowing them to trace the letters. Although this isn't a handwriting lesson, students should not practice forming the letters incorrectly. Pace the lesson as needed and remember that you may not have time to go through all five letters each day. Based on observations, focus on the letters that are most difficult for students if time is short.

◇◇

Teacher: Let's practice writing some of these letters.

(The teacher distributes dry-erase boards. The five uppercase and lowercase letters are left on the tabletop chart because this group is still struggling with letter formation and identification.)

Teacher: Is everybody ready? The first letters I want you to write are the uppercase and lowercase *S*. If you aren't sure what an *S* looks like, look at the letters on the board. First write the capital *S*, and then write the lowercase *s*.

(Several students immediately write the letter S *while other students search the cards on the board.)*

Teacher: Susan, do you need a little help getting started?

(The teacher reaches over and makes an S *for Susan. Then she asks Susan to make another* S*.)*

Teacher: Good!

(The teacher monitors and assists when needed. As students become more confident in recognizing and writing these letters, the letter cards can be removed.)

Cut-Up Sentences: This daily activity reinforces alphabet recognition in the context of words in a sentence. Additionally, high-frequency words are included to address automaticity. This also allows students to observe the teacher writing the sentence and reinforce conventions of print. First, post a blank sentence strip so it is easily visible to the group. Read the sentence aloud for the group at least three times before you start writing. Then have students repeat the sentence with you. Point to your fingers in a left-to-right progression and count the number of words in the sentence. Then have students touch each finger as they repeat the sentence with you.

Ask, "What is the first word in the sentence?" Write the word on the strip. As you continue writing the words, emphasize conventions such as capital letters, spacing between words, and punctuation. Model your thinking. For example, you could state, "This is the first letter of the first word in the sentence, so it should begin with a capital letter." After completing the sentence, cut apart the words in a jigsaw fashion and give individual students a word or punctuation mark from the sentence. Make sure each student has a part of the sentence. Then ask, "Who has the first word in the sentence?" Continue until the sentence is reassembled. Point out high-frequency words that are part of the group's developing vocabulary word bank.

Teacher: Listen to our sentence for today: *The cat is black.* Listen again: *The cat is black.*

(The teacher touches a finger to each word in the sentence as it is read aloud.)

Teacher: Now you say the sentence with me and touch each word on your fingers.

(Students repeat the sentence with the teacher and touch their fingers. Repeat.)

Teacher: Now I'm going to write the sentence. What is the first word in the sentence?

Laura: *The.*

Teacher: Yes, and it is in our word bank. *The* is the first word in the sentence, so it must start with a capital letter.

(The teacher writes a T*.)*

Teacher: What letter is this?

Hannah: That's a *T.*

Teacher: Right, and *the* has two more letters.

(The teacher focuses on letter recognition.)

Teacher: Now I need to leave two finger spaces before I write the next word.

(The process continues as the sentence is completed.)

Teacher: Now I'm going to cut the sentence apart. What word am I cutting off first?

(The teacher continues cutting up the sentence.)

Teacher: I'm going to mix all the words up and give each of you part of the sentence.

(The teacher gives each student a word or end punctuation mark.)

Teacher: Who has the first word?

Suzanne: I have the word *The.*

(The activity continues as the sentence is put back together and reread.)

Teacher: Now I'm going to put our sentence pieces in a plastic bag and write the whole sentence on the outside of the bag. It will be in your sentence basket so you can practice taking it apart and putting it back together. Tomorrow, you will get your own cut-up sentence to put back together.

(On the second day of this lesson, the teacher brings out this cut-up sentence for students to review. Then he or she gives each student an individual cut-up sentence to cut, put in order, and glue into a journal. After that, students will copy the sentence below the glued sentence and draw a picture about the sentence. As students become confident with their own cut-up sentences, this can become an extension activity to complete independently, outside the small group. Students cut the sentence apart, glue the sentence down, and copy the sentence. After this, the students draw a picture to illustrate the sentence. Figure 4.10 illustrates a completed cut-up sentence activity.)

Figure 4.10
Sample Cut-Up Sentence

! Independent word study extension activities include the following ideas:

- Make letter cards available for partners to play Memory. Students turn the cards over and take turns making matches with uppercase and lowercase letters.

- Have dry-erase boards and markers available for students to practice writing the letters being studied.
- Use letter tiles, magnetic letters, sandpaper letters, and so forth to reinforce the letters being studied. These formats provide the kinesthetic support young children often need.
- Have students complete a letter hunt. In this activity, students search through old magazines and newspapers for the focus letters. Students cut them out and glue them on a piece of paper. This activity helps students recognize letters in various fonts.
- Have letter stamps available so students can stamp and match uppercase and lowercase letters.

Vocabulary

High-frequency word recognition is the basis for vocabulary instruction with Emergent readers and writers. Using the 100 most frequent words as a guide, begin a word bank for the group. It is important for Emergent readers to automatically recognize at least 15 high-frequency words before advancing to the next book level, which includes books that no longer have patterned text. Begin with the first 5–10 words on the list, and never include more than 20–25 words in the bank. After the teacher reviews the bank of high-frequency words, the group can play a game called Fish Pond. Word cards are placed face up on a table, and individual students are asked to "fish" for a word. If they cannot identify a word, the teacher asks them to find a specific word. If students are still struggling, they can be shown a word card and then find the matching word in the pond.

In the following scenario, the group's word bank has 10 words. The teacher has two copies of each word in the bank so students will get more practice. This activity is appropriate when students know fewer than 10–15 high-frequency words.

Teacher: Let's take a quick look at our word bank. I think that we have ten words now.

(Students respond chorally as teacher reviews word cards.)

Teacher: Now let's play Fish Pond.

(The teacher places the cards face up on the table to create the "Fish Pond.")

Teacher: Rose, can you fish for any word in the pond?

(Rose does not respond, so the teacher offers the next layer of support.)

Teacher: Can you find the word *is*?

(Rose still has difficulty finding the word, so the teacher adds another layer of support and holds up her card for is.*)*

Teacher: This is the word *is*. Now can you find a card that says *is* like mine?

Rose: Here it is! It looks just like yours.

Teacher: Yes, and this word is *is* like "It is a good day."

(The teacher goes to the next student and repeats the process, always starting with the lowest level of support.)

❗ Independent vocabulary extension activities include the following ideas:

- Put word bank words in a sealable plastic bag so partners can practice reading them.
- Make copies of the high-frequency word cards for each student to take home.
- Post a list of the word bank words. Color-code each group's words.
- Have students complete word hunts, looking for the focus words in newspapers and magazines. Then have students cut the words out and glue them on a piece of paper or in a word work journal.
- Make two sets of the words and have partners play Memory. Students take turns turning over the cards and trying to make matches.
- Provide magnetic letters so students can build high-frequency words and then write them.

Comprehension

Realistically, the books that Emergent students are reading have very little in the way of storyline, so comprehension opportunities are admittedly limited. Therefore, the teacher should focus on strategies that will support students in a successful read of the book. The group depicted in the following scenarios is reading a new book at a higher level than the reread; therefore, the teacher is skillful in pointing out text changes that might be unfamiliar or difficult.

Before Reading

Before reading, the teacher begins with a short introduction of the front cover, discusses the author and illustrator, and conducts a complete picture walk of the book to familiarize students with the story. The teacher should also point out words that Emergent readers are not expected to read without heavy picture support, along with two or three high-frequency words, and write the words on index cards. These words will be presented and placed on the tabletop board. Finally, the purpose for reading the book is presented.

◇◇◇

Teacher: Our new book is called *The Parade*. Let's take a look at the front cover. It says that the author and illustrator is Beverly Randall. So what jobs did she have?

D'Marcus: She did the story.

Teacher: Yes, she wrote the story, so she is the author of the story, and she is also the illustrator. What does that mean?

Ella: She drew the pictures.

Teacher: Yes, she did. She is a good illustrator. The name of our new book is *The Parade*. Have you ever been to a parade or seen one on television? What kinds of things can you see in a parade?

(The teacher helps students make connections to the text.)

Meredith: You can see big balloons, and clowns, and bands!

Teacher: Yes! Anything else?

Robert: I saw old cars and people dancing.

Teacher: So you can see a lot of different things in a parade. Let's take a look at the pictures in our book and see what was in this parade. Take a look at this picture. What does it show us?

Leo: Horses. There are horses in the parade.

Teacher: Yes, and here is the word *horses*. I notice something new on this page. Does anyone see something different?

Joao: There are a lot of words on this page.

Teacher: Yes! We have two lines on every page. When we have two lines, we have to move our fingers down to the next line to finish reading the sentence.

(The teacher continues the picture walk through the book, pointing out picture clues and making text connections that will support students in a successful read of the new book. If students have a copy of the book during the picture walk, they are often distracted. The teacher controls the picture walk by holding up his or her book and waiting to hand out student books until the walk is complete.)

During Reading

During reading, the teacher carefully selects reading strategies to support Emergent readers, such as echo reading, lead reading, and choral reading. The teacher poses questions to support understanding and the purpose for reading.

Teacher: Now let's read *The Parade*. Turn to the first page. Let's look at the picture. What do we see in the picture?

All: Clowns!

Teacher: So we already know we will be reading about clowns in the parade. The pictures help us read the book. I'll read the first page, and you point to the words in your books while I read. When I finish reading, you will read the page with me. You will be my echo.

(The teacher reads the first page aloud.)

Teacher: Now it's your turn. Put your finger under the first word, and get ready to read.

(Students read the first page with the teacher.)

Teacher: On this page, I see some high-frequency words that are on our cards. Can you find the word *the?*

(The teacher observes as students point to the word. During the read, the teacher makes sure the focus words are pointed out.)

Teacher: Let's turn the page. Take a look at the picture. What will we be reading about on this page?

Students: Horses.

Teacher: I think you are ready to choral read with me. Put your finger under the first word.

(The teacher and students finish reading the book using choral reading.)

After Reading

After reading, the teacher should return to and discuss the purpose for reading. Students then review the high-frequency words that were presented before reading. Finally, the teacher discusses a follow-up writing activity that students will complete independently.

Teacher: We read this book and found a lot of new things. Let's make a list of everything you can remember in the parade.

Laura: There were clowns and bands in the parade.

Teacher: Good. Let me write those on our list.

(Students continue to recall, and teacher writes all suggestions on a list, focusing on the letters and strong consonant sounds in the words.)

Teacher: Let's take a look at the high-frequency words we saw in the book.

(The teacher reviews three high-frequency words she reviewed prior to reading.)

Teacher: I think we have this word in our word bank. Do you know this word?

(The teacher points to the word here. *Student responds correctly, so the teacher returns to the text and points out the word* like. *Students cannot identify this word.)*

Teacher: We can figure out this word if we whisper read up to this word. Let's try it. Do you remember how it started? *We like the clowns.* Yes, this word is *like.* We will read this book again tomorrow. After you leave the group, I want you to take your book and a piece of paper with you. Watch me fold my paper. First, I will fold it in half.

(Students observe the teacher as she folds the paper.)

Teacher: Now I am going to open my paper. How many boxes did I make?

D'Marcus: Four. 1, 2, 3, 4.

Teacher: Yes, there are four boxes. Now I want to see you fold your paper.

(The first time students are asked to do this activity, it is appropriate to model the process in the small-group setting. Afterward, students should be able to complete the activity independently.)

Teacher: Now you are going to choose your four favorite things that were in the parade. Go back and look at the pages. Watch me. I am choosing clowns, so I am going to copy the word *clowns* in my first box. Now I am going to draw and color a picture of a clown.

(The teacher continues the demonstration.)

Teacher: When you leave the group, I want you to return to your table and choose four words from the book and then draw those things in the parade. [See student sample in Figure 4.11.]

The day after the lesson discussed in the previous section, the teacher asks students to respond with drawing and writing about their favorite part of the book. Figure 4.12 is an example of such a written response. Notice that the drawing is discernable, but the letter strings are not. In this case, the teacher asks the student to read his or her writing, and the teacher writes the sentence at the bottom of the page. Then she touches each word while reading the sentence before asking the student to do the same. If students cannot read their own writing, allow them to dictate a sentence about their favorite part, and then write that sentence below the drawing.

Figure 4.11
Sample Four-Square Vocabulary Activity

Figure 4.12
Drawing and Writing About a Favorite Passage

When to Move to the Next Stage

Many students will skip the Emergent Stage 1B because they already recognize and are able to write more than half the letters when they finish the ELFS lessons. There will also be students who pass a letter assessment with 80 percent or greater accuracy and will need to be assessed in the next assessment (Beginning stage 2A), which assesses beginning consonant sounds. Students who pass the 2A assessment can start at the Beginning Stage 2B, which focuses on beginning digraphs and blends. All students will need to go through Stage 2B, so there is no need for further assessment.

In some instances, there will be "borderline" students who do not fit neatly into established groups. For example, a student might score 70 percent on the Stage 1B assessment, while the rest of that group scores below 50 percent. Provide additional individual assistance with a tutor, or allow the borderline students to meet with both an Emergent and a Beginning group for a period of time to determine if they can move ahead successfully. Intervention may also be helpful with some students; they can go back through the Emergent stage 1B while the rest of the group moves to Stage 2A. Remember that the lesson plan is based on word study assessments, not book levels. Therefore, it would be realistic to see Beginning students reading a Level A or B book.

Conclusion

Emergent readers and writers face unique challenges, including phonemic awareness, recognizing and producing letters, learning to track print, and acquiring high-frequency words. These are critical understandings and should not be underestimated. As teachers, we are laying the conceptual groundwork for the early reading and writing processes. No matter what grade a student is in, if he or she is an Emergent reader, someone must take the time to lay the foundation for future literacy success.

There is one word of caution in implementing small-group instruction. Keep the lessons interactive and watch your lesson pacing. The fast-paced lessons and activities presented in this book should keep all students engaged and enthusiastic about learning to read and write. Remember that you can use this as a basic guide and adjust based on your students. All support materials for both Emergent 1A and 1B—including lesson plans, assessment, high-frequency word cards, letter cards, and activities—can be downloaded from www.beverlytyner.net.

Chapter 5

The Beginning Reader and Writer

Characteristics of Beginning Readers and Writers

The criteria for entering the Beginning stage include the ability to recognize and produce at least half the alphabet. Beginning readers and writers have started to develop print-related understandings that underpin the reading and writing process. Many students may already know how to track print with a return sweep and possess a strong understanding of print concepts. Additionally, Beginning readers and writers have some basic high-frequency word knowledge that will be instrumental in advancing their text levels at this stage. Another characteristic of Beginning readers and writers is their ability to see printed words as discrete units with recognizable letters. Finally, they also use picture clues to support comprehension. With these foundational skills in place, students are ready to do some simple writing in response to the texts they read. Figure 5.1 shows expectations in reading levels, high-frequency words, word study, comprehension, and writing about reading for the Beginning stage.

Beginning readers and writers will quickly advance their literacy abilities, building on the foundational skills mastered at the Emergent stage. For the first time, these readers will learn to read text that is less patterned. They will continue to build their high-frequency word knowledge and quickly recognize 40–50 words by the end of this stage. As they focus on beginning consonant sounds, they will be able to apply these skills and begin to decode text. As the text levels advance, there will also be a stronger focus on comprehension.

Figure 5.1

Stage 2: Beginning Reader and Writer

Fluency	Vocabulary	Word Study	Reading Comprehension	Writing About Reading
• Typically, mid- to late K • Book levels EI 3/4/5, F&P C/D • Out of patterned text • Rereading to develop fluency	Recognizing first 50 high-frequency words	• Recognizing and producing initial consonant sounds (2A) • Cut-up sentences focusing on initial consonant sounds (2A) • Recognizing and producing initial blends and digraphs (2B) • Cut-up sentences focusing on initial blends and digraphs (2B)	• Using initial consonant sounds in decoding • Reading simple text • Using sentence context and pictures or word recognition cues to decode • Summarizing simple text	• Completing alphabet recognition and production • Using correct consonant letter sounds in writing • Using some sight words in writing • Showing spaces between words • Drawing and writing about the book • Student begins to "read" own writing • Writing purpose is addressed in drawing and writing with teacher support

EI: Early Intervention   F&P: Fountas and Pinnell

Word study for Beginning readers and writers is multifaceted. Students work on completing alphabet recognition and production (if necessary), and they focus on recognizing and producing initial consonant sounds at Stage 2A. After students complete the alphabet sequence, the alphabet activities should be discontinued. The focus of word study at this stage should be hearing and writing initial consonant sounds in words. The process of assigning and writing a letter name to its sound marks the point of moving from phonemic awareness to phonics. After the completion of Stage 2A, students move to Stage 2B, where they focus on hearing and writing initial blends and digraphs. This sequence is critical as Beginning readers and writers build foundational word study knowledge.

My extensive experience has shown that the vast majority of on- and above-level kindergarten students breeze through the 2B stage. With struggling kindergarten students, you might consider skipping Stage 2B, especially if it is near the end of the year. Most kindergarten standards require that students correctly write most three-letter words. Many struggling kindergarten students are in the last quarter of the school year before successfully completing initial consonant sounds

(Stage 2A). In this situation, you might consider going directly to 3A and focusing on three-letter words. Why would you do this? Blends and digraphs are generally included in 1st grade standards. Therefore, it might be better to introduce the patterns in terms of word families at the Fledgling stage. First graders who begin the year with exposure to blends and digraphs in isolation only will quickly get further behind. Therefore, Stage 2B might be best utilized in intervention while the teacher begins word families at 3A in 1st grade.

There will be significant writing progress at the Beginning stage. Students begin to group letters and move left to right in their writing. Students also begin to leave spaces between letter groups to represent spaces between words. At this stage, writing and drawing (in response to a text) is appropriate. In the early part of the stage, students may need to dictate their thoughts; however, always encourage each student to make an attempt to write. It's a good idea to ask students to write for a specific purpose, such as "Draw your favorite character and tell why it is your favorite."

By the end of the Beginning stage, students should demonstrate mastery of consonant sounds and recognize that words have a medial sound. Along with extending their knowledge of high-frequency words, students' writing will become more legible, and they will be able to "read" their own writing. These basic skills will prepare students to write more complex sentences in the future developmental stages of writing.

At the Beginning stage, short, leveled books are the texts of choice. They are no longer patterned but still contain high picture support and numerous high-frequency words. Look for books that have several lines of print per page. Books at this level should have little repetitive text, because Beginning readers have already mastered the skill of tracking print with a return sweep. Keeping students in heavily patterned text for too long hinders their growth as readers, because they are simply practicing a skill they have already mastered. Once students can track print and automatically recognize at least 15 high-frequency words, they should be moved out of patterned text.

Remember that if students can recognize and produce at least half the alphabet at the end of the ELFS lessons, they will skip the Emergent stage and move straight to the Beginning stage. Therefore, this stage may be the first opportunity for these students to read a book. If this is the case, Beginning readers will need to start at Level A or 1 and practice reading until they can track print with a return sweep and recognize 15 high-frequency words. In Chapter 4, Figure 4.1 includes a correlation between number of known high-frequency words and the instructional book level students should be capable of reading with teacher support (p. 64).

Remember, these are just approximates; students won't always fit neatly into our boxes! I cannot stress enough the importance of this correlation process. I can, with a great deal of certainty and experience, say that this chart has been powerful in advancing students' literacy levels.

Beginning stage standards are basically addressed in prekindergarten and kindergarten. Common standards that support each lesson model component can be found in the Appendix.

There are numerous prekindergarten and kindergarten standards that are addressed or could be addressed in these small-group lessons. I included these standards so you could easily reference them as you are planning and ensure your lessons are on track with these standards.

Lesson Plan Components for the Beginning Stage

The Beginning stage lesson plan is found in Figure 5.2 and provides instruction in fluency, word study, vocabulary (high-frequency words), comprehension, and writing about reading. Although these same components are found at the Emergent stage, the strategies and activities in the Beginning lesson plan are differentiated to meet the developmental needs of these more advanced readers and writers.

Fluency

For Beginning readers, fluency becomes more important to understanding the text. These readers must recognize a wide range of punctuation and command appropriate levels of speed and accuracy when recognizing words. Rereading, therefore, is the main strategy in developing fluency. Practice—both in and out of small groups—should be important parts of the classroom routine. If necessary, echo read the first page or two of a story to get students started and then let them choral read with you. Additionally, students can take turns being the lead reader while other students whisper read. This activity gives teachers the opportunity to assess individual reading competencies while engaging other students.

The group of kindergarten students represented in this chapter's scenarios are Beginning readers and writers working at Stage 2A. They are reading Level 4 (C) books and working on beginning consonant sounds /b/, /s/, and /m/.

◇◇

Teacher: Yesterday we read a book called *Red Puppy*. Do you remember why the little puppy was sad?

Figure 5.2

Lesson Plan: Beginning Stage

FLUENCY	FLUENCY EXTENSION
Text Level: _____ Reread: ☐ Choral Reading ☐ Teacher-Led Reading ☐ Student-Led Reading ☐ Whisper Reading	☐ Reread with a partner. ☐ Buddy read. ☐ Other
WORD STUDY	**WORD STUDY EXTENSION**
Alphabet Focus: _____ Beginning Consonants: Lesson # _____ Diagraphs/Blends: Lesson # _____ ☐ Card Sound Sort ☐ Writing Sort ☐ Group Cut-Up Sentence	☐ Cut, sort, and paste picture cards. ☐ Write the letter sound for each picture. ☐ Find pictures in magazines with the same beginning sounds. ☐ Work on individual cut-up sentences. ☐ Other: _____
VOCABULARY	**VOCABULARY EXTENSION**

High-Frequency Words (HFW)
   ☐ 15–35
   ☐ 35–50
   ☐ _____
☐ Word Wizard Game
	☐ Make and write high-frequency words (magnetic letters).
	☐ Beat the clock (with partner): how many words can you read in 30 seconds?
	☐ Work on four-square vocabulary.
	☐ Other: _____

COMPREHENSION	**COMPREHENSION EXTENSION**

New Read: _____ Text Level: _____
 	
Before Reading
☐ Build background knowledge (if needed).
☐ Preview high-frequency words from text.
☐ Set the purpose.
 	
During Reading
☐ Stopping points/text-dependent questions
•
•
•
•
 	
After Reading
☐ Revisit high-frequency words.
☐ Revisit purpose for reading (summarize).
☐ Discuss writing extension.
	Draw and write about reading *(with teacher support as needed)*.
	   ☐ Story elements
	   ☐ Favorite part
	   ☐ Retell in writing
	   ☐ Main idea (i.e., what I learned)
	   ☐ Other:

Laura: He didn't have a home, and that made him sad.

Teacher: That's right. Who finally took the little red puppy home?

Harrison: The girl in the wheelchair did.

Teacher: Why do you think that the girl chose the little red puppy?

Tommy: Because they were both lonely.

Teacher: Although we don't know for sure, I think that is a very good guess.

(The teacher distributes individual copies of the book to students.)

Teacher: Please remember to keep your books flat on the table. Let's read the title of the book together as we touch the words. Be sure to use your magic reading finger!

Students: *Red Puppy.*

Teacher: Now let's turn to the first page. I'll read the first page to get us started, and you follow along.

(The teacher reads the first page.)

Teacher: Now let's read this page together.

(Students all choral read the page.)

Teacher: Turn to page 5. Katherine, will you be the lead reader on this page? We will be your back-up readers and whisper read with you.

(Katherine leads as the group whisper reads.)

Teacher: Turn the page. Look at the picture. Which toy will the story talk about on this page?

Eric: The teddy bears.

Teacher: Who took the teddy bears?

Laura: The boys took the teddy bears out of the basket, and now their mom is paying the man.

Teacher: Good. The picture can help us read the story, so we always need to look at the pictures before we read. Ethan, it's your turn to be the lead reader on this page. We are ready to whisper read with you.

(Ethan reads out loud while the others whisper read.)

Teacher: Now let's turn the page and look at the picture. What did the girls take out of the basket?

Katherine: They took the rabbits.

(Students finish reading the book with variations of choral reading, lead reading, and whisper reading. The reread is intended to focus on fluency practice, so very little time should be spent on comprehension. The comprehension portion of the lesson takes place with the new read.)

Teacher: You did a really great job reading that book. When we finish in group today, I want you to reread this book with your partner. Then put the books in your small-group extension folder.

! Independent fluency extension activities include the following ideas:

- Assign each student a reading partner with whom they can reread away from the small group. As one student lead reads a page, the other whisper reads. Partners continue to switch roles until they finish the book.
- Provide a basket of "reading telephones" (PVC pipes) in the classroom. Students use them as they reread independently to reduce the noise level and stay focused.
- Create individual reading boxes for each student or for the reading group. The reading box should include all the books that students have reread in and out of group.
- Have students keep a weekly Buddy Reading Log. In this activity, students may choose any other student to listen to them read. On the log, students record the titles of books they read to their reading buddies during the week. The reading buddies must sign the log to document the day that he or she listened to the reader. The teacher might, for example, require that each student have three entries in every week's Buddy Reading Log.
- Students can record themselves reading one book per week. Ask students to listen to themselves read and reread the book to see if they improve.

Word Study

Continue the alphabet recognition and production sequence from the Emergent stage if it has not yet been completed. You may choose to readminister the

Alphabet Recognition and Production assessment to get a current status of students' knowledge so you can customize and focus the study on letters they have not mastered. Begin word study with a quick match of the uppercase and lowercase letters, focusing on the names and sounds of each. This should only take a couple of minutes. If time permits, mix up the letters and flash them to the group for automatic recognition. When students attain 80 percent or greater on the assessment, suspend the alphabet activities and have students work with picture cards and initial consonant sounds. Alphabet recognition and production can still be woven into the lesson, but it shouldn't be the focus. The scope and sequence for Beginning word study is found in the Appendix and gives a day-by-day focus for sounds, blends, and diagraphs to be studied.

Beginning readers and writers will follow the word study scope and sequence, which focuses on presenting initial consonant sounds in sets of three with systematic review lessons. On the first day, review all the pictures to make sure students can identify each (don't use pictures that continually confuse the group). This ensures that the activity is truly focused on phonemic awareness and phonics and not on picture vocabulary. The first day of new consonant sounds can be a picture sort only. Distribute three pairs of picture cards to each pair and monitor as students match the cards according to the initial consonant sound. Another way to do this activity is to distribute cards and ask students to find the picture that begins with one of the sounds. Card sorting should only be used on the first day. After that, students should always write the beginning sounds in a writing sort, which you then check by placing the cards in the correct category on the sorting chart. It's a good idea to sort three picture cards across and two or three down in each lesson. Using more pictures will take too much time away from the other important parts of the lesson. Also remember, this activity has students sort by beginning sound and letter name, thereby making a solid transition from phonemic awareness to phonics.

Follow the scope and sequence and don't remain on letter sets longer than is indicated. You are, however, encouraged to skip lessons if students are automatically producing the correct beginning sounds. This is especially important in the review lessons. Students will be assessed at the end of the sequence, and there will be an opportunity for review at that point. Developmentally, Beginning readers and writers are capable of producing the initial sound of a word. During a writing sort, call out a picture card name that begins with one of the focus sounds and ask students to write the letter that correctly represents that beginning sound into the correct category. Writing is the key. If the teacher continues sorting cards, then students will never directly experience the connection of a picture with the actual letter that represents the beginning sound. I cannot emphasize this enough.

I once had a frustrated teacher tell me that her students would never get out of 2A! When I asked her to show me the assessments, I noticed that she was asking students to write entire words rather than the beginning sound for each word. They weren't proficient enough to do that correctly, but they were getting a lot of the individual sounds correct, which told me this group should have moved on long ago. Students should score close to 80 percent on the initial consonant sounds assessment while at Stage 2A. If they fail to reach that level, analyze the mistakes made and go back and reteach around the mistakes. After students master initial consonant sounds, proceed to the scope and sequence for Stage 2B, which includes consonant blends and diagraphs. The activities for 2B mirror the ones discussed above, with the exception of picture cards that demonstrate beginning blends and digraphs (see Figure 5.3). The assessments for both Beginning Stages 2A and 2B can be found in the Appendix. All word study materials needed for this stage, including picture cards and activities, can be downloaded from www.beverly tyner.net.

◇◇

(The following group of kindergartners completed the ELFS lessons and skipped the Emergent stage because they could already recognize and produce most of the letters. They are just finishing up the last few letters, followed by a lesson on initial consonant sounds /b/, /s/, and /m/ using a writing sort.)

Teacher: We are just about finished with our alphabet letters. Let's look at the last five letters.

(The teacher displays five capital letters and asks students to identify them.)

Teacher: Now let's match the lowercase letters with the capital letters.

(The teacher slides the lowercase letters underneath and asks students to give a thumbs up when she gets to the correct capital letter. The teacher controls the cards rather than giving them to students to sort. This keeps all students engaged in the activity.)

Teacher: I am going to give each of you a writing sort board and a marker. Today, we are going to look at some picture cards that have the same beginning sound. If we want to write the word *bird*, the first letter would be a *b*. The letter *b* stands for the first sound we hear at the beginning of *bird*. Write *b* in your first sorting box.

(The teacher places the Bb *letter card on the board and the* bird *picture card underneath the letter card.)*

Teacher: The *s* stands for the first sound we hear in *sun*, so I am going to put the *S* card here and the sun under it. Write the letter *s* in your middle box. Our last letter is *m*, and it stands for the first sound we hear in *man*. Write the letter *m* in your last box.

(The teacher places the letter card and picture card on the pocket chart and completes the minilesson.

Teacher: Please show me ready position.

("Ready position" is when students put their elbows on the table, hold their hands together, and rest their chins in their hands. This position keeps busy hands away from others and elevates the head so students are eye-to-eye with the teacher.)

Teacher: Now we are going to listen for the beginning sounds in some words, and you are going to write the beginning letter on your writing boards under the correct letter. The first picture is *book*. Say *book*. Now write the letter sound you hear at the beginning of *book*.

(The teacher observes that a student has difficulty with his attempt.)

Teacher: Caleb, listen: *book… bird*. Say those words with me. What do you hear at the beginning of those words?

Caleb: I hear /b/.

Teacher: That's right. Now write the letter that /b/ stands for.

Teacher: Good job. Aiden, where does this picture go?

Aiden: It goes under the bird.

Teacher: Why does it go there?

Aiden: It has the /b/ sound.

(The teacher places the picture of the book under the bird on her chart. The teacher then points to the Bb letter card.)

Teacher: Let's read the *Bb* column. The sound for *Bb* is /b/.

(Students respond together.)

Teacher: Now let's name the picture cards.

(Students respond together.)

Teacher: Do they all begin with the same sound? Give me a thumbs up or thumbs down.

(The activity is completed when there are two cards under each header picture card sort and students have successfully written the correct letters in each category.)

Figure 5.3
Picture Card Sort

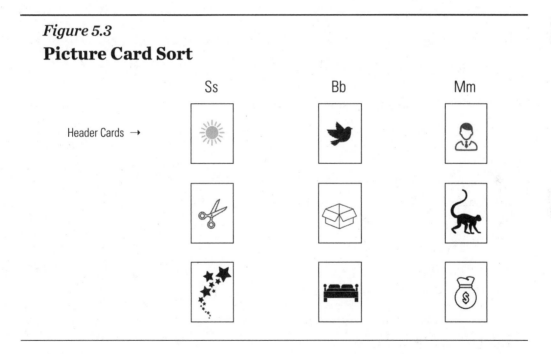

I also want to include a scenario for a group of students at Beginning Stage 2B. Word study for Stage 2B focuses on beginning digraphs and blends taught in isolation. Although the assessment for 2B is included in the Appendix, I suggest using it to gather additional information about students—not as an actual assessment. The scope and sequence serve as an introduction to these letter patterns, but mastery is not the goal at this stage. Students need to recognize that two letters can make one sound and that other letter pairs retain their individual sounds but blend together. As students move to Stage 3A and focus on word families, these blends and digraphs will be seen in some of those words.

◇◇◇

(This group of students has just begun Stage 2B and is being introduced to the digraphs sh, ch, *and* th. *The group is completing a closed sort with the teacher.)*

Teacher: Today, we are going to look at some letter pairs that hang together and make only one sound. We call these letter pairs *digraphs*.

(The teacher puts sh *on the pocket chart.)*

Teacher: When we see the letters *sh* together, they make the sound we make when we want someone to be quiet: /sh/. *Sheep* is a word that begins with the digraph *sh*.

(The teacher places a picture of sheep under the sh *digraph.)*

Teacher: The next digraph is *ch*, which sounds like /ch/. We hear this sound at the beginning of *chair*. Say *chair*.

(The teacher places a picture of a chair under the ch *digraph.)*

Teacher: The last digraph we have today is *wh*. This makes the /wh/ sound we hear at the beginning of *whale*.

(The teacher places a picture of a whale under the wh *digraph.)*

Teacher: I am going to give each of you two picture cards. Look at your cards and make sure you know the name of each picture.

(The teacher assists with picture names, if necessary.)

Teacher: Now, let's look at the digraph *sh*, which sounds like /sh/. Who has a picture that begins with this sound?

Simon: I have the shirt. It sounds like that.

Teacher: Good! Let's put the picture of the shirt under the sheep. Do *sheep* and *shirt* sound the same at the beginning?

Suzanne: Yes. They both sound like /sh/.

Teacher: Does anyone have a picture card that begins like *chair*?

Martha: I have cherries, and they go under the chair.

(This process continues until two picture cards are placed under each header card.)

Figure 5.4 shows an example sorting board for the digraphs *ch*, *sh*, and *wh*.

Figure 5.4
Digraph Sorting

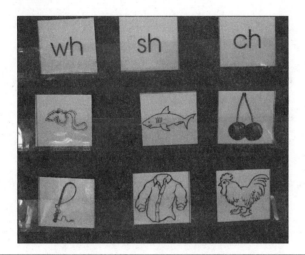

The purpose of cut-up sentences is to allow students to see words that have the focus sounds, digraphs, and blends in an authentic context. High-frequency words should also be included in these sentences. At the Beginning stage, the sentences are completed over a two-day span. On the first day, the teacher writes the sentence on a sentence strip with student input before cutting apart and mixing up the words. Then the teacher gives each student a part of the sentence, which is then reconstructed.

◇◇

(This small group of Beginning readers and writers is focusing on the initial consonant sounds /b/, /s/, and /m/. Therefore, the sentence contains words that begin with these focus sounds.)

Teacher: Today, we're going to be working with a new sentence. Listen: *The boy is mad.*

(This sentence was selected because it has several word bank words and two words with initial sounds that match the word study focus. The teacher repeats the sentence while touching her fingers in a left-to-right progression as students watch.)

Teacher: Listen again: *The boy is mad.* Now hold up your left hand and touch your fingers while we say this sentence together.

Students: The boy is mad.

Teacher: How many words do we have in our sentence today?

Students: Four.

Teacher: What is the first word in our sentence?

Beth: *The.*

Teacher: Yes. *The* is the first word, and it is one of our word bank words. Who remembers how to spell the word *the*?

Andy: *T-h-e.*

(The teacher writes the word on a sentence strip as students watch.)

Teacher: What kind of letter should we use at the beginning of a sentence?

Jill: A capital letter.

Teacher: Yes, we always start a sentence with a capital letter. Let's leave two finger spaces before we write the next word. What word comes next?

Nick: Boy.

Teacher: Yes, *boy.* How does *boy* sound at the beginning?

Jill: /b/

Teacher: Yes, and that sound is represented by the letter *b.* I will write the rest of the word, and you tell me the letters.

(Students name letters as the teacher writes the word on a sentence strip. They listen for and identify other strong consonant sounds in the middle or at the end of words. The teacher continues in this manner for the rest of the words. The sentence is then cut into individual words, which are distributed to the group for students to study and reassemble.)

This activity is excellent for Beginning readers and writers because it allows them to see how words come together to form sentences. It also provides a framework for the appropriate use of capital letters, spacing between words, and ending punctuation.

On the second day, students have individual cut-up sentences that are the same as the group sentence from the previous day. They independently cut apart the sentence and then put it back together and glue it in a journal. Finally, students copy the sentence and draw an illustrative picture. These individual cut-up sentences can be downloaded from www.beverlytyner.net. Figure 5.5 shows an example of an independent activity with cut-up sentences.

Figure 5.5

Cut-Up Sentence for Stage 2A

The cut-up sentences for Stage 2B are structured similarly, substituting words with blends and digraphs to accommodate for the focused patterns. Figure 5.6 shows some of the sentences that can be downloaded from www.beverlytyner.net.

❗ Independent word study extension activities for Stages 2A and B include the following ideas:

- Ask students to find pictures in magazines or draw pictures of things that begin with the focus beginning sounds, blends, or digraphs.

- Make copies of the picture cards so each student has a set. Students can cut up the picture cards and put them in a plastic bag to work with each day. Several activities can be completed with the cards, including sorting by initial sound or writing the beginning sound for each picture card.
- Have partners play a game of Memory. Using the focus picture cards, students turn over cards and try to make matches.
- Ask students to sort and paste the cards in journals. This activity could also be used as a form of assessment.
- Have students complete individual cut-up sentences (cut, paste, copy, draw).

Figure 5.6

Cut-Up Sentences for Stage 2B

The	sheep	are	in	the	grass	.
The	wheel	is	on	the	floor	.
The	cherries	are	in	the	glass	.
Do	sharks	eat	cheese	?		
The	sheep	was	thirsty	.		

Vocabulary

The high-frequency word list (see Figure 2.7, p. 33) lists words in order of how frequently they are seen in beginning text and should serve as the scope and sequence for introducing the words. These words have been chosen because they represent the order in which readers generally encounter words in early books. When the word bank gets to 20–25 words, retire 10 of the words for independent practice. Then add 10 new words to the word bank. The word bank should always contain at least 10 words that students know automatically, along with new words. Avoid the practice of working on 20 words at a time, retiring that group, and then working on another set of 20. I find that students learn new words more efficiently if they have some familiar words peppered among the unknown words.

Remember that students should recognize high-frequency words automatically and quickly. Begin by reviewing all the words in the word bank as a group. Students should say the words as soon as they are presented. Then shuffle the word cards to play Word Wizard. Add the words *zap* and *skip* to make the game more interesting. If students get the word *zap,* they must return all the words they have claimed so far. If they get the word *skip,* they must skip their turn.

(This small group of Beginning readers and writers has mastered most of the first 25 high-frequency words. The teacher dropped the 10 words they knew well and has added the next 10 words.)

Teacher: Your word bank has really been growing! Let's quickly flash through the word bank and see how quickly you can say the words. Remember, many of these words are new, so watch carefully.

(The teacher flashes the cards for group responses.)

Teacher: Now let's play a game of Word Wizard. I am going to add a new card to the deck today that says *skip.* If you get this word, you must skip your turn. I will still have the card *zap* in the deck. You don't want that card because if you get it, you must give me all your cards. I'm going to set the timer for two minutes. When the buzzer goes off, the person with the most cards wins the game and will be our Word Wizard for the day. Remember that you only have three seconds to say the word. If two of you miss the same word, that word will go in the fish pond and you will get a chance to fish for it when we finish. Ready?

(Students play Word Wizard.)

! Independent vocabulary extension activities include the following ideas:

- Play Beat the Clock using retired word bank words. All you need is a timer. Let students see how many words they can correctly identify in one minute. Each student can keep a record of his or her best time for fun.
- Create high-frequency word bingo cards, and let the group play independently. It's good practice to have students write the words and make their own cards.
- Students can complete word hunts using newspapers and magazines. They can look for and cut the focus words out and glue them in a journal. Let students have a contest to see who can find the most words. Anything that adds an element of competition leads to more interest!
- Choose five words that are particularly difficult for students. Ask them to make the words with magnetic letters and then write each word.

Comprehension

Reading a new text allows Beginning readers to practice their reading strategies. The teacher should carefully structure the discussion to support students' comprehension. Introduce the book by conducting a picture walk and encouraging students to look at the pictures while you verbalize important parts of the story. It is important to point out words that might be difficult for students and help them relate the words to the pictures. Build background knowledge only if necessary to understand the story. Do not build background that is discussed and revealed in the story. Next, select several high-frequency words from the text and introduce them on index cards. Set a purpose for reading that is personal and relevant to that particular book. Begin by reading the text aloud while students whisper read along with you. After a few pages, let the students choral read along with you. Be careful not to read too fast; keep their fluency levels in mind. This approach is appropriate until you feel confident calling on students to be lead readers while you and the rest of the group whisper read along with them.

Beginning readers will continue to need the support of an in-depth picture walk before reading the text. These readers are able to read text that is no longer patterned, so a picture walk provides them with information that is necessary for a successful reading.

The small group represented in the following scenarios is reading an informational book called *The Seasons*. With informational text, it is important to introduce all vocabulary with picture support during the picture walk. There may be words with which students are unfamiliar. Remember that the skill level for Beginning readers means they will not be able to recognize specialized vocabulary. The teacher should, however, encourage students to use picture support along with their knowledge of initial sounds to read the words. If students seem to be struggling, the teacher should wait until the next stage to introduce informational text.

(Before Reading)

Teacher: We're going to begin a new book today that is a little different from the other books we have read so far. The book is called *The Seasons*. Look at the front cover. Do you notice anything different about the picture?

Susan: It has real children on the cover, and they are at the beach. It looks like they are pictures from a camera.

Teacher: You're right. This is a story about real children and real things. We call this kind of book a nonfiction book. We have four seasons each year. What season is it right now?

Jill: It's fall.

Teacher: Yes, it is. Another name for the fall is autumn. Let's look at the pictures in the book and see what other seasons they show us.

(The teacher completes a picture walk of the book, pointing out pictures and words that will be important for a successful read of the story.)

Teacher: I want to show you a few words that we are going to see in our book today.

(The teacher writes three high-frequency words from the book on index cards. This is an excellent way to increase student knowledge of sight words beyond the group word bank.)

Teacher: Let's read this book to find all the things the children enjoy doing in the different seasons of the year.

(While reading, the teacher asks questions to increase students' comprehension. The teacher uses the illustrations for many of her questions.)

(During Reading)

Teacher: Let's read the title together. Everyone put your finger under the first word.

(The teacher and students read chorally.)

Teacher: Let's turn the page. Look at the picture. Do you remember what season this is?

Peter: Summer. The boys are playing at the beach.

Teacher: Great! Now let's read this page together.

(The teacher and students read.)

Teacher: Let's look at the next page. What clues do we have that it is still summer?

Joan: The girl has ice cream, and it looks like it's melting, so it's still summer.

Teacher: Good. Now I am going to start reading with you, but if I stop reading, I want you to keep going. Let's see if you can read this page together without my help.

(Students read the rest of the page.)

Teacher: You did a good job! Turn the page. Take your magic reading finger, and find the word *we*. Good! Now be a word detective and find the word *like*.

(Students finish reading the book with choral and stop-and-go reading. In stop-and-go reading, the teacher begins choral reading with students and then drops out as students continue reading. This allows the teacher to evaluate how well students are handling the text.)

(After Reading)

Teacher: Let's take a look at the three high-frequency words we saw in the story.

(The teacher shows the appropriate word cards as students identify them.)

Teacher: We read this book to find out all the things that the children like to do during each season. Who remembers what the children liked to do during the summer?

Anna: Oh, they liked to eat ice cream.

Teacher: Yes, they did.

Alexa: And I like to go swimming.

Teacher: We do like to go swimming, but did the book tell us about that?

Alexa: No.

Teacher: Remember, we only want to talk about things that we read in the book.

(The teacher continues to build students' ability to support questions with evidence from the text, which will be critical as they matriculate through the grades.)

Comprehension: Writing About Reading

Beginning writers will be drawing and writing some sentences about their favorite season. They will identify the season (e.g., I like spring) and draw and write a sentence about their picture or dictate a sentence to the teacher (e.g., I like flowers. I like to fly kites). This sentence dictation can take place after the picture is drawn out of group. See Figure 5.7 for a sample of a student's writing. If some students are unable to write sentences on their own, guide them by reminding them to apply their knowledge about letters, sounds, and high-frequency words. Provide support as needed.

◇◇

Teacher: Today, we read about the seasons. I want you to pick your favorite season. I want you to name two things you like about that season. So, if your favorite season is winter, you might draw a snowman and a Christmas tree. You can find the seasons in the book by looking at the pictures. Write the name of your season on your paper above your drawings. Use this sentence to write about your favorite season: *I like* _____. You can fill in the blank with the name of the season. Go back and look in the book for the pictures and the name of your favorite season.

Figure 5.7
Student Writing Response

When to Move to the Next Stage

Several skills should be mastered before students are ready to begin the Fledgling stage. Along with complete alphabet recognition and production, students should be able to identify and write most initial consonant sounds. Students should score close to 80 percent on the Stage 2A assessment (see Appendix). If students don't meet this score, analyze their mistakes and go back and reteach. Students will have progressed through the 2B lessons that focus on initial digraphs and blends, but they do not need to master these skills to proceed to the Fledgling stage. You may administer the Stage 2B assessment to assess students' progress, but do not repeat Stage 2B. Whatever the score, students should move directly to the Fledgling stage.

Remember that the decision to move to the next stage is based on word study and not high-frequency word recognition. Students should be fluent and confident in finger-point reading of simple texts, but continue to look at the overall progress of the group. Students will continue to review initial and final sounds in the context of words—instead of pictures—in the next phase of word study. It is better to move ahead than to remain with material that is not challenging. Look for common areas of weakness and plan to reteach those skills. Keep in mind that instructional decisions should be based on the majority of students' needs and not on the lowest student in the group.

Conclusion

The Beginning reader and writer is like a sitting rocket being fueled. These students are now equipped with the basic strategies that will launch them into the world of literacy. It is at the Beginning stage that many slower learners and ELLs may need extra time. The diligent work done at this stage is well worth the effort, because the Fledgling stage is one of great excitement for both students and teachers.

Chapter 6

The Fledgling Reader and Writer

Characteristics of Fledgling Readers and Writers

Fledgling Readers and writers are typically mid-kindergartners to mid-1st graders and can best be described as novice, inexperienced, or learning a new skill. Pay close attention to the word *typically*. A number of students will fall out of this typical grade-level range, and you need to look closely at their characteristics and consider using assessments to make this determination. Many kindergartners are Fledgling readers and writers, and some students with disabilities may be at the Fledgling stage in 2nd grade or beyond.

Although students at the Fledgling stage bring some basic literacy knowledge to the table, they are still relatively new to the reading and writing processes. In the beginning of this stage, students are reading simple texts and have generally mastered around 30–50 high-frequency words. They are also capable of writing simple sentences. With solid initial consonant knowledge supported by strong phonemic awareness, students are ready to learn about word families and one-syllable words with short vowel sounds. Expectations for students at the Fledgling stage—in terms of text levels, word study, vocabulary (including high-frequency words), comprehension, and writing—are presented in Figure 6.1.

For teachers who have carefully laid a solid foundation, the work at previous reading stages is fully realized at the Fledgling stage. These students, although inexperienced, are equipped with the knowledge necessary to begin applying their decoding and comprehension strategies.

Fledgling readers can easily read text featuring simple sentence structures with significant picture support. About halfway through this stage, students will complete their study of the first 100 high-frequency words, and vocabulary will transition to the study of words selected from the text. Supported by this increased high-frequency word knowledge, Fledgling readers will also make great advances in their instructional book levels.

Figure 6.1

Stage 3: Fledgling Reader and Writer

Fluency	Vocabulary	Word Study	Reading Comprehension	Writing About Reading
• Typically, early to mid-1st grade • Book levels EI 6–11, F&P E/F/G • Out of patterned text • Repeated reading of simple text	Recognizing 100 high-frequency words	• Recognizing and using word families (3A) • Recognizing and using blends and digraphs in word families (3A) • Recognizing and using short-vowel one-syllable words (3B)	• Using word family knowledge in decoding • Reading simple text • Self-correcting reading errors • Using sentence context and pictures or word recognition cues to decode • Summarizing the text	• Using word family and short-vowel knowledge to write words • Writing 3–5 sentences to respond to the book or text • Using correct capitalization and punctuation

EI: Early Intervention   F&P: Fountas and Pinnell

The difference between Stages 3A and 3B is solely with word study. This stage is divided into two parts: Stage 3A focuses on common word families, and Stage 3B is centered on one-syllable words with short-vowel sounds (in the predictable CVC pattern) that no longer rhyme. This stage is particularly exciting for new writers. Fledgling writers bring with them solid alphabet and sound knowledge, along with the knowledge of numerous high-frequency words. By the end of the stage, students will be able to write four or five sentences that show understanding of a text. They will also respond to text for a specific purpose, such as writing about a problem and solution, writing to summarize the story, writing to discuss character traits. or writing about the main idea and supporting details.

Using carefully leveled books continues to be critical for success in early reading. For Fledgling readers and writers, choose texts that contain a variety of sentence patterns and punctuation. Both narrative and informational texts with moderate picture support should be considered. Books that contain high-frequency words and easily decodable words are also important when making text selections. These texts will increase in difficulty and provide a foundation for deeper reading comprehension.

Fledgling readers will generally complete the first 100 high-frequency words by the end of this stage. Once they do this, don't waste time moving on to another word list. These students will continue to practice automatic high-frequency word recognition as they read the text. Focus instead on reading the text and selecting vocabulary words for intentional focus.

Fledgling readers and writers essentially address common kindergarten and 1st grade language arts standards. As we reach this stage, the number of standards that are addressed in the lesson plan increase. Standards that support the lesson components for the Fledgling stage can be found in the Appendix. I provide this list for busy teachers so they can easily identify the standards that support or could support the lesson plan model.

Lesson Plan Components at the Fledgling Stage

The lesson plan that supports this stage continues to support fluency, word study, vocabulary, and comprehension and is supported by familiar strategies used at earlier stages. Figure 6.2 shows the lesson plan model for both Stages 3A and 3B. Remember, the distinguishing feature between these two levels is seen in the focus vowel patterns and will be discussed in depth later in this chapter. You will also see text levels and writing skills increase as students progress through this Fledgling stage. In the following sections, each lesson plan component will be discussed followed by a vignette that follows students working through this stage.

Fluency

Common fluency standards at the Fledgling stage include reading and understanding 1st grade text. This is a very general standard and must be further defined as you plan for the specific needs of your students. Kindergarten and 1st grade standards vary from state to state in terms of reading expectations. Many states require kindergarten students to read texts that other states consider 1st grade text. The point is, students need to be reading at an appropriate instructional level apart from those dictated by standards.

For Fledgling readers, rereading continues to be an important lesson element. Each lesson begins by rereading the book that was introduced in the previous lesson. Fledgling readers are practicing appropriate reading speed, accuracy, and expression. Phrasing is a central focus of these lessons and should be teacher modeled.

The students in the following scenarios are rereading a book called *Eggs and Dandelions*, which is appropriate for mid-1st grade students who are reading on grade level. The purposes for the reread are to practice reading simple text and develop fluency. Students will reread text using varied strategies, such as choral reading, teacher-led reading, student-led reading, and whisper reading (discussed in Chapter 2).

Figure 6.2

Lesson Plan: Fledgling Stage

FLUENCY	FLUENCY EXTENSION
Text Level: _____ Reread: ☐ Choral Reading ☐ Teacher-Led Reading ☐ Student-Led Reading ☐ Whisper Reading	☐ Reread with a partner ☐ Buddy read ☐ Other
WORD STUDY	**WORD STUDY EXTENSION**
Word Families (3A) Lesson # _____ Short Vowels (3B) Lesson # _____ ☐ Card Sort ☐ Sound Boxes ☐ Writing Sort ☐ Word Scramble ☐ Sentence Dictation	☐ Cut and sort cards. ☐ Write the sort in a notebook. ☐ Write sentences with words from each pattern. Circle parts of speech. ☐ Word hunts: find words in books that have the same patterns. Add them to the list. ☐ Other: _____
VOCABULARY	**VOCABULARY EXTENSION**

High-Frequency Words (HFW)
   ☐ 40–60
   ☐ 60–80
   ☐ 80–100
   ☐ _____
☐ Word Wizard Game
	☐ Make and write high-frequency words (magnetic letters).
	☐ Beat the clock (with partner).
	☐ Play Memory.
	☐ Read and write sentences with high-frequency words.
	☐ Other: _____

COMPREHENSION	COMPREHENSION EXTENSION
New Read: _____ Text Level: _____ **Before Reading** ☐ Build background knowledge (if needed). ☐ Introduce story vocabulary. ☐ Set the purpose. **During Reading** ☐ Stopping points/text-dependent questions • • • • **After Reading** ☐ Review vocabulary (oral sentences using words in context). ☐ Revisit and discuss purpose for reading. ☐ Discuss writing extension.	Write sentences with each vocabulary word as used in text. ☐ Write to summarize ☐ Main ideas/details ☐ Problem/solution ☐ Compare/contrast ☐ Cause/effect ☐ Writing checklists ☐ Other:

◇◇

(An in-depth discussion to enhance comprehension was conducted the previous day, so very little time is spent in comprehension discussion with the reread. The purpose for rereading is to develop fluency, so keep this in mind.)

(Before Reading)

Teacher: Yesterday, we read the book *Eggs and Dandelions*, and today we are going to reread the book for practice. We found out something very interesting about dandelions yesterday. Luke, what do you remember?

Luke: Bears like to eat dandelions, and some people like to eat them in salads.

Teacher: I'm not sure if I would like them in my salad, but I may try that sometime. What was the problem that the bears were trying to solve?

Brian: Mother Bear wanted Father Bear and Baby Bear to find some food. They found some eggs, but they smelled bad.

Teacher: How did they solve the problem?

Jennifer: They kept looking, and then they found some good eggs and some dandelions.

Teacher: OK. I think we are ready to reread this book. Let's try to read the story today to make it sound like it is really happening. Let's read the title together.

(The teacher and students read the title aloud.)

(During Reading)

Teacher: Turn to page 3. I'm going to be the lead reader on the first page to get us started. Who is doing the talking on this page?

Harrison: Mother Bear, because it says, "said Mother Bear."

Teacher: There are two question marks on this page. I know that my voice needs to go up when there is a question. I also see a comma in the last line, so I need to pause there. Whisper read along with me while I read this page.

(The teacher reads with speed, accuracy, and expression, but she also makes sure she is not reading too quickly and dragging students through the text.)

Teacher: This time, you choral read with me.

(The teacher and students read together.)

Teacher: Now let's turn to page 5. Luke is going to be the lead reader on this page, and we will be the whisper readers. I see some quotation marks on this page. Can you find them? What do they tell us?

Susan: They tell us that someone is talking.

Teacher: Now Luke, will you get us started?

(The book is completed and each student has an opportunity to be the lead reader.)

(After Reading)

Teacher: Please put your book in your folder. When we finish group today, I want you to reread this book with your reading partner. When you finish, put your copy of the book in your independent reading box.

! Independent fluency extension activities include the following ideas:

- Have students reread books with a partner from their reading group.
- Assign students to read a certain number of books per week with a buddy. Using a Buddy Reading Log, students should record the name of the book,

and the buddy must sign the log to indicate that he or she listened to the student read the book.

- Let students record themselves reading at least once a week. After listening to the recording, students read the text again and try to improve.

Word Study

Word study for Fledgling readers and writers involves the systematic study of word families and one-syllable words with short-vowel sounds. This phase of word study will be long but important. Let me explain the difference between Stages 3A and 3B in word study. Whereas stage 3A focuses solely on word family patterns, Stage 3B focuses on the study of one-syllable words that no longer rhyme. Students should commit a good number of these words to sight memory and develop competence in spelling these patterns.

There are five activities that support Fledgling readers' word study: card sorts, writing sorts, sound boxes, word scrambles, and sentence dictation. These activities are discussed in depth in Chapter 2. Rotate among the activities since each addresses these patterns in a different way and helps students solidify their phonics knowledge. You will not have time to complete each activity; you should expect to do one of the activities and a sentence dictation daily. The suggested scope and sequence and spelling assessment for stages 3A and 3B can be found in the Appendix. Progress through the sequence as suggested, reteaching as indicated by assessment. Again, all word study materials can be downloaded from www.beverlytyner.net.

Card Sorts: There are two different types of card sorts: open and closed sorts. With an open sort, the teacher shows students all the cards, and they work together to figure out the common patterns. This activity takes a great deal of time, so I therefore recommend using closed sorts, where the teacher shows and discusses each pattern. This activity should only be used on the first day when introducing new word patterns. Begin with three header cards for the short *a* word family: *cat*, *man*, and *cap*. The words should be ones that students recognize.

Demonstrate the card sort process to students. Start with the word card *mat*. Ask students in which column the word should be placed. Slide the card under each header word and finally place it under *cat*. Students shouldn't be required to say the word first and then sort it. If students know the header card and sort the word correctly, they can identify the new word by substituting the initial sound (see Figure 6.3).

Figure 6.3
Card Sort

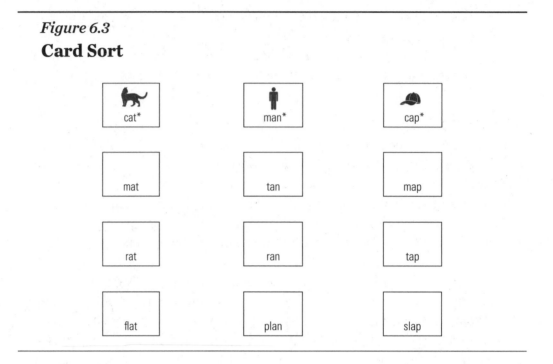

Continue to take turns, allowing students to sort the cards in the appropriate columns. After each card has been sorted, have students read all the words in each column to determine if they are placed correctly. Use no more than two or three cards in each category per lesson; there will not be time for more. This activity should be fast paced. Follow the same procedure for other short-vowel sounds. After completing this activity for the short *a* and short *i* word families, review the two families together. This ensures that students can clearly distinguish between the two sounds (e.g., *man-big-cat-hit*). Do the same thing for other pairs of short-vowel sounds.

(The following dialogue follows a group of 1st graders as they participate in a closed sort at the beginning of Stage 3A. The teacher clearly establishes the word family patterns rather than asking students to discover the patterns in an open sort.)

Teacher: Today I have three words I want you to look at.

(The teacher places the words cat, man, *and* cap *on the pocket chart.)*

Teacher: What do you notice about these three words?

Beth: Well, they all have an *a* in them.

Teacher: Good. How are they different?

Rick: The first and last letters are different.

Teacher: Yes, good observation. Now I'm going to give each of you a word. They all have the letter *a* in them. Your job is to figure out which category your words need to go in.

(The teacher distributes word cards to students.)

Teacher: What word do you have?

Laura: I'm not sure.

Teacher: Let me help you figure it out. Where do you think your word would go? Does it look the same as another word?

Laura: I think it looks like the one that ends with a *t*.

Teacher: Why?

Laura: My word ends with a *t*.

Teacher: OK. Put the word under the other word. This first word is *cat*. So what letter sound do you have at the beginning of your word?

Laura: *S*. It sounds like /s/. Oh, I know! It's *sat*, and it rhymes with *cat*.

(The activity continues with the other students' words.)

Writing Sorts: Writing sorts provide students with ample opportunities to both sort and write words. During traditional card-sorting activities, only one student is sorting while the others are observing. In my experience, this lack of interaction leads to boredom and off-task behavior. The writing sort requires all students to write the words in the correct category, so everyone is busy. Students can use the writing sort templates for this activity (see Appendix). These sheets can be placed in sheet protectors and used multiple times. Figure 6.4 shows a completed writing sort for a student reviewing the *at*, *it*, and *ot* word families. The dictated sentence at the bottom of the page is discussed at the end of the stage.

Figure 6.4

Sample Writing Sort

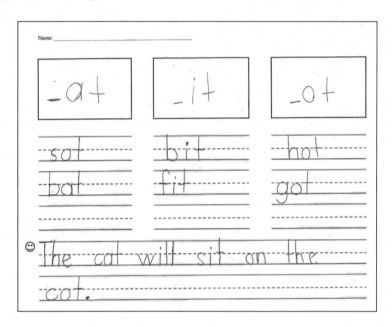

(The following group of Fledgling readers is reviewing the a, i, *and* o *word families. The teacher begins with a short minilesson, followed by a writing sort.)*

Teacher: Today, we are going to do a writing sort with the *a, i,* and o word families.

(The teacher places header cards for cat, hit, *and* hot *in the pocket chart. She then distributes the writing sort template and a personal whiteboard to each student.)*

Teacher: Write these header words on top of the three boxes: *cat, hit,* and *hot.* Then write the word family for each word in the box.

(The teacher monitors as students write and assists when necessary.)

Teacher: The first word is *pot.* Say *pot.*

Students: *Pot.*

Teacher: Which family does *pot* belong to? Write the word under the correct family.

(Students look for the pattern in the boxes and write the word pot *under the* ot *word family. When all students have this written correctly, the teacher continues.)*

Teacher: Yes, *pot* goes under the *ot* family. Let's read the words in this family together.

All: *Hot ... pot.*

Teacher: The next word is *flat.* Say *flat.*

Students: *Flat.*

Teacher: Which family does *flat* belong to? Write the word under the correct family.

(If a student starts looking around at other students, you know that they need help, so lean in and assist. This teacher continues to sort the word cards on a tabletop sorting board as a way for students to check their work. She continues this process and calls out four more words for students to sort and write.)

Sound Boxes: Sound boxes are particularly useful for Fledgling spellers. They help students isolate and blend sounds to read simple, one-syllable words. For this activity, use the sound box template found in the Appendix. The sound boxes can also be constructed on heavy cardstock and placed in sheet protectors so they can be reused. You can use this activity for three-, four-, and even five-letter words with short vowels. Figure 6.5 shows examples of sound boxes used with words that have a digraph and blend. I have provided "cheat sheets" online that show examples of all patterns suitable at the Fledgling stage. I was never taught basic phonics in elementary school, so I know there must be other teachers who also need this support. I found that some teachers were not using sound boxes as an activity because of their fear of not using them correctly. These are for you.

With the sound boxes in front of each student, call out a word (such as *fat*).

Ask students to touch their fingers to each sound in the word *fat* and then write the letters that make those sounds in the appropriate boxes. Remind students that they should use only one box for each sound they hear. Finally, help students segment and blend the sounds back together. Remember that a digraph (e.g., *sh, ch, th*) is placed in one box because the two letters make one sound. Consonant blends (e.g., *bl, cr, st*) retain both letter sounds and should be written in two separate boxes.

Figure 6.5

Sample Sound Boxes

(The following students are doing a mixed review lesson for the o *and* u *word families. The teacher begins each activity with a short minilesson.)*

Teacher: We have already completed the *o* and *u* word families, and today we are going to mix some of these families.

(The teacher turns to the tabletop pocket chart.)

Teacher: The first word family we will review today is the *o* family, like in the word *hot*.

(The teacher places the hot *header card on the chart.)*

Teacher: We also have the *u* word family, like in the word *nut*.

(The teacher places the hit *header card on the chart. The minilesson continues until four words are discussed and placed on the pocket chart.)*

Teacher: Today, we are going to work in our sound boxes. Remember that only one sound can go in each box, but when we have two letters together that make a new sound, the two letters go in one box.

(The teacher distributes sound boxes, dry-erase markers, and erasers.)

Teacher: The first word is *shut*. Say *shut*.

Students: *Shut.*

Teacher: Let's touch the sounds we hear in *shut*.

(The teacher and students touch each sound on their fingers.)

Teacher: So how many sound boxes do we need to write the word *shut*?

Students: Three.

Teacher: Pick up your markers, and write the word *shut*.

(The teacher monitors and assists if needed. The teacher then guides students in pronouncing each sound individually as they place their fingers under the respective letters.)

Teacher: Now let's go back and do this the smooth way.

(The teacher slides her finger under letters as the entire word is pronounced.)

Teacher: Here is my card for *shut*. Where does it go?

Erica: It goes under *nut* because it belongs to the *ut* family.

Teacher: Good. Now let's read these words.

(The teacher points to nut *and* shut *while students say the words aloud.)*

Rosa: Those are rhyming words.

Teacher: Yes. Look at the two words. How are they the same?

Kate: The last two letters are the same.

Teacher: Right! That makes these two words rhyme.

(This process continues until two words for each pattern are written in the sound boxes. After each word, the teacher always places it on the chart and reads the entire column. This helps students see the relationship among the words.)

Word Scrambles: In word scrambles, students physically move letters to spell (and then write) words. This helps students make connections between patterns and solidify their word knowledge. Word scramble activities for Fledgling readers should be geared to the scope and sequence. For example, if students are reviewing the short vowels *a* and *i*, then the word scramble will involve students making words with these short-vowel sounds. After students make a word, they should write it underneath. This writing part is critical!

◇◇◇

Teacher: Today, we are going to make words from the word families we have been studying: the *o* family as in *pot*, the *u* family as in *cut*, and the *e* family as in *pet*.

(The teacher places these words on the pocket chart and distributes the following letter cards: o, u, e, h, t, s, b.*)*

Teacher: You will need these letters to make the words. Line your letters up at the top of your paper. Make the word *hot*. Say *hot*.

Students: *Hot.*

Teacher: Let's touch the sounds in *hot* with our fingers. Now make the word *hot*. After you make the word, write the word *hot* underneath.

(The teacher observes students and assists those who are having difficulty. Reduce the support of touching the individual sounds as quickly as possible. Oversupporting students will hold them back in the long run. Start by giving the least amount of support and add support only if needed.)

Teacher: Where does the word *hot* go on the board?

(The teacher sorts the word correctly on the chart.)

Teacher: Now add one letter to make the word *shot*. Which letter will you need to change?

Luke: You add an *s*.

Teacher: Yes! Now write the word *shot*.

(The teacher monitors and assists students as needed.)

Teacher: Where should we put the word card for *shot*?

Marcus: It goes under *pot*.

Teacher: Good. Let's read the column for this word family.

Prewritten word scramble activities that support students at the Fledgling stage are provided at www.beverlytyner.net. Figure 6.6 gives an example of a word scramble activity.

Sentence Dictation: This activity gives students the opportunity to apply their word study knowledge in the context of real writing. The teacher should select a short sentence that incorporates some high-frequency words with the focus patterns. The teacher then dictates the sentence so students can write it. Although this is included on the writing sort template, it should be included every day after the activity is completed. Remember that the other activities rotate, but the dictated sentence is daily. Alternatively, you could use a writing journal for the dictated sentences.

Figure 6.6
Example Word Scramble Activity at the Fledgling Stage

Word Family: *a*

Letters: *t, b, f, l, a, p, c, s*

1. Make the word *bat.*
2. Change one letter to spell *fat.*
3. Change one letter to spell *cat.*
4. Change one letter to spell *cap.*
5. Change one letter to spell *lap.*
6. Add one letter to spell *flap.*
7. Change one letter to spell *slap.*
8. Change one letter to spell *clap.*

Teacher: The sentence for today is *The hen will hop on the truck.* Let me repeat the sentence. *The hen will hop on the truck.* Now you say the sentence with me and touch your fingers as you say each word. How many words are in this sentence?

Joan: There are seven words in the sentence.

Teacher: Yes. Now let's say the sentence again so you can remember all the words when you write the sentence.

(Students may need to repeat the sentence several times to commit it to memory. Do not complete this activity by having students write one word at a time. Students should commit the entire sentence to memory. If a student gets stuck, simply have him or her start from the beginning of the sentence and recite up to the unknown word.)

Teacher: Pick up your markers and write the sentences. I am looking for a five-star sentence. That means it should have a capital letter at the beginning, punctuation at the end, and spacing between words. All words should be spelled correctly, and the sentence should make sense and not be missing any words.

(This activity also gives teachers an opportunity to observe things such as punctuation, capitalization, and spelling in an authentic context. Rather than telling students they forgot a capital letter or period, simply say, "You have a three-star sentence. Go back and look for ways to make it a five-star sentence." This allows students to become editors of their own writing.)

Word study in Stage 3B is short in nature and focuses on short vowels in one-syllable words that are no longer associated with word families. The same activities used in Stage 3A will apply to Stage 3B. It is important to use the words *vowel patterns* as new patterns are introduced. Therefore, as students are identifying words, the teacher would ask, "What is the vowel pattern in this word?" Remember that in Stage 3A, we use the term *word families*. At this stage, the vowel pattern will be CVC. I find that many students get confused when they look at these letters and then try to remember what they stand for, so I say that the vowel is closed up on both sides by consonant letters. When we see this pattern, we know the vowel sound will be short. The same activities (sorting, word scramble, sound boxes, and dictated sentences) used in Stage 3A of word study are also appropriate for Stage 3B.

As you finish the Stage 3A scope and sequence, administer the stage 3A assessment. Review students' results and customize a review based on common mistakes. The entire sequence does not need to be repeated unless half the students score less than 60 percent. Then readminister the assessment and consider grouping options. Students who still score poorly may need to be placed in another group. Finally, begin the short-vowel sequence with words that no longer rhyme (i.e., Stage 3B). Establishing effective routines for word study is important for success in developing decoding skills. See the Appendix for these word study assessments.

⚠ Independent word study extension activities include the following ideas:

- Have students go on a word hunt using books, newspapers, and magazines. Students should look for words that have the same vowel patterns they are currently studying.

- Ask partners to play Memory, making matches with word families or words with short-vowel sounds.
- Have students sort individual word cards and write the sorts in a small-group notebook.
- Have students cut, sort, and glue words in word study journals.
- Ask students to choose two words from each pattern and write a sentence with each word.
- Ask students to use letter cards to make as many words as they can that fit the word study patterns. Let students work with a partner to complete the activity out of group for higher student engagement.

Vocabulary

As students progress to more complex text selections, automaticity in word recognition and knowledge of vocabulary words will be valuable. Fledgling readers and writers should be able to commit the first 100 high-frequency words to memory by the end of the stage. After the high-frequency words have been mastered, vocabulary should be preselected from the text. Refrain from continuing with more high-frequency words after students master the first 100 words.

(This small group is working on the last 25 high-frequency words. When they complete these words, they will move to focusing on vocabulary from the text that is important to comprehension.)

Teacher: Let's play Word Wizard. First, let's all review the words together.

(The teacher flashes words to the whole group, and students respond chorally.)

Teacher: Today, I'm going to add a few more cards to the deck to make the game a little more interesting. We already have *zap* and *skip*. So now I am going to add *reverse* and *pass*. If you get *reverse*, we will switch the direction of play, and if you get *pass*, you will pass all your cards to the next player. Ready? I'll set the timer for two minutes, and when the buzzer goes off, whoever has the most cards will be the winner.

(Students complete the game.)

⚠ Independent vocabulary extension activities include the following ideas:

- Choose five high-frequency words that seem to be particularly difficult for students. Ask students to write at least an eight-word sentence with each of the troublesome words. The more students see these high-frequency words, the more likely they will recognize them.
- Students play Word Wizard with a small group, but assign one student to be the teacher.

Comprehension

The numerous comprehension strategies that can be addressed in this component are listed in the Appendix. Although fluency and decoding—rather than deep comprehension—is still the primary focus for Fledgling readers and writers, there are several strategies to focus on before, during, and after reading. These strategies will begin to lay the foundation for more in-depth comprehension instruction at future reading and writing stages.

◇◇

(This group of mid-1st grade students is near the end of the Fledgling stage and reading a level 10 book. This is an informational text and includes some content-specific vocabulary. These students completed the first 100 high-frequency words earlier in the stage. Before reading, the teacher briefly introduces the book by focusing on the cover of the book. These students are close to knowing 100 high-frequency words and do not need a picture walk.)

(Before Reading)

Teacher: Today, we are going to read a book called *When the Wind Blows*. Let's look at the front cover to see if we can get some more clues about what this book will be about.

Adam: This looks like a real story about the wind because the children are flying kites.

Teacher: What kinds of things does the wind help us do?

Jennifer: It can make the kite fly, and it can also help dry clothes.

Harrison: I saw some windmills, and the wind makes them blow.

(Content-related words make informational text difficult for many Fledgling readers. Providing upfront vocabulary support is an important step to a successful first read of any book.)

Teacher: Let's look at some of the words we will see in the book. I see *windmill*, *millstone*, and *wind pump*. Some of these words may be new to you.

(The teacher displays the words on index cards on the pocket chart and tells students they will learn what these words mean by reading the book.)

Teacher: Let's read this book to find out how wind can help but also hurt us.

(The teacher gives each student a book. During the first read, the teacher uses questioning strategies to enhance students' comprehension.)

(During Reading)

Teacher: Let's read the title of the book together.

(The teacher and students read the title aloud.)

Teacher: Look at page 3. The little girl is flying a kite, and it looks like the wind is blowing. Have you ever tried to fly a kite on a day when the wind wasn't blowing?

Luke: Yeah, and I had to run and run and keep running to keep my kite up.

Teacher: How do you think that helped keep the kite go up?

Laura: It made wind when he ran.

Teacher: Yes, now let's read the first page together.

(The teacher and students choral read the first page.)

Teacher: On the next page, we are going to read about how strong wind can help us. How is it helping in the picture?

John: It's making the sailboat move because it doesn't have a motor.

Teacher: Can a strong wind also hurt us? How?

Ken: Strong wind can blow down trees or blow things down like in a hurricane or tornado.

Teacher: Right. On this page, we are going to read about some more ways that wind can be helpful.

(The teacher uses choral reading and lead reading techniques to complete the book.)

(After Reading)

Teacher: Let's go back and take at a look at our vocabulary words. The first word is *windmill*. Who can give us a sentence using the word *windmill* that tells something that we learned in the story?

Jackie: The windmill can create electricity.

Teacher: Great job, Jackie!

(The process continues with the other vocabulary words.)

Teacher: Today, we read about different ways that wind can help us and hurt us. Let's see how many things we remember about these two topics.

(The teacher records students' thoughts and suggestions on a dry-erase board.)

Comprehension: Writing About Reading

Teacher: When you leave group today, I want you to write about how wind helps us and hurts us. I am going to write your first sentence: *Wind can help and hurt us.* Use your journal, and write this as your first sentence. Then write at least two more sentences that tell how wind helps us and at least two sentences that tell how wind hurts us. These examples must come from the book. The last sentence should tell again that you are writing about how wind helps and hurts us.

(The concluding sentence can also be given to students, if necessary. See Figure 6.7 for an example student response to this writing prompt.)

! Independent writing extension activities include the following ideas:

• Use a graphic organizer to write a short summary based on the story.
• Write a short story summary.

- Write a sentence with each vocabulary word that tells something that happened in the story.
- Illustrate the vocabulary words.
- Complete a story map based on the story.
- Choose an illustration from the story and ask students to write about the event shown in the illustration, using specific details from the picture.
- Write about what you learned.
- Write about the problem and how the problem was solved.
- Sequence the events in the story.
- Write about your favorite character.

Figure 6.7

Sample Student Writing Response: How Wind Helps Us and Hurts Us

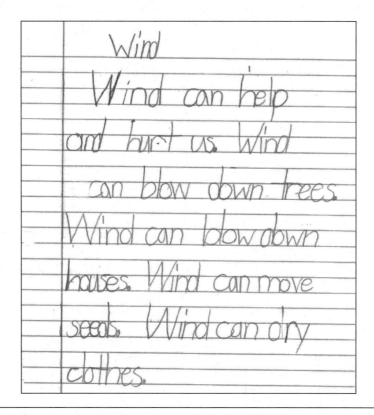

When to Move to the Next Stage

There are several milestones to consider before advancing to the Transitional stage. Students should be able to automatically recognize and write many words with short-vowel sounds. Students should also be able to recognize at least 100 high-frequency words. At this point, completion of a quick Reading Review is feasible to determine if students are reading at an appropriate level (see Chapter 3 for more information). This assessment should provide ample information to determine students' readiness for the next stage. Additionally, students should have successfully passed the spelling assessments for word families (Stage 3A) and short vowels (Stage 3B). These assessment scores give teachers the affirmation they need to move to the next stage. As students move to the next stage, they will rely on this foundational knowledge to navigate more complex reading and writing.

Conclusion

The Fledgling stage allows students to improve and extend their existing range of skills. By orchestrating experiences with vowel patterns, writing, vocabulary, and comprehension, students are able to exhibit greater confidence as readers and writers. Fledgling readers and writers are capable of enjoying reading and writing about simple texts. In the next stage, the Transitional stage, students will advance toward fluency in both reading and writing.

Chapter 7

The Transitional Reader and Writer

Characteristics of Transitional Readers and Writers

Transitional readers and writers are typically mid- to late 1st graders. These students have mastered the skills necessary to begin this important stage of literacy development—including the study of word families and one-syllable words with short-vowel sounds. For the first time, Transitional students are able to read and write independently for specific purposes with little teacher modeling. As you navigate through the lesson plan sequence, you will notice that these students will be reaching higher literacy levels in both reading and writing. Expectations for students at the Transitional stage—in terms of text levels, word study, vocabulary (including high-frequency words), comprehension, and writing—are presented in Figure 7.1.

Although they still rely on significant teacher support, Transitional readers are working toward reading and writing independence. Additionally, they can confidently read and decode one-syllable words with short-vowel sounds, consonant blends, and digraphs. Although learning to read and process text has been the primary focus for Emergent, Beginning, and Fledgling readers, there is an increased emphasis on comprehension at this stage as Transitional students begin to orchestrate decoding and comprehension strategies. Students will automatically use decoding skills to unlock new words. These foundational phonics skills will play an important part as students read more difficult text. Finally, writing in response to reading becomes critical at this stage since it supports comprehension of increasingly difficult texts.

Figure 7.1

Stage 4: Transitional Reader and Writer

Fluency	Vocabulary	Word Study	Reading Comprehension	Writing About Reading
• Typically, mid- to late 1st grade • Book levels EI 12–17, F&P H/I • Rereading to develop fluency	• Identifying words from text • Summarizing text with selected vocabulary	• Recognizing and using common vowel patterns • Writing dictated sentences using words with common vowel patterns	• Using common vowel pattern knowledge in decoding • Developing independent reading using decoding and simple comprehension strategies • Beginning to read for a purpose	• Using common vowel patterns correctly in writing • Writing most high-frequency words correctly • Using punctuation and capitalization correctly • Writing a simple paragraph for a specific comprehension purpose • Using some text evidence in writing

EI: Early Intervention   F&P: Fountas and Pinnell

At this stage, Transitional readers and writers are ready to study another important aspect of word recognition—the teaching of common, one-syllable vowel patterns. Success in mastering common vowel patterns depends on previous success in mastering consonant sounds, word families, and short vowels. Each stage builds upon the prior stage. For example, mastery of initial consonants prepares students for word families since students recognize that the first letter is the only thing that changes as word families are built. Success in reading and spelling short vowels naturally leads to work on the five short-vowel patterns, and mastery of words with short vowels brings essential knowledge to common one-syllable vowel patterns.

The differentiation at the Transitional stage is embedded in word study in 4A and 4B. Word study for the Transitional lesson plan begins at Stage 4A—common vowel patterns. The study of common vowel patterns is long and often frustrating for both teachers and students. The easier patterns are presented at Stage 4A; at

Stage 4B, some of the more difficult vowel patterns are presented—along with a review of vowel patterns addressed in 4A.

Text levels will obviously advance through this stage based on your observations and assessments. In addition, writing skills will vastly improve, and you will adjust writing assignments accordingly. Visually, though, there will be a distinct difference noted in the word study section of the lesson plan to address the patterns at both 4A and 4B. This is the reason these two levels are noted.

Transitional writers are quickly honing skills that allow them to write in a much more sophisticated way as they respond to text. Students focus on writing a well-constructed paragraph for specific comprehension purposes that is supported by specific evidence from the text. They will consistently use their word study skills and basic writing fundamentals as they demonstrate their understanding of text, and you should hold students accountable for the correct use of previously taught vowel patterns in their independent writing. It is here that we see how reading and writing develop hand in hand.

The leveled texts used for Transitional readers and writers should include longer text pieces, both narrative and informational, that encourage growth in both reading and writing. Using a wide variety of genres is increasingly important for Transitional readers and writers because they present opportunities to write for varying purposes. When selecting texts, be sure to include poetry, fairy tales, biographies, and narrative text (to name just a few). Informational text should include support for grade-level standards in both science and social studies. The texts should also rely less on illustrations and visual support as students begin to read more closely and find clues to make meaning in context. Common standards that support or could be supported at the Transitional stage can be found in the Appendix. As you plan for your group, I thought it would be important to have these standards readily assessible. So many teachers worry about addressing standards in small groups, especially when it comes to struggling readers and writers, when in fact many of these standards can be addressed in lower-level texts.

Lesson Components of the Transitional Reader and Writer Stage

The Transitional lesson plan is found in Figure 7.2 and accommodates both Stages 4A and 4B. The word study section differentiates 4A and 4B and will be discussed in depth as the lesson plan unfolds. In the following sections, you will find a short discussion of each component, followed by dialogue from a small group of Transitional readers and writers.

Figure 7.2

Lesson Plan: Transitional Stage

FLUENCY	FLUENCY EXTENSION
Text Level: _____ Reread: ☐ Choral Reading ☐ Teacher-Led Reading ☐ Student-Led Reading ☐ Whisper Reading	☐ Reread with a partner. ☐ Buddy read. ☐ Other
WORD STUDY	**WORD STUDY EXTENSION**
Stage 4A: Lesson # _____ Stage 4B: Lesson # _____ Word Sort: ☐ Open ☐ Closed ☐ Writing Sort ☐ Sound Boxes ☐ Word Scramble *(choose one of the above)* ☐ Sentence Dictation	☐ Conduct a writing sort (with partner). ☐ Word cards: cut/sort/write sorts in notebook. ☐ Write sentences with words from each pattern. (Circle nouns, verbs, adjectives.) ☐ Add prefixes or suffixes. ☐ Make words plural or past tense. ☐ Use words in sentences. ☐ Write sentences to show meaning. ☐ Word hunt: find words with the same patterns. ☐ Other: _____
COMPREHENSION	**COMPREHENSION EXTENSION**
New Read: _____ Text Level: _____ **Before Reading** ☐ Build background knowledge (if needed). ☐ Preview vocabulary from text. ☐ Set the purpose for reading (make it personal to the text). **During Reading** ☐ Stopping points/text-dependent questions • • • • **After Reading** ☐ Revisit vocabulary (use in a sentence that tells something about the text). ☐ Revisit purpose for reading. ☐ Discuss writing extension.	Writing Checklist: ☐ Main ideas/details ☐ Character traits ☐ Problem/solution ☐ Compare/contrast ☐ Cause/effect ☐ Sequencing ☐ Write a sentence with each vocabulary word that tells something about the story (text). ☐ Write your own sentence with the vocabulary words. ☐ Other: _____

Fluency

The ability to read and understand text in 1st grade is the common fluency standard for Transitional readers. Rereading continues to play an important role in developing reading fluency. Although most Transitional readers can read text fairly accurately, they may be rather slow or choppy at doing so, and they may pay little attention to punctuation. Without mastery of speed, accuracy, and expression, it is difficult to comprehend a text's message. One way to address this concern is for you to become a part of the rereading process by alternating turns with students. This oral reading provides a fluent model for students to emulate. By choral reading with students, you have the opportunity to "pull" students through appropriate phrasing and expression. Additionally, Transitional readers can benefit significantly from listening to and whispering along with the teacher. Rereading can be conducted using these techniques, along with other strategies previously mentioned, such as lead reading.

As the texts get longer, there probably will not be time to reread along with a new read each day. Therefore, the reread can be completed the day after a new read. At this level, the teacher has options for various reading groups. For students who are reading above grade level, rereading can be completed out of group. For an on-level group, the teacher can make observations as students read for the first time. If you feel that a reread will be successful out of group with a partner, you may choose to do so. However, you might want to reread the entire book the next day because of the lack of fluency on the first read. For groups reading below grade level, the texts must be read and reread in their entirety during the small-group lesson. For example, if you are working with a 2nd grade group who is reading at this Transitional stage, rereading would be necessary because they are reading below grade level. After rereading a text, partners could conduct a third read out of group. To increase fluency, students must have ample time to reread text they can read comfortably.

(This small group of Transitional readers and writers is well into this stage of development and is currently reading a Level 15/16 (Level I) book, which is typical for an end-of-year 1st grader. In this lesson, students are rereading a book they read the day before. Although these are on-level readers, the teacher felt that students were struggling with fluency. For this reason, she has decided to reread the entire book and focus on fluency.)

(Before Reading)

Teacher: Yesterday, we read the book *The Secret Cave*. Today, we are going to reread this book so we can try to make it sound like a real story. There is a lot of dialogue where the characters are talking to one another, so we will have to pay close attention to that as we read. How will we know when the characters are speaking?

Maye: We will see those quotation marks on both sides of where they are talking.

(During Reading)

Teacher: You are right, Maye. Everyone turn to the first page. I will start by being the lead reader, and you whisper read along with me. Pay attention to how I change my voice when I come to the quotation marks. You also need to see how I read differently at the end of the sentence depending on the punctuation. If we don't pay attention to the punctuation, it makes the story hard to understand. It's important to read the story about the same speed that we talk.

(The teacher lead reads while students whisper read along with her.)

Teacher: What did you notice about my voice when I read the page?

Mary: You changed your voice a little when you saw the quotation marks, so it sounded different, sort of like the person was really talking.

Katie: And you also made your voice go up at the end when you read questions.

Teacher: Good! Now this time, let's read this page together so you can practice using expression.

(The teacher and students choral read the page together.)

Teacher: Now I want you to take turns being the lead reader. Remember, the rest of us need to be back-up readers and whisper read along with our leader. John, will you be our first lead reader?

(The teacher and students finish reading the book using various reading strategies.)

(After Reading)

Teacher: Today, when you leave group, I want you to reread this story with your partner. Please take turns being the lead reader. Remember to make it sound like a real story.

! Independent fluency extension activities include the following ideas:

- Have students continue reading and rereading with a partner and independently. Each student or reading group should maintain an independent reading box. At this level, it is much easier to keep the box stocked with books previously read in group, rather than new reads. If you choose to add new books that have not been read in small groups, chose carefully and at independent levels well below the group's instructional reading level.
- Establish a poetry box or folder of favorite poems read numerous times in whole group. Students can select a poem to reread or practice with a partner for a class performance.
- Have students record their reading on a regular basis. This allows them to listen to themselves and work on improving their oral reading fluency.

Word Study

Word study standards in most 1st grade curricula are based on the mastery of basic vowel patterns that are supported at the Transitional stage. Students working at Stage 4A have mastered the study of one-syllable words with a short-vowel sound. The word study now advanced to the study of other common vowel patterns. A day-by-day scope and sequence for the Transitional stage is located in the Appendix. Each number represents one day of study. Make adjustments as needed based on observations and assessments. Each vowel pattern lesson begins with a minilesson that the teacher delivers while explaining the vowel patterns being studied. This is followed by one of the suggested activities—card sorts, writing sorts, sound boxes, or word scrambles—and each word study lesson ends with a dictated sentence.

Card Sorts: The card-sorting technique used with word families lends itself nicely to vowel patterns. This activity should only be used on the first day of a new set of words. Begin with a minilesson that introduces the vowel patterns, and place header word cards in a tabletop pocket chart (e.g., *cat, make, day*). Use word cards to illustrate the vowel patterns in isolation and put them under these header words. Next, model the task by showing students one word in each category and explaining why the word fits the pattern (e.g., *cat*—CaC, *make*—aCe, *day*—ay). Remind students that they must not only look at the words but also listen for the sound the vowel makes in each word. Finally, give each student two words to sort on the board and have them explain why each word goes in the category they select.

This is an example of a closed sort, meaning that you establish the patterns prior to giving students cards. In an open sort, there is no introduction and you hand out cards to see if students can identify the patterns and organize them into categories. An open sort takes more time to complete, but you could have partners sort the words before coming to group and then explain the categories while in small groups. You might want to give students the cards prior to small-group work and let them work with a partner in an open sort to discover the vowel patterns.

Over the years, I have found that many students are confused by CVC notation. They have trouble remembering that *C* represents a consonant and *V* represents a vowel. Although I do mention the words *vowel* and *consonant* in discussions, students seem to do much better when I represent the pattern by leaving blanks for consonants.

Teacher: Today, we are going to review the vowel patterns that were introduced yesterday. We have already learned two of these patterns, so this will be a review. In the word *cat*, the vowel pattern *_a_* lets us know the vowel will be short. When the vowel is all closed up on both sides with consonants, the vowel will make the short sound.

(The teacher places the cat *word card in the pocket chart and the card with the isolated vowel, which illustrates the CVC pattern.)*

Teacher: In the word *make*, what vowel sound do we hear?

LaDonna: You can hear the *a* saying its name.

Teacher: Yes, that's the sound for long *a*. When we see the vowel pattern that has *a_e*, we know the vowel will make the long sound and the *e* is silent. In the word *day*, what vowel sound do we hear?

Lisa: It sounds like its name, *a*.

Teacher: Yes, and we have another pattern that has the same sound. Turn to your partner and talk about which pattern that might be.

(Students turn and talk while the teacher listens in.)

Teacher: Paul, share what you and Joe were talking about.

Paul: Well, the word *make* has the same long *a* sound, so how will we know which pattern it will be?

Teacher: When you hear the long *a* sound at the end of a word, that will usually be the *ay* pattern.

(After three patterns are discussed and placed in the pocket chart, the teacher distributes two cards for each student. The teacher then calls for all words that fit a particular pattern, and the cards are placed in the correct columns. When all the cards are sorted, the closed sort is completed.)

Writing Sorts: This writing sort activity follows the same guidelines as the writing sort for word families and short vowels. In this activity, students write the sorts as the teacher calls out words that contain the focus patterns. As previously mentioned, there are two writing sort templates: one for sorting three patterns and one for sorting four patterns. Use the four-pattern box pattern template because it is useful as students review and mix several vowel patterns. You could also put the three-box template on one side and the four-box version on the reverse. Again, put these in sheet protectors that make them easily erasable. As a way to check and reinforce the focus vowel pattern, the teacher sorts the cards on a tabletop sorting board after each student has successfully written the word in the correct category. Figure 7.3 shows a completed writing sort for three of the *a* patterns: short *a*, long *a*–consonant–*e*, and *ar*.

Teachers should follow the word study scope and sequence provided for lesson pacing (see Appendix). You may choose to skip lessons if the group masters the patterns before the suggested sequence is completed, but do not remain on patterns longer than suggested. Transitional readers and writers need to be exposed to all the common vowel patterns as they navigate more complex text. Keep in mind that many students will need to repeat the sequence for vowel patterns more than once. Much of what students will read and write in the future will include words derived from these basic patterns, so be diligent, consistent, and patient as students work toward vowel pattern mastery. The "gift" of basic vowel pattern knowledge is crucial to continued decoding in reading and writing success.

Figure 7.3

Sample Writing Sort

ă	āСе	ar
flat	make	farm
clap	plate	car

Dictated Sentence(s):

1) Dad made a trap for the shark.

2) _____

(These 1st grade students are beginning the study of vowel patterns. In this lesson, students will be completing a writing sort.)

Teacher: We are going to do a three-box writing sort today with our vowel patterns. Write the word *cat* on the first line under the first box and then write the vowel pattern in the box.

(The activity continues until the three words and patterns are completed.)

Teacher: The first word is *flat*. Say *flat*. Listen for the vowel pattern, and write the word under the correct pattern.

(The teacher observes while the students visually sort and write the word.)

Teacher: Where does this word go? Which word has the same vowel pattern?

Bethany: It goes under *cat*.

Teacher: Why does it go there?

Bethany: Because it has the same vowel pattern and has the short *a* sound.

Teacher: Thumbs up, thumbs down. Do you agree with her?

(All agree with the word card placement.)

Teacher: The next word is *plate*. Say *plate*. Where does *plate* go?

(The teacher observes and sees that Andre has written the word plate *in the correct category but has forgotten the* l. *The teacher then leans in toward Andre.)*

Teacher: Andre, look at the word *plate* again. Do you see something wrong with the way you spelled it? Does it look right?

(Andre looks at the word and cannot identify the mistake, so the teacher pushes sound boxes in front of Andre and helps him by focusing on the initial pl *blend. The activity is completed when there are two words for each pattern.)*

Word Scramble: Word scrambles at this stage are still a powerful activity to help students see relationships among patterns (such as long *a*–consonant–*e*, long *i*–consonant–*e*, and long *o*–consonant–*e*). This activity enhances students' abilities to see relationships among words. Prewritten word scramble activities for each of the word study patterns at the Transitional stage can be downloaded from www.beverlytyner.net. Figure 7.4 shows an example of a word scramble activity available to you.

Figure 7.4

Example Word Scramble Activity at the Transitional Stage

Word Family: *a*
Letters: *a, e, r, t, d, p, g, y*

1. Make the word *drag*.
2. Drop one letter to spell *rag*.
3. Add one letter to spell *rage*.
4. Change one letter to spell *page*.
5. Drop two letters and add one letter to spell *pay*.
6. Change one letter to spell *ray*.
7. Add one letter to spell *tray*.

Teacher: We are going to do a word scramble activity today with the *u* patterns. Let's review those patterns before we start.

(The teacher completes a short minilesson on the u *vowel patterns. She then distributes eight letter cards to each student:* u, n, e, r, t, g, h, b.*)*

Teacher: Now you are going to make some words with *u* patterns. Listen carefully to my directions. Make the word *rug*.

(Students pull the correct letters to make the word.)

Teacher: Now write the word *rug*.

(Students write each word after it is constructed. Writing the word solidifies the process of recognizing and using vowel patterns.)

Teacher: Change one letter to make *hug*. Now write the word *hug*. Now add one letter to make the word *huge*. Now write the word *huge*. Change two letters to make the word *tune*. Write the word *tune*. Drop one letter and change one letter to make *bun*. Write the word *bun*. Add one letter to make the word *burn*. Write the word *burn*.

(Students make each word, and the teacher monitors and assists when necessary. Writing the word is critical for students to use these patterns automatically in reading and writing.)

Sound Boxes: The sound boxes used at the Fledgling stage continue to be instrumental in the development of common vowel patterns. Use the template for four sound boxes at this stage. Choose two words from each pattern currently being studied, and pronounce the words for students. Then ask students to write the sounds using one sound in each box. This means that two letters might go in one box, as in the word *day*. You would only use two boxes for *day* because it only has two sounds. The *d* goes in the first box and the *ay* goes in the second box because the two letters together make the sound for long *a*. I have provided a "cheat sheet" for those teachers, like me, who were never taught phonics in elementary school (see Appendix). Don't skip this valuable activity just because you aren't sure about the correct boxes.

Teacher: Today, we are going to use our sound boxes to write the sounds we hear in some words with the vowel patterns we have been studying.

(The teacher distributes a sound box template to each student along with a dry-erase marker. I really encourage you to use these templates with sheet protectors. Students can erase easily when they make mistakes or get ready for the next word.)

Teacher: The first word is *shake*. Write the word *shake* using one box for each sound you hear. Remember, sometimes two letters make one sound. Silent letters must be included, but add a slash mark across the silent letter. Silent letters obviously don't make a sound, so they will not stand alone in a box.

(The teacher observes as students write the word in the sound boxes.)

Teacher: Now turn to your partner and explain how you decided to write the sounds in the word *shake*. Beth, what did you and Joan come up with?

Beth: We used three boxes because *shake* has three sounds. In the first box, we wrote *sh* because these two letters together make one sound. In the next box, we just wrote the letter *a* because it is a long *a* sound. In the last box, we wrote the letters *ke*, but we put a line through the *e* because it is silent and doesn't deserve its own box.

(Asking students to verbalize their thinking can serve as an informal assessment of mastery of this skill. Use partners frequently so students have more opportunities to talk about their choices. You can listen in to the conversations and pick and choose the reporting team.)

Sentence Dictation: Sentence dictation for students at this stage is quick and straightforward. The goal is to provide students with an opportunity to practice the focus word patterns in the context of writing complete sentences. To transfer students' word study skills into real reading and writing, it is critical to point out words in sentences that contain vowel patterns that have been introduced. In addition, call attention to word patterns in content-area texts and student-generated writing. Repeat each sentence several times and ask students to repeat the sentence with you. As students write the sentence, assist as necessary.

Teacher: Our sentence today is *She rode a huge bus to her club*. Listen again: *She rode a huge bus to her club*. Now say the sentence with me and count each word on your fingers.

All: She rode a huge bus to her club.

Teacher: Now pick up your markers and write the sentence. Think about all the *u* vowel patterns as you write the sentence.

(Students begin writing. The teacher reaches over to assist one student.)

Teacher: Lauren, do you remember the *u* pattern in the word *huge*?

Lauren: Is it the long *u* sound?

Teacher: Yes, it is. Which pattern would that be?

Lauren: Is it long vowel, consonant, *e*?

Teacher: Very good!

(Figure 7.5 shows an example of the dictated sentence. The student drew the illustration out of group. Don't waste group time drawing pictures!)

Figure 7.5

Example Dictated Sentence: Transitional Stage

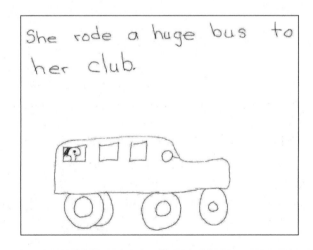

❗ Independent word study extension activities include the following ideas:

- Have students play Memory using vowel pattern cards.
- Ask students to complete speed drills with a partner. Speed drills can be used to increase students' automaticity in recognizing word patterns. Often, students can sort patterns but have trouble writing them. This process requires visual memory of what the words and patterns look like so students will be automatic in applying their knowledge in decoding new words. Students work in pairs and flash a stack of vowel pattern words to their partners. They count the number of words read correctly in one minute and try to beat their personal scores.
- Give each student a copy of the vowel pattern cards being studied. Have students sort the cards by pattern and write them in a word study notebook.
- Have students choose two words from each pattern and write a complete sentence. Students can exchange their sentences with a partner to check for errors.
- Have students complete a word hunt to find words in previously read texts that have the same vowel patterns.

Comprehension

A new read provides students with an opportunity to develop and apply decoding and comprehension skills. Specific strategies are used before, during, and after reading a text to support comprehension. Prior to reading, the book is introduced, preselected vocabulary is shown on index cards, and a purpose is given for reading the text. If important background knowledge is not revealed in the text that students will need for comprehension, that information can be given quickly.

There are a variety of oral reading alternatives to consider as students read the text selection, including choral reading, whisper reading, and lead reading. At this point, begin to use an independent whisper reading activity. In this activity, you set a purpose for reading, and students whisper at their own speed. When everyone is whisper reading, all students are active readers with support as needed. Keep the text short so readers will not be waiting on one another to finish.

Transitional readers begin strategic work on identifying text evidence to support their answers to text-dependent questions. Giving each student a small sticky note to use for tagging evidence gives every student a chance to be interactive with the text. At strategic points in the story, stop to ask questions about what has happened so far, giving specific evidence from the text to support a prediction or summary. Ask students to tag specific text evidence to support an answer to a specific question. Other questions might address illustrations and how they are used to support the text.

After reading, you can use a variety of strategies outlined in this section to help students discuss the comprehension focus given before reading. Additionally, the vocabulary presented prior to reading is used when summarizing the text.

◇◇

(Before Reading)

Teacher: Today, we are going to begin reading a book called *Stormy Weather*. We have had a lot of stormy weather in the last few months.

Lucas: Yes, we had a big rainstorm and it also had thunder.

Teacher: Yes, we did, and that is unusual in the winter.

(Prior to reading the book, the teacher preselects and introduces vocabulary that is important to understanding the text's message.)

Teacher: There are a couple of words in the text today that we need to look for as we read. The first one is *hurricane*.

(The teacher has written the vocabulary words on note cards.)

Michael: Oh, I've heard of those before, but I didn't think about them being storms.

Teacher: We will find out why hurricanes are dangerous storms as we read today. Here are two more words: *tornadoes* and *dangerous*. Based on the title of our book, it makes sense that we will see this word in the book today.

(The teacher quickly presents the vocabulary and distributes the books to students. Do not spend time prior to reading trying to define these words. Save that time to examine the words while reading, using context clues, and again after reading to summarize the text.)

Teacher: Let's read this book to find out about different kinds of storms and what makes them dangerous.

(During Reading)

(The teacher has identified several strategic stopping points to ask text-dependent questions. It's important for the teacher to support the comprehension focus with appropriate questioning. Make every question count. There are many occasions when teachers ask too many questions. Creating fewer but more powerful questions allows students to think deeply about the text. It also provides the opportunity to read more text during small-group time.)

Teacher: What kind of storm is shown on the front cover of the book?

Harrison: It looks like a thunderstorm, but now I am thinking that it could also be a hurricane or tornado.

Teacher: Turn the page to the inside cover. Here we have the table of contents. How can this help us read and understand the book?

Lucas: It tells us what kind of stuff we are going to read.

Teacher: Yes, and it can help us see how the author organized the information he will share in the book. There is something at the end of the table of contents called a glossary. Does anyone know what a glossary is?

Michael: It's kind of like a little dictionary that just has hard words from the book in it.

Teacher: Yes, and it can help us if we run into a word and aren't sure what it means. If we see some words while we are reading today and we don't know what they mean, we can look them up in the glossary. Let's all turn to pages 2 and 3. Take a look at the picture at the top of page 2. What's happening?

Harrison: Well, it looks like a rainy day. Maybe they are thinking about what they can do since they can't go outside.

Teacher: All right. So what do you think is happening in the picture at the bottom of the next page?

Helen: It looks like they decided to play on the computer since they couldn't go outside.

Teacher: Can you tell what is on the computer screen?

Lucas: I think it's a picture of the world, but it's really hard to see.

Teacher: Let's read these two pages together and find out why the children are using the computer.

(The teacher and students read chorally.)

Teacher: Were we right? Tag the sentence on the page that tells us what the children were doing.

(Students use sticky notes to find the sentence while the teacher monitors.)

Teacher: Helen, what did you find?

Helen: They weren't playing on the computer. They were looking on the computer to find out about the weather.

Teacher: Read that sentence to us.

(Helen reads the sentence.)

Teacher: Turn to pages 4 and 5. What kind of storm do you see here?

Valerie: It looks like a snowstorm. I've never seen a snowstorm like that. We don't ever get much snow here.

Teacher: Let's all choral read these two pages to find out how a snowstorm and a blizzard are different.

(Notice that the teacher poses a quick purpose for reading the next page. This leads to a logical question after reading.)

Teacher: The story tells us that snowstorms can be dangerous, but it doesn't tell us why. Use what you already know in your head and answer the question. Turn to your partner and share your thoughts.

(Partners discuss.)

Teacher: Lauren, what did you and Adalyn talk about?

Lauren: Well, for one thing, you could freeze to death if your car broke down.

Teacher: Yes, and that has happened to a lot of people when they get stuck on the road without warm clothes and food. What does the book tell us about the difference between snowstorms and blizzards?

Monica: A blizzard is a big snowstorm that has a lot of wind.

(The teacher guides students through the text by using teacher questioning, guiding student comprehension, and a variety of oral reading techniques.)

(After Reading)

Teacher: Let's go back to the vocabulary words we talked about before reading. Let's look at the word *dangerous*. I want you to think of a sentence using the word *dangerous* that tells something about what we read in the book today.

Harrison: We learned that some storms can be dangerous, like snowstorms and hurricanes and tornadoes.

Teacher: Good. The next word is *hurricane*. Turn to your talking partner. Use the word *hurricane* in a sentence that tells something you learned in the text.

(Partners discuss.)

Teacher: Valerie, will you share the sentence you and Harrison came up with?

Valerie: We learned today that hurricanes start over the water before they come on land.

Teacher: You really learned a lot today.

(The teacher finishes reviewing the other vocabulary words. The primary comprehension focus after reading is to revisit the purpose set prior to reading. The teacher will orchestrate a comprehension conversation. The purpose for reading usually requires students to summarize the text with information, including putting events in the proper sequence, comparing and contrasting, identifying main ideas and details, and so forth.)

Teacher: We read the book to find out about different kinds of storms and why they are dangerous. Turn to your partner and talk about one kind of storm we read about and why it is dangerous.

(The teacher listens in while partners discuss.)

Teacher: Anna, what did you talk about with your partner?

Anna: We talked about tornados. They have such strong winds that they can pick up houses and cars. Sometimes people don't have enough time to get away from them because they can start quickly and they get trapped.

Teacher: That was great information.

(Discussion continues as the main points are discussed.)

Comprehension: Writing About Reading

◇◇◇

Teacher: When you leave group today, I want you to write a sentence with each vocabulary word that tells about something you learned by reading the text. After that, I want you to write a summary paragraph that tells what you learned today. Your first sentence should be: *Storms can be very dangerous.* Then write about three ways that storms are dangerous. Your paragraph should have at least five sentences. I am going to give you a checklist for Main Ideas and Details to make sure that you include everything in your paragraph. When you finish, I want you to exchange your paragraph with your partner and edit for capital letters and punctuation. Then look at the checklist and see if your partner included all the things on the list.

(Figure 7.6 shows a student product based on this assignment. The next time students come to small groups, the teacher may decide to collect the paragraphs for further review or have students share their paragraphs with a partner.)

When to Move to the Next Stage

Moving to the Fluent stage is an important milestone as readers prepare to enter the upper elementary grades. To be prepared to move ahead, students need to automatically recognize numerous high-frequency words and specialized vocabulary. Students should be able to write dictated sentences containing varied vowel patterns with accuracy and confidence. Additionally, they should have mastered a short well-constructed paragraph written for a specific purpose. Before progressing to the next stage, Transitional readers and writers must take the Stage 4A and 4B spelling assessments and pass with near 80 percent accuracy or better. Fluent readers and writers often choose to read and write by themselves; therefore, students at the Transitional stage should begin to show some independence in reading and writing. Finally, a Reading Review or other more detailed Running Record should be completed to confirm that students are reading at the appropriate instructional level, generally around late 1st grade or early 2nd grade.

Figure 7.6

Sample Writing Checklist and Student Summary

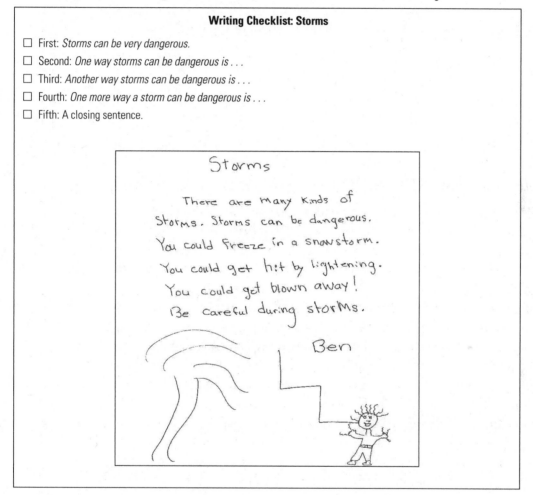

Writing Checklist: Storms

☐ First: *Storms can be very dangerous.*
☐ Second: *One way storms can be dangerous is . . .*
☐ Third: *Another way storms can be dangerous is . . .*
☐ Fourth: *One more way a storm can be dangerous is . . .*
☐ Fifth: A closing sentence.

Conclusion

Students' accomplishments at the Transitional stage are extensive. They have been transformed from being heavily dependent on the teacher to being confident readers and writers with less teacher support. Developing strategies in decoding and comprehension has increased students' abilities to read and write independently. As these students transition to the Fluent stage, they will continue to focus on increasing their competencies in fluency, word study, and comprehension in higher levels of text complexity.

Chapter 8

The Fluent Reader and Writer

Characteristics of Fluent Readers and Writers

Fluent readers and writers bring with them some beginning characteristics of more mature readers. They read with more speed, accuracy, and proper expression, and they read independently from a variety of genres and for a variety of purposes. The Fluent stage is typically representative of a beginning to late 2nd grade student. As texts become longer, a new read may take more than one day, and a larger part of the lesson plan will focus on comprehension. Along with increasing text difficulty, these students are digging deeper into reading comprehension. Fluent readers learn how to skim text quickly to retrieve information and make inferences. Without conscious attention, these students perform multiple reading tasks—such as word recognition and comprehension—at the same time. Vocabulary within the text will be an important focus as it relates to understanding the text.

Systematic word study will progress to the study of less common vowel patterns and common word features, which will support these readers and writers with new text challenges. As with the previous stages, the differentiation is obviously in text levels and writing as students advance through the stage. In addition, word study is differentiated with two distinct stages (5A and 5B). Note that the lesson plan accommodates for both levels of word study. Fluent stage readers and writers use their word study skills, are grounded with the knowledge of common vowel patterns, and consistently use this knowledge in their decoding and writing. The word *fluent* is an appropriate word to describe the transition seen at this stage. As students master less common vowel patterns and word features, they become prepared to use this knowledge as they read and write to respond to texts in a wide variety of genres.

Expectations for students at the Fluent stage—in terms of text levels, word study, vocabulary, comprehension, and writing—are presented in Figure 8.1.

Figure 8.1

Stage 5: Fluent Reader and Writer

Fluency	Vocabulary	Word Study	Reading Comprehension	Writing About Reading
• Typically, early to late 2nd grade • Book levels EI 16–22, F&P J/K/L/M • Rereading to develop fluency	• Selecting key vocabulary from text • Summarizing the text using key vocabulary	• Recognizing and using less common vowel patterns (5A) • Recognizing and using common word features (e.g., contractions, prefixes, suffixes, homophones, compound words) (5B) • Writing dictated sentences using words with common features (5B) • Writing dictated sentences using words with less common vowel patterns (5B)	• Developing more diverse comprehension strategies • Using knowledge of common word features in decoding and understanding a text • Developing fluency in a variety of texts for comprehension purposes • Reading for a purpose and finding evidence to support purpose	• Using less common vowel patterns correctly in writing • Using common word features correctly in writing • Using word study knowledge to spell new words • Writing a well-constructed paragraph for a variety of comprehension purposes • Supporting writing with evidence from text • Using capitalization and punctuation correctly

EI: Early Intervention   F&P: Fountas and Pinnell

At this stage, readers use diverse strategies as they cope with challenges in more difficult text. Although they still need your support at their instructional levels, they are capable of decoding and understanding text at their independent levels.

As students progress through this stage, the increase in text complexity becomes more apparent. Texts become longer and more complex, and a variety of texts should be used with Fluent readers and writers. Consider text with a range of topics, formats, text types, and illustrative styles. Longer stories and chapter books with rich vocabulary and more fully developed plots are also an option. Avoid choosing too many long chapter books, which limits the selection of other genres. As educators, we sometimes feel that more accomplished readers simply need longer books. As reading maturity develops, readers will benefit from a wide variety of shorter pieces, including a variety of narrative and informational text selections including poetry, magazine articles, fables, tall tales, biographies, mysteries, and cultural fairy tales. These are all genres required in many state-mandated assessments (e.g., Common Core State Standards). It is also important for the teacher to preread texts to decide if they are at an appropriate level of difficulty. Teachers should always be mindful of the supports and challenges presented in each text selection.

Students write with increasing sentence length, and they use multiple paragraphs in their responses by the end of this stage. Fluent writers also focus on using more descriptive vocabulary, and using correct capitalization and punctuation correctly also becomes routine. Fluent writers focus on more sophisticated writing in all genres, which is supported by a solid word study foundation and more advanced reading levels. The standards that are or could be supported in the lesson plan at the Fluent stage are found in the Appendix.

Lesson Components of the Fluent Reader and Writer Stage

Fluency

Figure 8.2 shows the lesson plan model for the Fluent reader and writer. In the following sections, each lesson plan component will be thoroughly discussed.

Fluency remains important to these readers, especially if students have not met grade-level benchmarks for speed, accuracy, and prosody. In consideration of this, rereading may require more time for some students. On the other hand, students who are meeting the benchmarks for reading fluency may not need to reread every day in small groups, but they should continue to practice with a partner or independently.

Another source for fluency practice is poetry. In my experience, students love the rhythm and rhyme of poetry, and it is helpful as students work on phrasing. I also find that poetry provides vivid vocabulary and a wide variety of comprehension opportunities. You may choose to work on a piece of poetry for the week. As you introduce a new poem, use it as a new read so there is time to look at both

Figure 8.2

Lesson Plan: Fluent Stage

FLUENCY	FLUENCY EXTENSION

Text Level: _____
Reread:
  ☐ Choral Reading
  ☐ Teacher-Led Reading
  ☐ Student-Led Reading
  ☐ Whisper Reading
	☐ Reread with a partner.
	☐ Reread independently.
	☐ Other

WORD STUDY	**WORD STUDY EXTENSION**
Stage 5A: Lesson # _____ Stage 5B: Lesson # _____ Word Sort: ☐ Open ☐ Closed ☐ Writing Sort ☐ Sound Boxes ☐ Word Scramble ☐ Meaning Discussions ☐ Dictated or Student-Created Sentence (5B)	☐ Conduct a writing sort (with partner). ☐ Use word cards: cut/sort/write sorts in notebook. ☐ Write sentences with words from each pattern. (Circle nouns, verbs, adjectives.) ☐ Add prefixes or suffixes. ☐ Make words plural or past tense. ☐ Use words in sentences. ☐ Write sentences to show meaning. ☐ Word hunt: find words with the same patterns.
COMPREHENSION	**COMPREHENSION EXTENSION**

New Read: _____   Text Level: _____
 	
Before Reading
☐ Build background knowledge (if needed).
☐ Preview vocabulary.
☐ Set the purpose for reading.
 	
During Reading
☐ Stopping points/text-dependent questions
  •
  •
  •
  •
 	
After Reading
☐ Revisit vocabulary.
☐ Revisit purpose for reading.
☐ Comprehension conversation.
☐ Discuss writing extension.
	Writing Checklist:
	  ☐ Main ideas/details
	  ☐ Character traits
	  ☐ Problem/solution
	  ☐ Compare/contrast
	  ☐ Cause/effect
	  ☐ Sequencing
	  ☐ Other: _____

vocabulary and comprehension. After the first day, the reread will take only a few minutes.

As with prose text selections, vary the poetry pieces to include humorous poems, seasonal poems, and even classical poetry. It is sometimes difficult to gauge the appropriate reading level with poetry, so teachers should always preview the selections prior to introducing them with students. If a particular piece provides too much challenge, simply replace the poem the next day with a less challenging piece. Continuing fluency practice, therefore, should remain an important reading component whether practiced in small groups, with a partner, or independently. Regardless, Fluent readers should be given ample time to read independently during the school day.

(The following group of late 2nd grade students is rereading a poem to practice fluency. The poem was introduced the day before, so the reread will take only a couple of minutes. You could also have students reread poems out of group with a partner.)

Teacher: Yesterday, we read the poem "Never Take Your Dog to School." I wrote this poem myself after we enjoyed reading a similar poem called "Never Take a Pig to Lunch." Today, we are going to read the poem again and tap out the beat of the poem with our pencils. One, two, ready, go!

(The teacher taps the table lightly with a pencil. Then she begins reading the poem as the students join her.)

All: "Never Teach Your Dog to Read"

Never teach your dog to read,

Unless he is a special breed.

One that schools permit inside,

Where you can show him off with pride!

Now that you have your dog at school,

He's bound to break most of the rules.

And even though your dog can read,

He'll be sent home with lightning speed!

Teacher: Please put your poem in your extension folder and practice it again with your partner.

🛈 Out-of-group fluency extensions include the following ideas:

- Practice rereading the poem with a partner.
- Have partners pick their own poems to practice and present to the class.

Word Study

In Stage 5A, the study of less common vowel patterns begins the sequence. After students complete their study of less common vowel patterns and pass the assessment, word study should move to the study of common word features. As with the earlier stages, teachers should administer spelling assessments to determine student readiness for Stage 5A in word study. After 5A is assessed and mastered, students move to Stage 5B, the study of common word features. The same spelling assessment format used in previous stages is still appropriate for Stage 5A. However, the assessment for Stage 5B is modified significantly to assess both the spelling and meaning of common word patterns. After the spelling assessment has been completed, students are asked to write a sentence for each word to demonstrate knowledge of how to use each word correctly in a sentence. Both spelling assessments for the Fluent reader and writer stage are located in the Appendix.

The activities that support the study of less common vowel patterns include card sorts, writing sorts, word scrambles, sound boxes, and sentence dictation. These activities were discussed in previous chapters and continue at this stage as the focus turns to less common vowel patterns. Cards and materials can be downloaded from www.beverlytyner.net.

There is a shift, however, in the activities that support common word features, as many of the previous activities are no longer meaningful. Think about what you want students to know about word features, and support this with activities that meet your objectives.

Contractions: Students should know which two words make up a contraction. They should also know how to use contractions correctly in their writing. A writing sort with the header cards *not*, *is*, and *are* could be used. Give students the two words that make up a contraction, and have them create the contraction and write it in the appropriate category. Along with the dictated sentence, students can create their own sentences out of group as a time saver and to show mastery of the use of the proper use of contractions.

Homophones: The purpose for studying homophones is for students to know what each homophone means and how to spell the correct form. There are two activities that make the most sense here. The most powerful, perhaps, would be to read a sentence using a homophone and based on the sentence, students write the correct form of the homophone. For example, you would read the sentence "I would like for you to do your homework. Write the word *would*." Alternatively, you might say, "We need some wood for the fire. Write the word *wood*." The teacher could also give students a homophone and ask them to write a sentence using each spelling correctly. This can be especially helpful for homophones that are more difficult for students. Again, students could write the sentences as an extension or write them independently to demonstrate mastery.

Compound Words: The focus here is for students to use the word parts to understand the compound words. I have found that students struggle with correctly using these words in context. Therefore, spend time discussing each word, and give examples of its correct use. Ask students to make oral sentences with these words to determine knowledge levels. In addition, asking students to write sentences with the compound words out of small group is a suitable activity. Focus on sentences with more difficult compound words in group and assign easier compound words as an extension activity.

Prefixes: The goal is for students to know the meaning of each prefix and how it affects the meaning of the base word. Students should be able to use the words correctly in their own writing. This is a great time to have in-depth conversations about the words and other words that have the same prefix. Sorting cards with the same prefix is mindless. The goal should be for students to discuss how these words are similar. Do not feel guilty if conversation rather than writing is the activity. Students can write sentences with these words out of group or find more words with the same prefix and define them.

Plurals: Students should know how to change a singular word to make it plural. As teachers, we know how important this skill is, especially in writing. There are a few standard rules that students need to know about making words plural, and then there are a slew of exceptions. I was 40 years old before I knew the rule about why you make *monkey* plural by only adding an *s*. (For those grammar-deprived people like me, you only add *s* because the *y* is preceded by a vowel.) Many of these plural exceptions are used daily in reading and writing, and students need this knowledge.

❗ Independent word study extension activities include the following ideas:

- Complete word hunts for other words that include the focus patterns.
- Choose two words from each pattern and have students write sentences.
- Have students sort the cards and then write the sorts in their word study journals.

- Write sentences with words at Stage 5B to show meaning.
- Find other words with the pattern you are studying (e.g., more words with same prefix, more compound words, more homophones).
- Complete the word study matrix (see Appendix) and have students manipulate the focus words, for example, by adding prefixes or suffixes or by finding synonyms, antonyms, and so on. This is especially appropriate for partners to work on during the week.

(The following group of end-of-year 2nd graders is studying plurals in word study Stage 5B. After reviewing some basic rules, the teacher engages students in a writing sort.)

Teacher: Today, we are going to look at ways to make words plural. What does the word *plural* mean?

Melissa: Plural means that there is more than one.

Teacher: Yes, and depending on the ending of the word, there are different ways we make the words plural. Take a look at my sorting board. We will sort words by the different ways to make them plural.

(The teacher completes a minilesson by discussing each pattern with an example. Students should compare the words and complete a spelling sort.)

Teacher: Fill out your writing sort sheet. I want you to write *s* in the first box, *es* in the second box, and *y/ies* in the last box.

(The teacher observes as students fill in the boxes on the writing sort sheets.)

Teacher: Now I am going to call out some words. They will be singular. You need to look at the three boxes and figure out how to make the word plural. Would you have to add an *s*, *es*, or change the *y* to *i* and add *es*? The first word is *box*. What do you have to do to the word *box* to make it plural? *(The teacher observes as students sort and write the word under the appropriate box.)*

Teacher: Chris, where did you write the word and why?

Chris: I wrote the word *boxes* under the *es* box because to make the word *box* plural, you have to add *es*. I think that there is a rule that says if a word ends in *x*, you always have to add *es* to make it plural.

Teacher: Great job! The next word I want you to make plural is *worry*. What do you have to do to *worry* to make it *worries*?

(The teacher continues the writing sort until there are at least two words under each category. Figure 8.3 shows a sample sort for plurals.)

Teacher: Now let's do a dictated sentence that includes some words that are in the plural form. The sentence for today is *The nurses took care of the babies.*

(The sentence contains two plurals that represent plural patterns that are the focus this week. The teacher observes and supports when necessary as students complete the dictated sentence. After students finish, the teacher points out the plural words and discusses the process used in making each singular word plural.)

Figure 8.3
Sample Writing Sort for Plurals

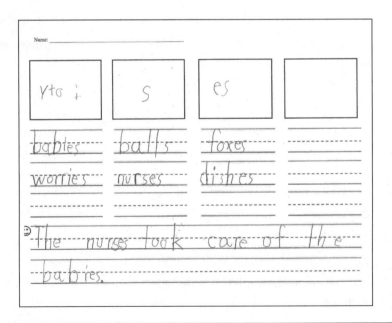

Comprehension

Fluent readers and writers spend a majority of their small-group reading time engaged in comprehending new text. The lesson plan framework provides explicit instructional recommendations for teachers as they guide students through before-, during-, and after-reading comprehension strategies and activities. Vocabulary is embedded in the comprehension process in the selection of focus words from the text.

The group in the following scenario is beginning an informational text called *Earthquakes and Tsunamis*. This book is on level for late 2nd to early 3rd graders. Because of the length of the book, it will take two days to complete.

◇◇

(Before Reading)

Teacher: Today, we are going to start reading a very interesting book called *Earthquakes and Tsunamis*. I am sure that you are familiar with earthquakes, and today we are going to also read about tsunamis. The book will give us a lot of information about both of these, so let's read to find out more.

(Rather than spending time discussing students' knowledge prior to reading, the teacher decides to spend more time in the text to help them gain the information. As a rule of thumb, there is no need to build background knowledge when the information is presented in the text. The teacher has also preselected vocabulary and written them on index cards: fault, collapse, jolt, earthquake, tsunami, plates, collapse, *and* jolt. *This informational text contains a number of vocabulary words that will be important for students to know and understand. The teacher has left some vocabulary so students can use context clues to discover their meanings.)*

Teacher: Let's look at some words we are going to see in this book about earthquakes and tsunamis. The first word is *fault*. As we read today, I think you will discover a new meaning for the word *fault*. We also have another word that has a new meaning for you, *plate*.

(The teacher quickly introduces the focus vocabulary words.)

(During Reading)

Teacher: We will read this book to find out how earthquakes and tsunamis are both similar and very different. When we finish reading the book, you are going to write about this topic. Let's take a look at the table of contents. It is important that we always look at this so we can see how the author organized the book. This will let us know what sequence we will see this information in the text. We know from the title that the book will discuss earthquakes and tsunamis. I'm interested to see if the author will talk about them in separate chapters, or if he will compare and contrast them in the same chapter. Look at the contents. What do you see?

Paul: The chapters look like the author first starts with chapters on earthquakes in the beginning of the book, and then the last part of the book is mostly about tsunamis.

Teacher: So we will need to remember that as we start reading the book. I also notice that the author has included a glossary and an index. Do you know the difference?

Rick: I know that the glossary is like a little dictionary with words from the book, but I'm not sure about the index.

Teacher: An index lists all the important words or topics covered in the book. For example, if I asked you to write a report about the San Andreas Fault, you could go to the index and see if it is an important topic in this book and which pages will be about that topic.

(For this portion of the lesson, the teacher uses a variety of questioning strategies to encourage comprehension. Remember that questioning includes summarizing text information at strategic points in the text.)

Teacher: We know from the title of the book and the table of contents that we are going to be learning about earthquakes and tsunamis. So, as we read the text, we are going to look for the important facts about earthquakes and tsunamis. We also want to examine how the two are similar and different. Let's all turn to page 4 and read the introduction together. I will be the lead reader, and you whisper read along with me. As we read, let's look for ways that earthquakes and tsunamis are alike and different.

(The teacher leads and provides a fluent framework while engaging students in the reading process as they all whisper read.)

Teacher: So, what causes a tsunami? Find the sentence in the text that answers that question. Tag that with your sticky note.

(Students return to the text to identify the sentence while the teacher observes.)

Teacher: Janet, will you read that sentence for us?

(Rather than going through the text prior to reading, it is more important for students to look at these text features and how the author uses them to increase comprehension.)

Teacher: Take a look at the picture on this page and the caption. I want everyone to whisper read this page to find out how this helped people know how bad the earthquake was going to be.

(Students all whisper read the two pages as the teacher listens to make sure they are able to handle the text.)

Teacher: Please turn to your talking partner and explain to them how this worked.

(The teacher listens in while students discuss.)

Teacher: Jennifer, will you share with us your thoughts?

Jennifer: Many years ago, people didn't have machines to tell them about earthquakes. They used to see how many balls fell down. If only one or two fell, it wasn't a bad earthquake. But if a lot of balls fell, it meant that it was a real bad earthquake.

Teacher: What did we read about what they use now to predict earthquakes?

Leslie: They have machines that measure them.

Teacher: On the next page, you are going to read about faults. Whisper read this page to find out what that word has to do with earthquakes.

(The teacher monitors as students read.)

Teacher: Use your sticky notes to mark the part that tells exactly what a plate is.

(The teacher monitors as students identify the sentence. The process continues as the teacher and students engage in the text.)

(After Reading)

Teacher: Let's take a look at the vocabulary we have seen so far in the book. The first word is *plates*. I want you to think of a sentence using the word that tells something you read about in the text. Turn and share that sentence with your partner.

(This partner strategy gives students more opportunities to respond to the question.)

Teacher: Jennifer, will you share the sentence you came up with?

Jennifer: OK. I had *plates*. The plates under the earth move and cause earthquakes.

Teacher: That was a great sentence.

(This process continues as all words encountered in the text thus far are discussed.)

Teacher: Today, we read the first part of the book *Earthquakes and Tsunamis*. Remember, we are reading this book to find out how earthquakes and tsunamis are alike and how they are also different. Turn to your partner and give one way that they are alike and one way they are different. Use information we have read so far.

(The teacher listens in for responses and then has students share.)

Writing About Reading

Consider extending the writing activity over a few days. Teachers often feel that an assignment must be completed the day it is assigned. On the contrary, if we expect students to produce better writing, they must have adequate time to write. At this level, have students use peer editing before they turn in a final copy to you.

Teacher: We are reading this book to compare earthquakes and tsunamis. We have already read some ways that earthquakes and tsunamis are the same and also how they are different.

John: Yes, like they both start with an earthquake.

Teacher: Good observation, John. I am giving each of you a writing checklist you will use as a guide for a writing assignment after we finish the book. When you leave group, I want you to go back to the text we read today and begin to gather information about how earthquakes and tsunamis are alike and different. There are several things you can record in your writing journal that you can use for your writing when we finish the book.

(Figure 8.4 shows the teacher-created writing checklist and a student writing example that resulted from this assignment.)

Figure 8.4
Sample Writing Checklist and Student Summary

- ☐ Include a topic sentence that tells what you will write about.
- ☐ Tell about what tsunamis and earthquakes are and what causes each one. (four sentences)
- ☐ Write about two ways earthquakes and tsunamis are alike, giving evidence from the text. (two sentences)
- ☐ Write about two ways earthquakes and tsunamis are different, giving evidence from the text. (two sentences)
- ☐ Provide a closing sentence that restates what you were writing about.
- ☐ Check your punctuation and capitalization. Review to make sure your sentences make sense and words are spelled correctly.

Earthquakes and Tsunamis

By Amelia

Earthquakes are alike but also different. Earthquakes are a big shaking of the earth. Earthquakes happen when plates under the earth collide. Tsunamis are when big waves from the ocean hit land. They happen when there is earth shaking under the water. Earthquakes and tsunamis are both earthquakes. Earthquakes and tsunamis cause a lot of damage. They are also different. Earthquakes happen under the ground and tsunamis happen under the water. These are some ways that earthquakes and tsunamis are alike and different.

❗ Independent writing extension activities include the following ideas:

- Have students complete a writing assignment that connects to the text and supports comprehension. For example, ask students to write about a main character. Have them choose three traits that made the character a hero and give an example of each from the story.
- Have students draw and write a sentence that tells how a new word was used in the text. Then have them draw a picture that represents the word and write a sentence that uses the word in another context.
- Use the 2nd grade writing checklists found in the Appendix. I created these simple templates, which are especially useful at the late Transitional and early Fluent stages.

When to Move to the Next Stage

The Fluent stage is appropriately named because as students complete this stage, they are truly fluent readers and writers. These students are now comfortable reading and writing about a wide variety of genres and are well prepared for the challenges of the upper elementary and intermediate grades—in both reading and writing. Fluent readers and writers have mastered common and less common vowel patterns, as well as common word features. Notice that students were asked not only to spell words correctly but also to write a sentence with each word to demonstrate meaning. This begins the study of the spelling/meaning stage of word study. Students must master the vowel patterns and word features before proceeding to the next stage. The Independent stage will be challenging with respect to text complexity, word study, and extensive reading and writing. Students leaving the Fluent stage must be competent in the study of vowel patterns and common word features.

Conclusion

The completion of the Fluent stage is critical as students move to the Independent stage. The next stage will have students dig deeper in more complex text and writing assignments, as students write to demonstrate comprehension. Fluent readers and writers have built a strong foundation and are well versed in both reading and writing comprehension supported by specific strategies and word study. The importance of successfully completing this Fluent stage cannot be underestimated.

Many students entering the upper grades often struggle because of weak foundational skills. Success at this stage ensures success in continued literacy learning, and it will open the doors for rich literacy experiences at the Independent stage of reading and writing.

Chapter 9

The Independent Reader and Writer

Characteristics of Independent Readers and Writers

The expectations for Independent readers and writers have risen dramatically over the past few years. A majority of state standards have increased the rigor required for these students, particularly those in the latter part of the stage. The texts that students are required to read in middle school, high school, college, and their future careers demand a sophistication for which many students today are unprepared. It is, therefore, critical that we begin honing their literacy skills in the early stages of development. Most Independent readers and writers are able to read to learn; however, they need continued support to fully engage with more complex texts.

Whereas students in the first five stages of literacy development are basically learning to read, Independent readers and writers are reading to gain knowledge from a variety of genres and writing to communicate that knowledge. Many of these Independent-level students have mastered fluency and will continue to hone this skill in independent practice. Word study advances in difficulty to support increasing text complexity, but comprehension is front and center throughout the stage, which generally correlates to 3rd, 4th, and 5th grade curriculum standards. To address this shift, more time in the lesson is devoted to comprehension in this Independent stage.

The Independent stage is generally differentiated by grade-level standards addressed most commonly in 3rd, 4th, and 5th grades. Therefore, the lesson plan components for Stage 6A focus on fluency, word study, writing, comprehension, and text levels appropriate for 3rd grade. Similarly, Stage 6B aligns with a 4th grade curriculum in these same areas. Finally, Stage 6C is more complex in both the text levels and the word study levels and is appropriate for 5th grade. These students will be expected to write across text genres in all types of written responses required by most 5th grade standards.

Figure 9.1 shows the three levels of the Independent stage and the specific expectations for those levels. Keep in mind that the writing is only addressed as students write about the text they have read.

For those of you who have used my previous book for Intermediate readers (Tyner & Green, 2009), these stages were addressed as the Evolving Year 1 and 2 and the Maturing Year 1. In this book, which address grades 3–5 only, I use the term Independent Stages 6A, 6B, and 6C to address these three grades.

Some students beginning this stage may need more time to build and refine fluency. For them, fluency will remain a lesson plan component, and you can decide the needs in your group. Poetry is a good choice for practicing fluency. On the other hand, more fluent readers will discontinue fluency as a lesson plan component. They should, however, practice rereading poetry or plays in independent practice.

Independent readers can decode fairly accurately, but as the text complexity increases, so does the need for more sophisticated decoding skills. Further, students use their knowledge of syntax (e.g., question marks, exclamation points, commas, apostrophes, hyphens) to understand the author's message. Thus, when students can focus on the author's meaning, expression naturally follows. As Independent readers become more fluent, they are able to focus on the meaning of words rather than on simply decoding words. The result is students who can read and decode words effortlessly and with sufficient speed to fully understand the text.

Understandably, much of the Independent lesson plan centers on comprehension. Independent readers largely determine the meaning of unknown words and phrases using context clues (e.g., definitions, restatements, examples, descriptions, illustrations) and grammatical structure. You must be skilled in asking text-dependent questions and threading students' conversations as they uncover meaning in text. Independent students continue to develop a wide variety of comprehension strategies as they navigate more complex text.

Figure 9.1

Independent Reader and Writer

Fluency	Vocabulary	Word Study	Reading Comprehension	Writing About Reading
Stage 6A				
• Typically, early to late 3rd grade • Book levels EI 23–30+, F&P N/O/P • Practice fluency with poetry or readers theater out of group	• Selecting vocabulary from text • Using selected vocabulary to summarize the text	• Recognizing and using multisyllabic words, compound words, syllabication, prefixes and suffixes, complex diagraphs, blends, and homophones • Beginning to make the spelling-meaning connection • Meeting word study standards for 3rd grade	• Learning and experimenting with before-, during-, and after-reading comprehension strategies • Reading a variety of text genres	• Writing multiple paragraphs to address the purpose for reading the text • Including evidence when responding to text • Writing a sequence of unfolding events • Writing to respond to text using narrative, informational, and opinion formats • Writing with evidence from text to support responses • Using time-order words in writing • Using some sensory words in writing • Meeting grade-level standards in writing for 3rd grade as they relate to text responses in narrative, informational, and opinion formats
Stage 6B				
• Early to late 4th grade • Book levels Rigby 16–28, F&P Q/R/S • Practice fluency with poetry or readers theater out of group	• Selecting vocabulary from text • Summarizing the text using vocabulary	• Making spelling-meaning connections • Learning about complex vowel patterns in multisyllabic words	• Reading longer texts in a variety of genres • Reading more text independently • Analyzing text • Reading multiple text pieces on the same subject	• Writing multiple paragraphs to respond to a text or text pieces in narrative, informational, and opinion writing

Stage 6B—(*continued*)				
		• Learning common Greek and Latin roots	• Reading and understanding a variety of text genres • Recognizing text structures	• Writing well-organized para-graphs in a logical sequence • Including quotes and definitions to support writing about text • Writing includes correct quotes to support writing purpose • Meeting grade-level standards in writing for 4th grade as they relate to respond-ing to text using narrative, informa-tional, and opinion response formats
Stage 6C				
• Early to late 5th grade • Book levels Rigby 29–30, F&P T/U/V • Practice fluency with poetry or readers theater out of group	• Selecting focus vocabulary from text • Using additional resources for defining words	• Recognizing and using more dif-ficult affixes • Increasing knowl-edge of more difficult Greek and Latin roots	• Reading much of the text indepen-dently and dis-cussing in small groups • Analyzing mul-tiple sources on the same topic • Explaining rela-tionships and interactions • Identifying and using text struc-tures to glean information • Integrating infor-mation from vari-ous sources • Interpreting the author's point of view • Developing inde-pendent use of before-, during-, and after-reading strategies	• Using complex syllable patterns in writing • Developing the topic with facts, definitions, con-crete details, quo-tations, or other information and examples related to the topic • Integrating information from multiple sources to respond to a topic • Using multiple media devices to support text response • Meeting grade-level standards in writing for 5th grade as they relate to respond-ing to text using narrative, informa-tional, and opinion response formats

Independent readers are also capable of reading an expansive range of genres, both narrative and informational. Reading content-area selections will be necessary as students access grade-level standards. By nature, informational text is more difficult than narrative text, and even on-level students may need more support to fully understand this text type. Independent readers should be comfortable using comprehension strategies interchangeably as needed for understanding.

Both in their classrooms and in everyday life, students must be immersed in different types of text, including novels, textbooks, reference materials, magazines, newspapers, and various forms of digital media. Exposure to these text types present unique challenges for readers and writers, as Independent students fine-tune their thinking about and comprehension of a given text. That said, these students must learn to adapt their thinking to promote understanding in a variety of text types. This is especially true with respect to digital literacy. As Independent readers and writers continue to use digital media to access information, they need to be able to sift through this information in an effective and efficient manner.

Although they are developing independence in reading and writing, these students still need leveled text selections to meet their wide range of abilities. Both the grade-level content and standards dictate that at least half the texts read by students be informational. Selecting texts based on grade-level content standards can also help teachers save time (since they are pushed to teach a multitude of standards). It is misleading to trust that any one basal text will be sufficient to cover these competing demands. Additional texts must be included; reading one story a week is not nearly enough to grow these readers.

Teachers, including myself, have often been misled into thinking that a basal program would cover everything needed at that grade level. We have to keep in mind that textbook publishers are businesses that need to make money. Choose carefully. I once went into a school district the fall after a new basal adoption. Unfortunately, the types of leveled texts offered with this basal were not of the quality or quantity needed to address a wide range of readers. I was less than popular when I suggested they needed to purchase more books and text pieces. Keep in mind that the Independent stage spans three grade levels, which requires many different text selections.

As Independent students hone their reading skills, they also advance their writing abilities. As students move to the upper elementary grades, the demands on their writing increase drastically, and grade-level standards include substantial writing, including narrative, informational, and opinion writing. If students can orally demonstrate a higher-level understanding of text, the expectation is that they can do the same thing in writing. This kind of in-depth writing requires extensive modeling by the teacher, guided practice, and writing opportunities with feedback.

Independent writers should be comfortable writing multiple paragraphs using varying sentence types and structures. The Independent stage spans three grade levels, with varying levels of difficulty that will be thoroughly discussed in this chapter. Independent writers adjust their writing for a variety of audiences and a number of different purposes. A truly self-regulated writer flexibly uses and internalizes processes and strategies. As students complete the Independent stage, they should be well prepared to enter middle school, where they will be asked to complete many high-level writing assignments connected to reading.

As students begin to read an increasingly wide variety of genres, they also begin to experiment with writing for different purposes. Independent writers need support to study the various elements of the writing process, and they need time to practice these elements independently. Many students fail to reach their writing potential when teachers expect them to write everything by hand. In this digital age, students need to be composing a majority of their pieces on a computer. Technology makes writing much less labor-intensive, and students have more energy for their writing tasks. The more proficient these students become as readers, the more they develop as writers. These two processes go hand in hand in literacy development.

As teachers, we are keenly aware of the grade-level standards for which we are held accountable. With this in mind, I felt it would be important to correlate the grade-level standards with these frameworks. My goal in including these specific standards is to reassure teachers that working in small-group instruction can also provide a platform to address a plethora of grade-level standards. As I reviewed many state standards documents, it became clear that most states use the Common Core State Standards as a base for developing their own standards with some adaptations. The Common Core State Standards that are addressed or could be addressed at the Independent stage are located in the Appendix. This reference will make it easy for you to use while planning for small-group instruction.

Lesson Components of the Independent Reader and Writer Stage

The Independent lesson plan is found in Figure 9.2. Included in this lesson plan are examples for activities that support each component and are intended to be out-of-group extension activities. The fluency component can be completed in small groups for students who continue to struggle with fluency. For most

Figure 9.2

Lesson Plan: Independent Stage

FLUENCY	FLUENCY EXTENSION
Poem: _____	☐ Reread poem. ☐ Utilize readers theater. ☐ Other: _____

WORD STUDY

Features: _____

Cycle: _____   Week: _____

Word Sort: ☐ Open   ☐ Closed

☐ Writing Sort

☐ Sound Boxes

☐ Meaning Discussions

☐ Student-Created Sentences *(oral or written)*

WORD STUDY EXTENSION

☐ Do a spelling sort with partner.

☐ Play Word Study Detectives.

☐ Write sentences to show meaning.

☐ Conduct a word hunt.

☐ Research words (e.g., words with the same pattern, root, prefix, suffix).

☐ Other: _____

COMPREHENSION

New Read: _____   Text Level: _____

Before Reading

☐ Build background knowledge (if needed).

☐ Preview vocabulary.

☐ Set the purpose for reading.

During Reading

☐ Stopping points/text-dependent questions

-
-
-
-

After Reading

☐ Revisit vocabulary.

☐ Revisit purpose for reading.

☐ Have a comprehension conversation.

☐ Discuss writing extension.

COMPREHENSION EXTENSION

☐ Write a sentence with each vocabulary word that tells something about the text.

Writing Checklists:

  ☐ Narrative: 6A, 6B, 6C

  ☐ Informative/Explanatory: 6A, 6B, 6C

  ☐ Opinion: 6A, 6B, 6C

☐ Other: _____

(Checklists available at www.beverlytyner.net)

☐ Teacher-created writing checklist

☐ Graphic organizer

students, though, the teacher can assign independent practice in extension activities that support fluency. Word study continues to be a consistent lesson element, and comprehension focuses on strategies that will be used before, during, and after reading. The final part of the lesson plan includes written comprehension responses students should complete as out-of-group extension activities.

Fluency

The fluency standards at this stage basically require that students be able to read and understand grade-level texts. That said, reading a 3rd grade level text (6A) versus a 5th grade level text (6C) with understanding are two different things. Generally, most Independent students are already fluent readers at their specified grade level, but they still need to continue fluency practice outside the small-group setting. For those students who still lack the fluency needed for comprehension, poetry or song lyrics serve several purposes. First, poetry is an important genre for Independent readers and can provide valuable vocabulary and comprehension development. Time constraints also make poetry a sensible choice. Beginning a lesson by reading or rereading a poem provides a warm-up and gets the lesson off to a quick start. Regardless, you should routinely include poetry as a text for comprehension focus.

Independent readers can sometimes become reluctant when asked to reread longer texts. For these readers, poetry is motivating, and there's an endless variety of seasonal, humorous, and classical poems. Song lyrics can also be used (and even sung) to develop fluency. A variety of out-of-group fluency extensions provide important independent practice. For example, students can build a fluency folder for all the poems and songs used in their small groups. Then students can practice the poems or songs for the week with a partner or go back and visit favorites. It would also be appropriate to ask students to reread a text or a part of a text with a partner outside their small groups.

◇◇

(Although this 3rd grade group is close to being able to practice fluency in independent practice, the teacher occasionally uses poetry to ensure the group can maintain this skill. The teacher has selected the poem "Sick" by Shel Silverstein to help students read a little faster. The poem is written in long phrases and sentences, so students must quickly look ahead to keep up with the rhythm of the poem. On the previous day, students looked at the structure of and vocabulary used in the poem.)

Teacher: Please get your poem out of your folder. Yesterday, we read the poem "Sick" for the first time. I hope you all had a chance to reread this poem out of group yesterday. Today, we are going to choral read the poem again. Please use your markers under each line so you can keep up. We will be reading quickly.

(The teacher and students reread the poem together.)

Teacher: When you leave group today, I want you to reread this poem again. Next week, you will work with a partner to pick your own Shel Silverstein poem to practice and share with the class.

Word Study

In word study, Independent students are learning to identify and use syllabication, multisyllabic words, synonyms, antonyms, homographs, and homophones. They also apply their knowledge of Greek and Latin roots and affixes, to name a few. With this in mind, word study at this stage is divided into three distinct levels, covering three grade levels: 3rd, 4th, and 5th. The scope and sequences for all three stages can be found in the Appendix. And as always, all support materials for the Independent stage—including word study cards, directions for lessons, assessments, and activities—can be downloaded from www.beverlytyner.net.

◇◇

(These students are exploring root words and affixes with three related prefixes: bi, tri, *and* quad. *In this exchange, students are starting an open sort to discover patterns and word meanings. This group of 4th grade students has successfully completed the 6A sequence in word study and is now working in Stage 6B.)*

Teacher: Today, we are going to start a new set of words. I am going to give you a set of words to sort with your partner. Decide how these words can be grouped together.

(The teacher distributes the word cards with the prefixes bi, tri, *and* quad. *She then observes while students discuss and sort words. This is an open sort because students have been given no information about the patterns. This is the first day of this word study where students are discovering and discussing the new patterns.)*

Teacher: Michael, tell us how you and David decided to sort the words and why.

Michael: Well, all the words begin with *quad*, *bi*, or *tri*.

Teacher: Does anyone remember what we call a group of letters that have direct meanings?

Nicole: It's either a prefix or a root word.

Teacher: It's one of those. Can anyone help her out?

Kevin: It's a prefix. A prefix can be added onto a root word or base word, but they have specific meanings and cannot stand alone as a real word.

Teacher: Good. You remembered a lot about prefixes. Let's start sorting the words into categories.

Ken: Sorting these words was really easy.

Teacher: I know, but it will be easier to think about the word meanings if they are separated. Now find a word you already know that has the prefix *tri*.

Janet: I see *tricycle*.

Teacher: What does that word mean?

Jessica: It's like a bicycle, but it has three wheels.

Teacher: So how does that help us know what the prefix *tri* means?

Jessica: Oh, *tri* means "three" because a tricycle has three wheels.

Teacher: So, what should we be looking for in each of the words that begins with *tri*?

Adam: Well, all the words in this category have something to do with three.

Teacher: You made a good connection.

  (The teacher goes through the same process with quad *and* bi. *The teacher then chooses two words from each category the students weren't familiar with for further discussion. She starts with the easier words and builds upon that knowledge during the week as other words are discussed. This lesson is completed after two words in each category are discussed.)*

Teacher: When you go back to your seats, I'd like you to work with a partner with two words that I am going to assign to you. I want you to find out what your words mean and explain how the prefix affects their meaning. Use your dictionary or go online if you need help. Write a sentence with the word and then draw a picture to show its meaning. When you come back to group, you are going to share this with the rest of the group.

❗ Independent word study extension activities include the following ideas:

- Write to explain the meanings of prefixes and how that helps when we are looking at other words with similar word parts.
- Complete a word hunt to find other words that fit these patterns.
- Provide students with a copy of the word cards for the week. Students will keep them in their extension folders as they work on various activities during the week.
- Write sentences to show meanings of the words.
- Keep a word study journal to record words, sentences, and other activities. This study of word parts is an important part of building vocabulary.

Comprehension

The number of standards that can be addressed in this model for Independent readers and writers is extensive (see Appendix). You will notice that the comprehension part of the lesson plan is subdivided into before-, during-, and after-reading sections. Prior to reading, the teacher should briefly introduce the text and give any background information needed to understand the text. Refrain from spending too much time discussing information that will be revealed in the text. Additionally, preselected vocabulary will quickly be presented but not defined. Students will search for these words (and the context clues that help define them) during reading. Perhaps the most important part of the before-reading routine is for the teacher to set a specific purpose for reading the text. During reading, the teacher will ask text-dependent questions to support this purpose and encourage student conversations to deepen comprehension. After reading, students will review vocabulary and write sentences that demonstrate an understanding of the words as used in the text. Finally, students will revisit and discuss the purpose for reading the text.

◇◇

(The following group of Independent students are reading a Level P book, which is appropriate for the end of 3rd grade. Talking partners have already been established for the week.)

(Before Reading)

Teacher: Today, we are going to read a myth called *King Midas and the Golden Touch*. It is retold by Laura Layton Strom and illustrated by Kirk Parrish. We have seen the word *retold* before in another genre. Turn and talk to your partner, what was that genre?

(The teacher listens as partners discuss.)

Teacher: Nick, tell us what you and John discussed.

Nick: Well, we remember that the folktale we read last week had another author that retold the story, and that meant she told it again.

Teacher: Yes, that's right. A folktale is a story that is handed down from generation to generation. Each time it is told, the next person usually adds to or leaves out some of the story told to them. Today, we are going to read a book that is from a genre we have not yet discussed this year. *King Midas and the Golden Touch* is a myth.

(The teacher knows that her students have virtually no background knowledge about myths, so rather than have students guess, she simply tells them about the genre.)

Teacher: Long ago, the people who lived in Greece used myths to explain their heroes, gods, and the world. They had hundreds of gods, and they all had special meanings. They were not real but imagined. The satyr in this story was one of their gods. Satyrs were known to cause trouble and looked like a goat man with a tail.

(The teacher has preselected vocabulary words from the story that are important to understanding. These words are written on index cards and posted so the words can be revisited both during and after reading. The teacher simply shows each vocabulary word and gives students a chance to say each word.)

Teacher: Here are some words that we will read in the story today.

(The teacher holds up the index cards and places them on a tabletop sorting board.)

Teacher: We have the words *evict, intruder, greedy, foretold, misery, wealth,* and *pitcher.*

(There is little discussion of the meaning of these words prior to reading the text. This valuable time will be spent both during and after the story has been completed.)

Teacher: Let's see how the author uses these words in this story. Let's also look for context clues to help us figure out what these words mean. Let's read this myth to find out what valuable lesson the king learned and how he learned that lesson.

(During Reading)

(During reading, the teacher poses text-dependent questions to students and asks them to find and tag evidence to support their answers. In-depth comprehension conversations during reading are essential for teachers to gauge student under-standing and help guide deeper comprehension. These questions are developed by the teacher prior to the lesson and support the purpose for reading.)

Teacher: I will be the lead reader for the first two pages, and you will be my back-up readers by whispering along with me. On these two pages, we will see two important character traits that will guide the king's later decisions.

(The teacher and students read.)

Teacher: Talk to your partner and discuss the character traits the king is showing us on these pages.

(Students discuss with partners while the teacher listens in. This is a short conversation and should last about 20–30 seconds.)

Teacher: Beth, tell us about what you and Jill discussed.

Beth: We thought the king was being very greedy because it said he already had a lot of wealth, and he still wanted more gold.

Teacher: I like your word choice *greedy.* Although the author didn't use that word, it certainly describes his behavior. The author makes the statement that "Although the king had a lot of wealth, he did not have a lot of wisdom." Use your sticky notes and tag evidence that supports this statement.

(The teacher observes students as they tag evidence.)

Teacher: Christopher, please read the sentence you found.

Christopher: It says, "There was only one thing he loved more than his daughter—gold." So this author thinks he wasn't too smart to say that.

Teacher: That is a very important point. Let's choral read together the next two pages.

(The teacher and students read.)

Teacher: So we see that the satyr has come to the castle. Why did the king call his soldiers to evict the satyr?

Monica: It says that the satyr is known to cause trouble, so he wanted to make him leave.

Teacher: Let's read on to see how the satyr reacts.

(Students choral read the next page.)

Teacher: Why is the satyr responding like this? Let's read on to find out. Laura, will you be the lead reader on the next page, please? We will be your whisper readers.

(Teacher and students read.)

Teacher: We now have some clues about his behavior. What is the satyr's motive for acting this way? Turn and talk to your partner.

(Partners discuss.)

Teacher: Nick, what did you two talk about?

Nick: The satyr wants to stall the king so he won't get kicked out.

Teacher: It sure looks that way. Gabby, will you be the lead reader on the next two pages?

Gabby: Sure.

(Gabby lead reads as others whisper read.)

Teacher: On this page, the satyr says to the king, "This statement is quite bold." What statement is he talking about? What does that mean?

Monica: He is talking about when King Midas said he loves gold more than anything.

Teacher: Why does the satyr use the word *bold*?

Christopher: I think that he uses that word because he doesn't think the king is too smart!

Teacher: I want everyone to whisper read the next two pages on your own to find out what the turning point in the story is. Remember, I need to hear you whisper reading.

(The teacher listens in while students whisper read.)

Teacher: Turn to your partner and talk about the event that made things begin to change for the king.

(The story is finished in this manner, with lead reading and whisper reading. The teacher continues to ask questions and lead students in comprehension conversations.)

(After Reading)

Teacher: Let's take another look at the vocabulary in the story. I am going to give each of you one of these words. Give us a sentence using that word that tells something important that happened in the story. I will go first. I have the word *evict*. So my sentence is "The king called his soldiers to evict the satyr from the palace." Who wants to go next? Will?

Will: I have the word *greedy*. The king was very greedy, and he wanted more gold even though he already had a lot.

Teacher: Well, that was certainly true.

(All students give a sentence with their word.)

Teacher: We read this book to find out what lesson the king learned and how his traits changed from the beginning to the end of the story. Turn to your partner. What lesson did the king learn, and how did he learn the lesson?

(Students discuss as the teacher listens in.)

Teacher: Jill, what did you two discuss?

Jill: Well, the king definitely learned there were things more important than gold, like his daughter.

Teacher: Yes, and how did he learn that lesson, Christopher?

Christopher: When his daughter touched him, she turned to gold. Then he realized that the gold was not as important as his daughter.

Teacher: Laura, what do you think?

Laura: At the beginning of the story, the king was greedy because he wanted even more gold.

Teacher: Good. Can you give us another character trait he showed at the beginning?

Jill: Well, he wasn't very loving when he said he loved gold more than his daughter.

Teacher: How did his character traits change by the end of the story?

Philip: He was grateful that he had his daughter back.

Teacher: Good, I didn't think about that one.

(The comprehension conversation continues as other character traits are explored, and students give evidence from the text to support each one.)

Writing About Reading

Students must be held accountable for length, depth, spelling, grammar, sentence structure, word choice, and voice in their writing. We sometimes mistake writing assignments as a text-based response when the assignment is actually a creative response. For example, asking students to write about what they would do if they had all the gold in the world is a creative writing activity instead of one focused on comprehension.

Teacher: This week, you are going to be writing about King Midas. When we discussed the story, we focused on the lesson King Midas learned. We have been writing all year, so I feel you are ready to do some more extensive writing. You are explaining to your audience about the lesson King Midas learned and how he learned that lesson. I am going to give each of you a writing checklist to help guide you in your writing. Refer to this as you write so you include all components. Make sure you address each of the categories. There are certain elements you will want to include. Please include at least two quotes to support your statements. You will also need to write at least two paragraphs to complete this assignment. Based on this assignment, which writing checklist would you need to use?

Lauren: I think it would be the informative/explanatory checklist because we need to explain how he learned the lesson.

Teacher: That's right! Again, please check your essay with this checklist to make sure you included all the needed parts.

[See Figure 9.3 for a sample student essay.]

Independent Readers and Writers: Informational Text

The Independent stage spans three grades of varied reading levels. Therefore, I felt that this warranted an additional scenario showing students engaged in the comprehension of informational text at a higher level. Please note that this only addresses the comprehension and writing sections. This group of advanced 5th graders is made up of accomplished readers and writers. The teacher decides to do a study of Martin Luther King Jr.'s famous "I Have a Dream" speech. Although students conduct most of the reading out of group, the teacher has decided to read and discuss the first part of the speech together.

Figure 9.3
Sample Student Essay

King Midas and the Golden Touch

King Midas learned a valuable lesson in this myth. He also changed the way he behaved from the beginning to the end of the story. King Midas had a lot of wealth, that meant he had a lot of gold. He was greedy when he said, "I wouldn't mind having even more gold!" He was not very loving when he said, "I only love one thing more than my daughter—gold."

King Midas began to change after the satyr arrived while he was counting his gold at the castle. Satyrs looked like half man and half goat. They were known to cause trouble. The king tried to evict the satyr, but the satyr heard the king say that he loved gold and wanted more. The satyr told the king that it might not be a good idea. He was trying to trick the king into letting him stay and it worked. One night, after much wishing, the king's wish to have more gold came true. When he woke up, everything he touched turned to gold. At first he was happy, but when he started to eat, the food turned to gold and he couldn't eat. Then the king touched his daughter and she turned to gold. This is when the king began to change. He realized that gold was not that important if he couldn't have his daughter. The king said, "I hate the very sight of that yellow stuff!" Luckily, the satyr was able to change his daughter back to normal. He told the satyr, "Please take everything I own! Only give me back my precious daughter!" I don't understand that because the satyr helped the king and was not causing trouble. Maybe he wasn't a true satyr. The king learned that gold was not as good as having his daughter.

Comprehension

◇◇

Teacher: We have already studied Martin Luther King Jr. this year in social studies. Today, we are going to start an in-depth reading of his most famous speech. Many people believe it is one of the best speeches ever given. As we read and discuss the speech, we want to find out what makes this speech so effective and powerful. This text is probably more difficult than many other texts we have read this year. When we read more difficult text, we need to remember several strategies. Do you remember any of those strategies?

Jewel: Yes. When the reading is hard, we will probably need to reread it a couple of times.

Teacher: Yes, and that's a strategy I use in my own reading. Does anyone remember another strategy?

Marcus: Well, if it gets too long, it makes it seem harder than it really is, so we need to chunk the text into parts.

Teacher: Absolutely, and that is what we will be doing with this speech. Yesterday, I asked you to watch the video clip of Dr. King giving his speech and write down words that you would use to describe Martin Luther King Jr. as he delivered his speech. Who would like to share?

Ellison: I thought he was very confident. He stood up straight and looked at the audience.

Gordon: Yes, and his voice kind of boomed. It was really loud and strong.

Mary Frances: Another thing I noticed is he showed a lot of passion when he talked. You knew that he meant what he said.

Teacher: You all made some good observations, and these points contributed to the success of the speech. You can include some of this information as you write an essay after we discuss this speech in depth. I want to show some words that are included in the speech. Look at these words: *languish*, *threshold*, *oppression*, *tribulation*, *segregation*, *sear*, *wither*, and *emancipation*. When you come to these words, look for context clues to help you figure out what they mean. When you are reading independently and can't figure out what a word means or you aren't sure, what could you do?

Laura: Well, you could always look in a dictionary or Google it.

Teacher: That sounds like a good plan. After we study the speech, you will be writing an essay discussing the reasons why Dr. King's speech was so effective and powerful. Today, we are going to read and discuss the first section of the speech. You have already watched this speech once, and today we are going back to the first part. I have given each of you a sticky note to tag evidence and important points as we go along. I will be lead reading and you will whisper read along with me. As we read, look for words or phrases that give us visual images. Also look for words that helped Dr. King connect to his audience. Finally, look for words that are repeated, and think about the effect that has.

(The teacher and students read the first two paragraphs together.)

Teacher: Let's start with repeated words. Turn to your partner and discuss any words or phrases that have been repeated so far.

(The teacher observes as partners discuss.)

Teacher: Brian, what do you and Josie find?

Brian: Just the words *I have a dream*. I wonder how many times he uses that phrase? When I watched the speech, it seemed like a lot.

Teacher: Did you find any words that helped Dr. King connect to his audience?

Cora: We thought the word *friends*, so he wanted everyone to know he thought of all of them as friends. He also used the word *brotherhood*, which kind of means we are in a group all together.

Teacher: Did anyone else get *brotherhood*?

Students: No.

Teacher: You will want to add that to your sheet when you get back to your desk. What about phrases that give us visual images?

Tommy: We loved the phrase *Lips dripping with words*.

(Discussion continues.)

Teacher: What do you think was the main idea Dr. King wanted to communicate in this part?

Denise: He wanted to tell us that African Americans should be treated like other people and we all should be a part of making them free.

Teacher: That's great. In the first part of the speech we encountered the word *languish*. What meaning did the word have in the context of the speech?

Paul: He didn't want to languish anymore. That meant that he did not want to wait any longer.

Teacher: I really liked the way you defined the word as it was used in the speech.

Tommy: When we watched the speech, we heard Dr. King use a booming voice. He was also very passionate. Would those be some of the reasons the speech was so effective?

Teacher: Absolutely.

Mary Frances: When we read the first part of the speech, he used words that helped him connect with the audience like *friends* and *brotherhood*.

Teacher: Yes, those are definitely some reasons why this speech is so effective. As we continue reading the speech this week, you will be identifying other things to add to your list.

Writing About Reading

Students finish reading and discussing the speech over the next three days and begin working on their essay. See Figure 9.4 for an example of a completed writing assignment. This advanced Independent lesson gives above-level students the chance to work with authentic literature at a high level of text complexity. The teacher gives ample support, knowing that the text is considerably more difficult than previous assignments. The key to student success with this reading and writing assignment is the strong foundation that has been built during the elementary school years. Although these students are well prepared to complete much of their reading and writing independently, they are still in need of a teacher to guide the comprehension of complex text.

Conclusion

The Independent stage concludes the six stages of reading and writing development in elementary school. During this last stage of development, Independent students continue to develop their literacy skills as more accomplished readers and writers. They assume more responsibility for their learning; but they still require teacher support as they learn to think critically about text. Students are now able to spend large blocks of time reading and writing. Independent readers and writers are developing literacy expertise that allows them to access and respond in depth to a wide variety of complex texts. The important literacy foundations established in the elementary grades are essential in preparing students for middle school and to be lifelong readers and writers. Without question, they will also thrive in their future educational and professional endeavors.

Figure 9.4
Sample Student Essay

I Have a Dream: A Powerful Speech

On August 28, 1963, Dr. Martin Luther King made a speech that changed our country. This very special speech was called, "I Have a Dream." Many people think that it was the best speech that was ever given. There are several reasons that made the speech so effective.

Dr. King made people all feel included in his speech. It was not just a speech for the black people. During his speech he used words including friends, brotherhood, and together. He hoped that these words would let people know that it was everyone's responsibility to give black people the same rights as other people.

One of the most powerful ways that his speech was effective was his word choice. His words, phrases, and sentences helped the reader create visual images in their minds. For example, as he was talking about black people he said, "we cannot wallow in the valley of despair." It made me see black people who had been in jail unjustly, children with no food, and black people sitting in the back of buses all together rolling in mud. I saw the mud as their despair. I also particularly like the phrase he used to describe what life would be with all privileges of white people, "an oasis of freedom and justice."

Finally, Dr. King repeated words and phrases such as, "I have a dream." He also repeated phrases like "let freedom ring" or "we can never." When he repeated these phrases, it was easy for the people hearing the speech to remember the words. He chose these words and phrases carefully so that he could use them multiple times. By repeating words and phrases, it made the speech more powerful.

This speech is memorable because of the words he chose to create visual images. Repeating important words multiple times was also powerful. Dr. King was also successful in using words that made everyone feel that they were a part of the answer to rights for black people. Dr. Martin Luther King's famous speech is still popular and meaningful today because of the way he wrote and delivered his speech, "I Have a Dream."

Conclusion

Building a Framework for Reading and Writing Success

Few would argue that the educational future for our students is grounded in early reading and writing success. Without solid research-based instruction delivered in a systematic, differentiated format, we will continue to miss the mark for many students. The teaching of reading and writing is a complex process at best. To become effective teachers, we must first be cognizant of the developmental stages through which readers and writers pass. Additionally, we must understand the importance of research that supports effective literacy instruction. With an ever-shrinking instructional day, teachers must carefully examine every literacy activity in terms of the research and the developmental needs of all students.

If we are to accomplish the lofty goal of giving every child the opportunity to reach his or her maximum literacy potentials, we must be diligent in designing and implementing comprehensive reading and writing programs. Small-group differentiated reading and writing instruction can be used to address the problems of struggling readers and serve the important purpose of reducing reading failure. Additionally, differentiated instruction launches on- and above-level students on a trajectory for additional growth.

Reading and writing instruction must be consistent and provide students with opportunities to engage in contextual reading, systematic word study, and writing opportunities that are carefully paced to maximize learning opportunities. When children have a strong literacy foundation, the educational opportunities become endless.

This book presents step-by-step lesson plans that reflect the developmental stages of the reading and writing processes. They will assist teachers in planning for meaningful literacy instruction. Although this book contains many familiar research-based strategies, it is not in these individual strategies alone that we find the strength of the small-group differentiated reading and writing models. That power is found in the ways in which these strategies are pieced together and structured to support one another.

There is no reading or writing manual that can accurately tell a teacher everything to say or do. In my attempt to simplify the complex reading and writing processes, I acknowledge and emphasize the unique needs of each student. I do, however, feel that the approach presented in this book might help lay the foundation on which teachers can begin to build effective reading and writing programs for all students.

Teaching students how to become proficient readers and writers in the elementary grades is not an easy feat. Elementary students require a teacher who recognizes both their individual strengths and areas of need and can effectively plan instruction that will meet those needs. Differentiated reading instruction must become the standard if we are going to provide an opportunity for all students to reach their potential.

My hope is that this book will be a tool teachers use to build their knowledge base, apply that knowledge in a variety of classroom situations, unlock literacy challenges, and begin to explore unlimited potential for all students. Reading and writing practices for students in the 21st century need to meet the demands of an incredibly fast-moving society. Literacy skills are necessary for survival. Although we know that the job of an elementary teacher can be underappreciated—as well as daunting—I have observed incredible teachers who do not let the negatives overshadow their dedication to their profession and their excitement about their students' literacy gains. These are the teachers who are committed to making a difference for all students. These teachers are our role models as we seek to continually increase our knowledge and improve our pedagogy.

Appendixes

Online Material

Available at www.beverlytyner.net.

Emergent Reader and Writer, Stage 1A (Early Literacy Foundational Skills)

- Letter Cards
- Sound Boxes
- ELFS Lesson Plans (1–5)
- ELFS Lesson Plans (6–10)
- ELFS Lesson Plans (11–15)
- ELFS Lesson Plans (16–20)
- ELFS Lesson Plans (21–26)
- ELFS Materials (Lessons 1–5)
- ELFS Materials (Lessons 6–10)
- ELFS Materials (Lessons 11–15)
- ELFS Materials (Lessons 16–20)
- ELFS Materials (Lessons 21–26)
- Options for Advanced Students

Emergent Reader and Writer, Stage 1B

- High-Frequency Word Cards
- High-Frequency Words Assessment
- Emergent Cut-Up Sentences

Beginning Reader and Writer, Stages 2A/B

- Beginning Lesson Plan
- Word Study Cards (Stage 2A)
- Word Study Cards (Stage 2B)
- Cut-Up Sentences (Stage 2A)
- Cut-Up Sentences (Stage 2B)

Fledgling Reader and Writer, Stages 3A/B

- Fledgling Lesson Plan
- Word Study Cards (Stage 3A)
- Word Study Cards (Stage 3B)
- Cut-Up Sentences (Stage 3A)
- Cut-Up Sentences (Stage 3B)
- Sound Boxes
- Writing Sort (3 Box)
- Writing Sort (4 Box)
- Dictated Sentences

Transitional Reader and Writer, Stages 4A/B

- Transitional Lesson Plan
- Word Study Cards (Stage 4A)
- Word Study Cards (Stage 4B)
- Writing Sort (3 Box)
- Writing Sort (4 Box)
- Make It, Write It!
- Word Scramble Activities (Stage 4A)
- Word Scramble Activities (Stage 4B)
- Dictated Sentences
- Text-Dependent Questions
- Setting the Purpose
- Sound Boxes

Fluent Reader and Writer, Stages 5A/B

- Fluent Lesson Plan
- Word Study Cards (Stage 5A)
- Word Study Cards (Stage 5B)
- Writing Sort (3 Box)
- Writing Sort (4 Box)
- Make It, Write It!
- Word Scramble Activities (Stage 5A)
- Dictated Sentences
- Word Study Matrix
- Second Grade Writing Checklists
- Sound Boxes

Independent Reader and Writer, Stages 6A/B/C

- Independent Lesson Plan
- Word Study Cards (Stage 6A)
- Word Study Cards (Stage 6B)
- Word Study Cards (Stage 6C)
- Word Sort Directions
- Writing Checklist: 3rd Grade Narrative
- Writing Checklist: 3rd Grade Informative
- Writing Checklist: 3rd Grade Opinion
- Writing Checklist: 4th Grade Narrative
- Writing Checklist: 4th Grade Informative
- Writing Checklist: 4th Grade Opinion
- Writing Checklist: 5th Grade Narrative
- Writing Checklist: 5th Grade Informative
- Writing Checklist: 5th Grade Opinion

APPENDIX A:
Emergent Reader and Writer, Stages 1A/B

Emergent Stage: Common Standards

Fluency
- Follows words from left to right, top to bottom, and page by page.
- Reads emergent-reader texts with purpose and understanding.

Word Study (includes phonemic awareness and phonics)
- Counts, pronounces, blends, and segments syllables in spoken words.
- Blends and segments onsets and rimes of single-syllable spoken words.
- Produces and expands complete sentences in shared language activities.
- Isolates and pronounces the initial, medial vowel, and final sounds (phonemes) in three-phoneme (consonant-vowel-consonant, or CVC) words.
- Demonstrates basic knowledge of one-to-one letter-sound correspondences by producing the primary sound for each consonant.
- Discriminates and identifies sounds in spoken language.
- Matches pictures that begin with a particular consonant sound.
- Recognizes alphabet letters and sounds of beginning consonants.
- Recognizes and produces rhyming words.
- Recognizes and names all uppercase and lowercase letters of the alphabet.
- Demonstrates an understanding of the organization and basic features of print.
- Recognizes that spoken words are represented in written language by specific sequences of letters.
- Understands that words are separated by spaces in print.

Vocabulary
- Reads common high-frequency words by sight (e.g., *the, of, to, you, she, my, is, are, do, does*).
- Uses words and phrases acquired through conversations, reading and being read to, and responding to texts.

Comprehension
- Reads emergent-reader texts with purpose and understanding.
- With prompting and support, asks and answers questions about unknown words in a text.
- Identifies the front cover, back cover, and title page of a book.
- With prompting and support, identifies the author and illustrator of a text and defines the role of each.
- Participates in collaborative conversations with diverse partners about texts with peers and adults in small groups.

Writing About Reading

- Prints many uppercase and lowercase letters.
- Uses a combination of drawing, dictating, and writing to compose opinion pieces in which they tell a reader the topic or the name of the book they are writing about and state an opinion or preference about the topic or book (e.g., My favorite book is...).
- Uses a combination of drawing, dictating, and writing to compose informative/explanatory texts in which they name what they are writing about and supply some information about the topic.
- Uses a combination of drawing, dictating, and writing to narrate a single event or several loosely linked events, tells about the events in the order in which they occurred, and provides a reaction to what happened.

ELFS Lessons: Scope and Sequence (Stage 1A)

Lesson	**Focus Letter** Starfall Presentation and Alphabet Production	**Guess My Word** (Left to Right, Top to Bottom)	**Sound Boxes** (Sound Segmentation with Elkonin Boxes)	**Letter Match** ("Cover the letter that _____ begins with.")	**Rhyming**
1	Bb	b-all, c-ake, m-an, s-aw, m-ap	cab, Sam, bam, mac	sandwich, bird, matches, ant, corn	mall-ball, make-cake, draw-saw, cap-map, tank-bank, track-sack, take-lake, trap-cap, pan-fan
2	Ss	b-ank, s-ack, l-ake, c-ap, f-an	bam, cab, Sam, mac	sofa, bowl, mouse, apple, car	mall-ball, make-cake, draw-saw, cap-map, tank-bank, track-sack, take-lake, trap-cap, pan-fan
3	Mm	st-ick, m-ice, p-ink, sl-ide, l-ight	cab, bam, mac, Sam	candy, salad, bird, ani-mal, mouse	mall-ball, make-cake, draw-saw, cap-map, tank-bank, track-sack, take-lake, trap-cap, pan-fan
4	Aa	ch-in, d-ice, f-in, n-ight, br-ick	Sam, cab, bam, mac	cow, sand, bubble, alli-gator, milk	mall-ball, make-cake, draw-saw, cap-map, tank-bank, track-sack, take-lake, trap-cap, pan-fan
5	Cc	s-ock, c-op, st-ore, r-ock, bl-ock	cab, Sam, bam, mac	bank, supper, candle, moon, aunt	mall-ball, make-cake, draw-saw, cap-map, tank-bank, track-sack, take-lake, trap-cap, pan-fan
6	Dd	h-op, cl-ock, l-ock, c-op, st-op	fit, bit, sit, mit, rid	duck, fish, top, ring, inch	sock-clock, hop-stop, bug-mug, luck-duck, beat-meat, well-bell, vest-nest, bump-hump, rest-vest
7	Ff	tr-unk, d-uck, h-ump, tr-uck, b-ug	bit, mit, fit, rid, tab	dog, fan, tire, rabbit, Indian	sock-clock, hop-stop, bug-mug, luck-duck, beat-meat, well-bell, vest-nest, bump-hump, rest-vest
8	Tt	h-ug, b-ump, d-ug, d-ump, m-ug	rid, sit, Tim, bit, fit	dive, five, ten, robin, if	sock-clock, hop-stop, bug-mug, luck-duck, beat-meat, well-bell, vest-nest, bump-hump, rest-vest

Lesson	Focus Letter Starfall Presentation and Alphabet Production	Guess My Word (Left to Right, Top to Bottom)	Sound Boxes (Sound Segmentation with Elkonin Boxes)	Letter Match ("Cover the letter that _____ begins with.")	Rhyming
9	Rr	m-eat, tr-eat, w-ell, b-ell, h-eat	rid, bit, mid, sit, fit	dishes, finish, turtle, red, is	sock-clock, hop-stop, bug-mug, luck-duck, beat-meat, well-bell, vest-nest, bump-hump, rest-vest
10	Ii	v-est, n-est, s-eat, r-est, y-ell	bid, fit, sit, rid, bit	doll, frog, tan, roof, in	sock-clock, hop-stop, bug-mug, luck-duck, beat-meat, well-bell, vest-nest, bump-hump, rest-vest
11	Ll	let-ter paint-er neck-lace, ham-burg-er, liz-ard pre-sent	mop, hot, cot, pot, lot	lamp, purple, nest, hand, octopus	better-letter, blizzard-lizard, lumber, number, pickle-nickel, muppet-puppet, riding-hiding, doodle-noodle, madder-ladder, locket-pocket
12	Oo	laun-dry pil-grim num-ber hid-ing nick-el pen-ny	dot, hop, mop, cop, pop	ladder, pie, nine, home, on	better-letter, blizzard-lizard, lumber, number, pickle-nickel, muppet-puppet, riding-hiding, doodle-noodle, madder-ladder, locket-pocket
13	Pp	lol-li-pop pa-per noo-dle heat-er nurs-er-y lad-der	lob, sob, hop, rob, cob	light, pink, number, half, October	better-letter, blizzard-lizard, lumber, number, pickle-nickel, muppet-puppet, riding-hiding, doodle-noodle, madder-ladder, locket-pocket
14	Nn	lip-stick pump-kin news-pa-per ham-mer pup-pet pock-et	sod, rod, cob, hop, hot	lion, page, napkin, ham, off	better-letter, blizzard-lizard, lumber, number, pickle-nickel, muppet-puppet, riding-hiding, doodle-noodle, madder-ladder, locket-pocket
15	Hh	o-cean pris-on neigh-bor hand-ker-chief hatch-ing oc-to-pus	rob, cob, mob, dot, hot	lake, pumpkin, neck, hair, office	better-letter, blizzard-lizard, lumber, number, pickle-nickel, muppet-puppet, riding-hiding, doodle-noodle, madder-ladder, locket-pocket

(continued)

ELFS Lessons: Scope and Sequence (Stage 1A) (*continued*)

Lesson	Focus Letter Starfall Presentation and Alphabet Production	Guess My Word (Left to Right, Top to Bottom)	Sound Boxes (Sound Segmentation with Elkonin Boxes)	Letter Match ("Cover the letter that _____ begins with.")	Rhyming
16	Ww	jun-gle gal-lop win-dow um-brel-la ketch-up kit-ten	jug, bun, hug, bus, bug	water, junk, game, kitchen, umbrella	witty-kitty, belly-jelly, hotter-water, hello-jello, wiggle-giggle, vanilla-gorilla, corsage-garage, harden-garden, fennel-kennel
17	Uu	jel-ly geck-o wag-on wa-ter kleen-ex wed-ding	hut, but, cup, fun, gum	wig, jar, goose, kitten, under	witty-kitty, belly-jelly, hotter-water, hello-jello, wiggle-giggle, vanilla-gorilla, corsage-garage, harden-garden, fennel-kennel
18	Jj	jel-lo ga-rage whis-per gi-ant gig-gle wash-ing	cup, run, bum, gun, hug	winter, juggle, gate, king, up	witty-kitty, belly-jelly, hotter-water, hello-jello, wiggle-giggle, vanilla-gorilla, corsage-garage, harden-garden, fennel-kennel
19	Gg	jel-ly-fish gui-tar wal-rus go-ril-la ken-nel wo-man	bun, run, gum, jug, pun	wash, jeep, gone, key, uncle	witty-kitty, belly-jelly, hotter-water, hello-jello, wiggle-giggle, vanilla-gorilla, corsage-garage, harden-garden, fennel-kennel
20	Kk	work-er gar-den wreck-er gas-o-line kay-ak kit-ty	bus, cut, run, bug, jug	white, jump, gallop, kangaroo, unlock	witty-kitty, belly-jelly, hotter-water, hello-jello, wiggle-giggle, vanilla-gorilla, corsage-garage, harden-garden, fennel-kennel
21	Qq	vi-sor yel-low ze-bra el-e-phant quar-ter vol-ca-no	Ben, bet, fed, beg, yet	quick, very, every, yak, zero	wiser-visor, mellow-yellow, border-quarter, hero-zero, gecko-echo, toga-yoga, skipper-zipper, begin-violin, diet-quiet
22	Vv	vi-o-lin yo-gurt zip-per el-bow ques-tion en-ve-lope	den, get, bed, keg, bet	question, valuable, echo, yellow, zebra	wiser-visor, mellow-yellow, border-quarter, hero-zero, gecko-echo, toga-yoga, skipper-zipper, begin-violin, diet-quiet

Lesson	Focus Letter Starfall Presentation and Alphabet Production	Guess My Word (Left to Right, Top to Bottom)	Sound Boxes (Sound Segmentation with Elkonin Boxes)	Letter Match ("Cover the letter that _____ begins with.")	Rhyming
23	Xx	veg-e-table yo-yo ze-ro qui-et e-lec-tric x-ray	hen, jet, led, peg, yet	quart, vandal, edge, yes, zoo	wiser-visor, mellow-yellow, border-quarter, hero-zero, gecko-echo, toga-yoga, skipper-zipper, begin-violin, diet-quiet
24	Ee	va-ca-tion el-e-va-tor ech-o vam-pire Es-ki-mo yo-ga	yet, fox, bet, den, jet	quarter, vanilla, elbow, year, zip	wiser-visor, mellow-yellow, border-quarter, hero-zero, gecko-echo, toga-yoga, skipper-zipper, begin-violin, diet-quiet
25	Zz	e-lev-en e-qual quar-rel va-cant your-self ven-om	box, yet, vet, hen, zap	quiet, vet, elephant, yard, zone	wiser-visor, mellow-yellow, border-quarter, hero-zero, gecko-echo, toga-yoga, skipper-zipper, begin-violin, diet-quiet
26	Yy	vic-tor en-er-gy East-er yum-my e-ras-er zig-zag	vet, beg, led, get, yet	zoo, young, voice, energy, year	wiser-visor, mellow-yellow, border-quarter, hero-zero, gecko-echo, toga-yoga, skipper-zipper, begin-violin, diet-quiet

Emergent Lesson Plan (Stage 1B)

In Group	
FLUENCY	**FLUENCY EXTENSION**
Reread _____ ☐ Choral Read ☐ Stop-and-Go Reading ☐ Lead Reading ☐ Whisper Reading	☐ Read with a partner. ☐ Buddy read. ☐ Other
WORD STUDY	**WORD STUDY EXTENSION**
Alphabet Focus: _____ ☐ Match Game (uppercase and lowercase letters) ☐ Alphabet Production ☐ Cut-Up Sentence	☐ Cut and paste focus letters in magazines. ☐ Trace the letters. ☐ Cut and paste alphabet letters (uppercase and lowercase). ☐ Work on individual cut-up sentence. ☐ Other
VOCABULARY	**VOCABULARY EXTENSION**
High-Frequency Words (1–15) ☐ Fish Pond	☐ Make and write words (magnetic letters). ☐ Trace words (rainbow words). ☐ Practice with a partner.
COMPREHENSION	**COMPREHENSION EXTENSION**
New Read: _____ Text Level: _____ **Before Reading** ☐ Build background knowledge. ☐ Preview three high-frequency words from text. ☐ Conduct a picture walk. ☐ Set the purpose. **During Reading** ☐ Stopping points. • • • • **After Reading** ☐ Revisit purpose of reading. ☐ Revisit high-frequency words from text. ☐ Discuss independent writing assignment.	Draw and write about reading *(with support if needed).* ☐ My favorite part of the book is . . . ☐ My favorite character is . . . ☐ I liked the book because . . . ☐ I did not like the book because . . . ☐ Other

Emergent Assessment
Stage 1: Alphabet Production

Write the uppercase and lowercase letters:

1. Ll	14. Zz
2. Rr	15. Pp
3. Vv	16. Yy
4. Bb	17. Ss
5. Mm	18. Oo
6. Dd	19. Ww
7. Uu	20. Jj
8. Ee	21. Aa
9. Xx	22. Gg
10. Qq	23. Hh
11. Ff	24. Kk
12. Ii	25. Nn
13. Cc	26. Tt

Emergent Word Study
Scope and Sequence (Stage 1B)

Alphabet Recognition and Production

Week 1: BSMAC

Week 2: TDLRI

Week 3: JGHON

Week 4: PUQWY

Week 5: ZXEVKF

APPENDIX B:
Beginning Reader and Writer, Stages 2A/B

Beginning Stage: Common Standards

Fluency
- Reads emergent-reader texts with purpose and understanding.
- Follows words from left to right, top to bottom, and page by page.

Word Study
- Prints most uppercase and lowercase letters.
- Demonstrates command of standard conventions of standard English.
- Demonstrates basic knowledge of the most frequent sound for each consonant.
- Understands that words are separated by spaces in print.
- Demonstrates basic knowledge of one-to-one letter-sound correspondences by producing the primary sound or many of the most frequent sounds for each consonant.

Vocabulary
- Reads common high-frequency words by sight (e.g., *the, of, to, you, she, my, is, are, do, does*).
- Identifies new meanings for familiar words and applies them accurately.

Comprehension
- With prompting and support:
  - Retells familiar stories including key details.
  - Identifies characters, settings, and major events in reading.
  - Names the author and illustrator of a story and defines the role of each.
  - Asks and answers questions about unknown words in the text.
  - Explores word relationships.

- With prompting and support:
  - Describes the relationship between the text and illustrations.
  - Compares and contrasts the experiences and adventures of characters in books.
  - Actively engages in group reading activities with purpose and understanding.
  - Understands and uses question words.
  - Recognizes that spoken words are represented in written language by a specific sequence of letters.
  - Reads beginning texts with purpose and understanding.

Writing About Reading
- Uses a combination of drawing, dictating, and writing to compose opinion pieces in which they tell a reader the topic or the name of the book they are writing about and state an opinion or preference about the topic or book (e.g., My favorite book is…).

- Uses a combination of drawing, dictating, and writing to compose informative/explanatory texts in which they name what they are writing about and supply some information about the topic.
- Uses a combination of drawing, dictating, and writing to narrate a single event or several loosely linked events, tells about the events in the order in which they occurred, and provides a reaction to what happened.

Word Study: Scope and Sequence (Stages 2A/B)
Initial Consonant Sounds, Digraphs, and Blends

Initial Consonant Sounds

Lesson　1:　BMS picture cards
　　　　　2:　BMS picture cards
　　　　　3:　BMS picture cards
　　　　　4:　BMS picture cards
　　　　　5:　BMS picture cards

Lesson　6:　CDF picture cards
　　　　　7:　CDF picture cards
　　　　　8:　CDF picture cards
　　　　　9:　CDF picture cards
　　　　10:　CDF picture cards

Lesson 11:　Review BCD (mixing)
　　　　12:　Review SDF (mixing)
　　　　13:　Review MCD (mixing)
　　　　14:　Review BDF (mixing)
　　　　15:　Review MDF (mixing)

Lesson 16:　TRL picture cards
　　　　17:　TRL picture cards
　　　　18:　TRL picture cards
　　　　19:　TRL picture cards
　　　　20:　TRL picture cards

Lesson 21:　Review: CRL (mixing)
　　　　22:　Review: DTL (mixing)
　　　　23:　Review: FTR (mixing)
　　　　24:　Review: BRL (mixing)
　　　　25:　Review: MRL (mixing)

Lesson 26: NPW: picture cards
        27: NPW picture cards
        28: NPW picture cards
        29: NPW picture cards
        30: NPW picture cards
        31: Review TPW (mixing)
        32: Review RNW (mixing)
        33: Review LPN (mixing)

Lesson 34: GHJ picture cards
        35: GHJ picture cards
        36: GHJ picture cards
        37: GHJ picture cards
        38: GHJ picture cards
        39: Review NHJ (mixing)
        40: Review PGJ (mixing)
        41: Review WHJ (mixing)

Lesson 42: ZKV picture cards
        43: ZKV picture cards
        44: ZKV picture cards
        45: Review GKV (mixing)
        46: Review HZK (mixing)
        47: Review JKV (mixing)
        48: Mixed review all: B, D, G, J
        49: Mixed review all: M, N, W, R
        50: Mixed review all: F, H, P, T

Administer Initial Consonant Assessment

Initial Digraphs

Lesson 51:	sh	th	wh
52:	sh	th	wh
53:	sh	th	wh
54:	sh	th	wh
55:	sh	th	th
56:	sh	th	th
57:	ch	th	wh
58:	ch	th	wh

Initial Blends

Lesson 59:	bl	cl	fl
60:	bl	cl	fl
61:	gl	pl	sl
62:	gl	pl	sl
63:	pl	fl	cl
64:	br	tr	cr
65:	br	tr	cr
66:	dr	pr	gr
67:	dr	pr	gr
68:	dr	pr	gr

Administer Initial Digraphs and Blends Assessment

Beginning Lesson Plan

FLUENCY	FLUENCY EXTENSION
Text Level: _____ Reread: ☐ Choral Reading ☐ Teacher-Led Reading ☐ Student-Led Reading ☐ Whisper Reading	☐ Reread with a partner. ☐ Buddy read. ☐ Other

WORD STUDY	WORD STUDY EXTENSION
Alphabet Focus: _____ Beginning Consonants: Lesson # _____ Diagraphs/Blends: Lesson # _____ ☐ Card Sound Sort ☐ Writing Sort ☐ Group Cut-Up Sentence	☐ Cut, sort, and paste picture cards. ☐ Write the letter sound for each picture. ☐ Find pictures in magazines with the same beginning sounds. ☐ Work on individual cut-up sentences. ☐ Other: _____

VOCABULARY	VOCABULARY EXTENSION

High-Frequency Words (HFW)
    ☐ 15–35
    ☐ 35–50
    ☐ _____
☐ Word Wizard Game
	☐ Make and write high-frequency words (magnetic letters).
	☐ Beat the clock (with partner): how many words can you read in 30 seconds?
	☐ Work on four-square vocabulary.
	☐ Other: _____

COMPREHENSION	COMPREHENSION EXTENSION

New Read: _____   Text Level: _____
 	
Before Reading
☐ Build background knowledge (if needed).
☐ Preview high-frequency words from text.
☐ Set the purpose.
 	
During Reading
☐ Stopping points/text-dependent questions
•
•
•
•
 	
After Reading
☐ Revisit high-frequency words.
☐ Revisit purpose for reading (summarize).
☐ Discuss writing extension.
	Draw and write about reading *(with teacher support as needed).*
	    ☐ Story elements
	    ☐ Favorite part
	    ☐ Retell in writing
	    ☐ Main idea (i.e., what I learned)
	    ☐ Other:

Beginning Assessment (Stage 2A)
Initial Consonant Sounds

Write the letter sound you hear at the beginning of:

1. seal

2. cold

3. doll

4. fish

5. toast

6. rabbit

7. little

8. night

9. pony

10. wagon

11. goat

12. house

13. jacket

14. zoo

15. kite

16. vase

17. bunny

18. yellow

19. mouse

20. queen

Beginning Assessment (Stage 2B)
Initial Consonant Blends/Digraphs

Write the letter blends or digraphs that you hear at the beginning of these words:

1. chop

2. wheel

3. sheep

4. thumb

5. sled

6. flower

7. glasses

8. present

9. bread

10. cracker

11. drum

12. train

13. clown

14. frog

15. chain

16. shell

17. blanket

18. drip

19. shop

20. chalk

APPENDIX C:
Fledgling Reader and Writer, Stages 3A/B

Fledgling Stage: Common Standards

Fluency
• Reads with specific accuracy to support comprehension for grade 1.

Word Study
• Distinguishes short-vowel sounds in spoken single-syllable words. Orally produces single-syllable words by blending sounds (phonemes), including consonant blends.
• Isolates and pronounces initial, medial-vowel, and final sounds (phonemes) in spoken single-syllable words.
• Segments spoken single-syllable words into their complete sequence of individual sounds (phonemes).
• Knows and applies 1st grade level phonics and word analysis skills in decoding words.

Vocabulary
• Determines or clarifies meaning of unknown and multiple-meaning words and phrases based on grade 1 reading and content, choosing flexibly from an array of strategies.
• Uses sentence-level context as a clue to the meaning of a word or phrase.
• Uses frequently occurring affixes as a clue to the meaning of a word.
• Identifies frequently occurring root words (e.g., *look*) and their inflectional forms (e.g., *looks, looked, looking*).

Comprehension
• Asks and answers questions about key details in a text.
• Retells stories, including key details, and demonstrates understanding of their central message or lesson.
• Describes characters, settings, and major events in a story, using key details.
• Identifies words and phrases in stories or poems that suggest feelings or appeal to the senses.
• Explains major differences between books that tell stories and books that give information, drawing on a wide reading of a range of text types.
• Identifies who is telling the story at various points in a text.
• Uses illustrations and details in a story to describe its characters, setting, or events.
• Compares and contrasts the adventures and experiences of characters in stories.
• Asks and answers questions to help determine or clarify the meaning of words and phrases in a text.

- Determines or clarifies the meaning of unknown and multiple-meaning words and phrases.

Writing About Reading

- Demonstrates understanding of the organization and basic features of print (e.g., first word, capitalization, ending punctuation).
- Writes opinion pieces, in which they introduce the topic or name the book they are writing about, state an opinion, supply a reason for the opinion, and provide some sense of closure.
- Writes informative/explanatory texts in which they name a topic, supplies some facts about the topic, and provides some sense of closure.
- Writes narratives in which they recount two or more appropriately sequenced events, includes some details regarding what happened, uses temporal words to signal event order, and provides some sense of closure.
- Demonstrates command of the conventions of standard English grammar and usage when writing.

Word Study: Scope and Sequence (Stages 3A/B)
Word Families and Short Vowels

Word Families

Lesson 1: A family: at/an/ap
        2: A family: at/an/ap
        3: A family: an/ap/ack
        4: A family: an/ap/ack
        5: A family: at/an/ap/ack
        6: A family: at/an/ap/ack

Lesson 7: I family: it/ig/in
        8: I family: it/ig/in
        9: I family: ig/in/ick
    10: I family: ig/in/ick
    11: I family: it/ig/in/ick
    12: I family: it/ig/in/ick
    13: Review (mixing A and I): at/it/an/in
    14: Review (mixing A and I): ap/ig/ack/ick

Lesson 15: O family: ot/op/ob
    16: O family: ot/op/ob
    17: O family: op/ob/ock
    18: O family: op/ob/ock
    19: O family: ot/op/ob/ock
    20: O family: ot/op/ob/ock
    21: Review (mixing A, I, and O): ack/ick/ock
    22: Review (mixing A, I, and O): at/it/ot

Lesson 23: U family: ut/ug/unb
    24: U family: ut/ug/unb
    25: U family: ug/un/uck
    26: U family: ug/un/uck
    27: U family: ut/ug/un/uck
    28: U family: ut/ug/un/uck
    29: Review (mixing A, I, O, and U): ack/ick/ock/uck
    30: Review (mixing A, I, O, and U): at/it/ut/ot

Lesson 31: E family: et/ed/en
    32: E family: et/ed/en
    33: E family: ed/en/ell
    34: E family: ed/en/ell
    35: E family: et/ed/en/ell
    36: E family: et/ed/en/ell
    37: Review (mixing A, I, O, U, and E): an/in/un/en
    38: Review (mixing A, I, O, U, and E): at/it/ut/et
    39: Review (mixing A, I, O, U, and E): ig/og/ug/ed
    40: Review (mixing A, I, O, U, and E): ack/ock/ick/uck

Administer Word Families Assessment

Short Vowels

Lesson 1: Short vowels: A, O, and I
    2: Short vowels: A, O, and I
    3: Short vowels: O, I, and U
    4: Short vowels: O, I, and U
    5: Short vowels: A, U, and E
    6: Short vowels: A, U, and E
    7: Short vowels: Review (mixing all)
    8: Short vowels: Review (mixing all)
    9: Short vowels: Review (mixing all)
    10: Short vowels: Review (mixing all)

Administer Short-Vowel Assessment

Fledgling Lesson Plan

FLUENCY	FLUENCY EXTENSION
Text Level: _____ Reread: ☐ Choral Reading ☐ Teacher-Led Reading ☐ Student-Led Reading ☐ Whisper Reading	☐ Reread with a partner ☐ Buddy read ☐ Other
WORD STUDY	**WORD STUDY EXTENSION**
Word Families (3A) Lesson # _____ Short Vowels (3B) Lesson # _____ ☐ Card Sort ☐ Sound Boxes ☐ Writing Sort ☐ Word Scramble ☐ Sentence Dictation	☐ Cut and sort cards. ☐ Write the sort in a notebook. ☐ Write sentences with words from each pattern. Circle parts of speech. ☐ Word hunts: find words in books that have the same patterns. Add them to the list. ☐ Other: _____
VOCABULARY	**VOCABULARY EXTENSION**

High-Frequency Words (HFW)
     ☐ 40–60
     ☐ 60–80
     ☐ 80–100
     ☐ _____
 ☐ Word Wizard Game
	☐ Make and write high-frequency words (magnetic letters).
	 ☐ Beat the clock (with partner).
	 ☐ Play Memory.
	 ☐ Read and write sentences with high-frequency words.
	 ☐ Other: _____

COMPREHENSION	**COMPREHENSION EXTENSION**

New Read: _____   Text Level: _____
 	
 Before Reading
 ☐ Build background knowledge (if needed).
 ☐ Introduce story vocabulary.
 ☐ Set the purpose.
 	
 During Reading
 ☐ Stopping points/text-dependent questions
   •
   •
   •
   •
 	
 After Reading
 ☐ Review vocabulary (oral sentences using words in context).
 ☐ Revisit and discuss purpose for reading.
 ☐ Discuss writing extension.
	Write sentences with each vocabulary word as used in text.
	     ☐ Write to summarize
	     ☐ Main ideas/details
	     ☐ Problem/solution
	     ☐ Compare/contrast
	     ☐ Cause/effect
	     ☐ Writing checklists
	     ☐ Other:

Fledgling Assessment (Stage 3A)
Word Families

1. wet

2. sick

3. duck

4. back

5. sit

6. jig

7. tin

8. van

9. spot

10. drop

11. mob

12. sock

13. shut

14. plug

15. bell

16. map

17. bat

18. shed

19. when

20. sun

Fledgling Assessment (Stage 3B)
Short Vowels

1. glad
2. black
3. sick
4. swim
5. chop
6. drop
7. truck
8. must
9. then
10. flat

11. glad
12. trick
13. pick
14. shop
15. job
16. shut
17. cup
18. less
19. let
20. stack

APPENDIX D:
Transitional Reader and Writer, Stages 4A/B

Transitional Stage: Common Standards

Fluency

- Reads on-level text orally with accuracy, appropriate rate, and expression on successive readings.

Word Study

- Knows the spelling-sound correspondences for common consonant digraphs.
- Decodes regularly spelled one-syllable words.
- Knows final *e*, common vowel teams, and common vowel patterns for representing vowel sounds.

Comprehension

- Determines or clarifies the meaning of unknown and multiple-meaning words and phrases based on grade 1 reading and content, choosing flexibly from an array of strategies.
- Asks and answers questions about key details in a text.
- Retells stories, including key details, and demonstrates understanding of their central message or lesson.
- Describes characters, settings, and major events in a story, using key details.
- Explains major differences between books that tell stories and books that give information, drawing on a wide reading of a range of text types.
- Uses illustrations and details in a story to describe its characters, setting, or events.
- Compares and contrasts the adventures and experiences of characters in stories.
- Asks and answers questions about key details in a text.
- Identifies the main topic and retells key details of a text.
- Describes the connection between two individuals, events, ideas, or pieces of information in a text.
- Asks and answers questions to help determine or clarify the meaning of words and phrases in a text.
- Knows and uses various text features (e.g., headings, tables of contents, glossaries, electronic menus, icons) to locate key facts or information in a text.
- Distinguishes between information provided by pictures or other illustrations and information provided by the words in a text.
- Uses the illustrations and details in a text to describe its key ideas. Identifies the reasons an author gives to support points in a text.
- Identifies basic similarities in and differences between two texts on the same topic (e.g., in illustrations, descriptions, or procedures).

Word Study: Scope and Sequence (Stages 4A/B)

Lesson 1:	A patterns	_a_	a_e	ay	
2:	A patterns	_a_	a_e	ay	
3:	A patterns	_a_	a_e	ay	
4:	A patterns	_a_	a_e	ay	
5:	I patterns	_i_	i_e	ir	
6:	I patterns	_i_	i_e	ir	
7:	I patterns	_i_	i_e	ir	
8:	I patterns	_i_	i_e	ir	
Lesson 9:	Mixing A and I patterns	_a_	a_e	_i_	i_e
10:	Mixing A and I patterns	_i_	ay	ir	a_e
11:	Mixing A and I patterns	_i_	ay	ir	a_e
Lesson 12:	O patterns	_o_	o_e	oo	
13:	O patterns	_o_	o_e	oo	
14:	O patterns	_o_	o_e	oo	
15:	O patterns	_o_	o_e	oo	
Lesson 16:	Mixing I and O patterns	o_e	i_e	ir	or
17:	Mixing I and O patterns	oo	o_e	_i_	ir
18:	Mixing A and O patterns	o_e	oo	ay	a_e
Lesson 19:	U patterns	_u_	u_e	ue	
20:	U patterns	_u_	u_e	ue	
21:	U patterns	_u_	u_e	ue	
22:	U patterns	_u_	u_e	ue	
Lesson 23:	Mixing O and U patterns	_u_	u_e	o_e	_o_
24:	Mixing O and U patterns	_u_	ue	o_e	oo
25:	Mixing I and O patterns	_o_	_i_	o_e	i_e
26:	Mixing A, I, and O patterns	ay	ue	oo	
Lesson 27:	E patterns	_e_	ee	_e	
28:	E patterns	_e_	ee	_e	
29:	E patterns	_e_	ee	_e	
30:	E patterns	_e_	ee	_e	
Lesson 31:	Mixing A, I, and E patterns	ee	a_e	i_e	_e
32:	Mixing U and E patterns	_e_	ee	u_e	_u_
33:	Mixing I and E patterns	_e_	ir	ee	i_e
34:	Mixing A, O, and U patterns	ay	_o_	ue	
35:	Mixing A and O patterns	ay	a_e	o_e	oo

Transitional Lesson Plan

FLUENCY	FLUENCY EXTENSION

Text Level: _____
Reread:
  ☐ Choral Reading
  ☐ Teacher-Led Reading
  ☐ Student-Led Reading
  ☐ Whisper Reading
	☐ Reread with a partner.
	☐ Buddy read.
	☐ Other

WORD STUDY	WORD STUDY EXTENSION
Stage 4A: Lesson # _____ Stage 4B: Lesson # _____ Word Sort: ☐ Open ☐ Closed ☐ Writing Sort ☐ Sound Boxes ☐ Word Scramble *(choose one of the above)* ☐ Sentence Dictation	☐ Conduct a writing sort (with partner). ☐ Word cards: cut/sort/write sorts in notebook. ☐ Write sentences with words from each pattern. (Circle nouns, verbs, adjectives.) ☐ Add prefixes or suffixes. ☐ Make words plural or past tense. ☐ Use words in sentences. ☐ Write sentences to show meaning. ☐ Word hunt: find words with the same patterns. ☐ Other: _____

COMPREHENSION	COMPREHENSION EXTENSION

New Read: _____   Text Level: _____
 	
Before Reading
☐ Build background knowledge (if needed).
☐ Preview vocabulary from text.
☐ Set the purpose for reading (make it personal to the text).
 	
During Reading
☐ Stopping points/text-dependent questions
  •
  •
  •
  •
 	
After Reading
☐ Revisit vocabulary (use in a sentence that tells something about the text).
☐ Revisit purpose for reading.
☐ Discuss writing extension.
	Writing Checklist:
	  ☐ Main ideas/details
	  ☐ Character traits
	  ☐ Problem/solution
	  ☐ Compare/contrast
	  ☐ Cause/effect
	  ☐ Sequencing
	  ☐ Write a sentence with each vocabulary word that tells something about the story (text).
	  ☐ Write your own sentence with the vocabulary words.
	  ☐ Other: _____

Transitional Assessment (Stage 4A)

1. foot	11. glue
2. stay	12. slip
3. first	13. seed
4. that	14. step
5. club	15. dime
6. she	16. hook
7. lake	17. mute
8. true	18. bird
9. lock	19. way
10. left	20. spoke

Transitional Assessment (Stage 4B)

1. birth	11. town
2. sport	12. float
3. tube	13. stay
4. barn	14. clerk
5. keep	15. born
6. drive	16. spoke
7. load	17. clue
8. frown	18. herd
9. shake	19. churn
10. crop	20. brook

APPENDIX E:
Fluent Reader and Writer,
Stages 5A/B

Fluent Stage: Common Standards

Fluency

- Reads with sufficient accuracy and fluency to support comprehension.
- By the end of the year, reads and comprehends literature, including stories and poetry, in the grades 2–3 text complexity band proficiently, with scaffolding as needed at the high end of the range.

Word Study

- Distinguishes long and short vowels when reading regularly spelled one-syllable words.
- Knows spelling-sound correspondences for additional common vowel teams.
- Decodes regularly spelled two-syllable words with long vowels.
- Decodes words with common prefixes and suffixes.
- Identifies words with inconsistent but common spelling-sound correspondences.
- Recognizes and reads grade-appropriate irregularly spelled words.

Vocabulary

- Describes how words and phrases (e.g., regular beats, alliteration, rhymes, repeated lines) supply rhythm and meaning in a story, poem, or song.
- Determines the meaning of words and phrases in a text relevant to a *topic or text*.
- Determines or clarifies the meaning of unknown and multiple-meaning words and phrases choosing flexibly from an array of strategies.
- Demonstrates understanding of word relationships and nuances in word meanings.

Comprehension

- Asks and answers such questions as *who, what, where, when, why*, and *how* to demonstrate understanding of key details in a text.
- Recounts stories, including fables and folktales from diverse cultures, and determines their central message, lesson, or moral.
- Describes how characters in a story respond to major events and challenges.
- Describes the overall structure of a story, including describing how the beginning introduces the story and the ending concludes the action.
- Identifies the main purpose of a text, including what the author wants to answer, explain, or describe.
- Compares and contrasts the most important points presented by two texts on the same topic.
- Acknowledges differences in the points of view of characters, including by speaking in a different voice for each character when reading dialogue aloud.

- Uses information gained from the illustrations and words in a print or digital text to demonstrate understanding of its characters, setting, or plot.
- Compares and contrasts two or more versions of the same story (e.g., Cinderella stories) by different authors or from different cultures.
- Asks and answers such questions as *who, what, where, when, why,* and *how* to demonstrate understanding of key details in a text.
- Identifies the main topic of a multiple-paragraph text as well as the focus of specific paragraphs within the text.

Writing About Reading
- Writes opinion pieces in response to texts which they introduce the topic or book they are writing about, state an opinion, supply reasons that support the opinion, use linking words (e.g., *because, and, also*) to connect opinion and reasons, and provide a concluding statement or section.
- Writes informative/explanatory texts in which they introduce a topic, use facts and definitions to develop points, and provide a concluding statement or section.
- Writes narratives in response to texts in which they recount a well-elaborated event or short sequence of events; include details to describe actions, thoughts, and feelings; use temporal words to signal event order; and provide a sense of closure.

Word Study: Scope and Sequence (Stages 5A/B)
Vowel Patterns and Common Word Features

Lesson 1: A vowel patterns: rain/ball/saw
2: A vowel patterns: rain/ball/saw
3: A vowel patterns: rain/ball/saw
4: I vowel patterns: right/by/find
5: I vowel patterns: right/by find
6: I vowel patterns: right/by/find
7: Review A and I vowel patterns (mixing): rain/saw/by/find
8: Review A and I vowel patterns (mixing): saw/ball/right/find
9: Review A and I vowel patterns (mixing): rain/ball/right/find

Lesson 10: O vowel patterns: told/moon/boil
11: O vowel patterns: told/moon/boil
12: O vowel patterns: told/moon/boil
13: O vowel patterns: low/loud/boy
14: O vowel patterns: low/loud/boy
15: O vowel patterns: low/loud/boy
16: O vowel patterns: Review (mixing)
17: O vowel patterns: Review (mixing)
18: Review A, I, and O vowel patterns: told/low/right/find
19: Review A, I, and O vowel patterns: ball/saw/low/loud
20: Review A, I, and O vowel patterns: rain/told/low/right

Lesson 21: E vowel patterns: he/meat/head
22: E vowel patterns: he/meat/head
23: E vowel patterns: meat/head/new
24: E vowel patterns: meat/head/new
25: E vowel patterns: Review (mixing): he/meat/head/new

Lesson 26: Review A, I, O, and E vowel patterns (mixing): rain/right/told/low
27: Review A, I, O, and E vowel patterns (mixing): boil/head/loud/saw
28: Review A, I, O, and E vowel patterns (mixing): he/told/rain/meat
29: Review A, I, O, and E vowel patterns (mixing): loud/low/right/by
30: Review A, I, O, and E vowel patterns (mixing): new/moon/low/ball

Administer Vowel Patterns Assessment

Common Word Features

Week 1:   Contractions
          is   not   had

Week 2:   Contractions
          would   are   have

Week 3:   Prefixes
          pre   re   un

Week 4:   Plurals
          s   *es*   *y* to *i* (add *es*)

Week 5:   Homophones
          ate-eight   hair-hare
          hall-haul   hear-here
          by-buy-bye   blew-blue
          their-there-they're   sun-son
          plane-plain   sail-sale

Week 6:   Homophones
          road-rode   tale-tail
          write-right   made-maid
          knot-not   one-won
          knew-new   no-know
          mail-male   deer-dear

Week 6:   Compound Words
          night   any   every

Administer Common Word Feature Assessment

Fluent Lesson Plan

FLUENCY	FLUENCY EXTENSION

Text Level: _____
Reread:
  ☐ Choral Reading
  ☐ Teacher-Led Reading
  ☐ Student-Led Reading
  ☐ Whisper Reading
	☐ Reread with a partner.
	☐ Reread independently.
	☐ Other

WORD STUDY	**WORD STUDY EXTENSION**
Stage 5A: Lesson # _____ Stage 5B: Lesson # _____ Word Sort: ☐ Open ☐ Closed ☐ Writing Sort ☐ Sound Boxes ☐ Word Scramble ☐ Meaning Discussions ☐ Dictated or Student-Created Sentence (5B)	☐ Conduct a writing sort (with partner). ☐ Use word cards: cut/sort/write sorts in notebook. ☐ Write sentences with words from each pattern. (Circle nouns, verbs, adjectives.) ☐ Add prefixes or suffixes. ☐ Make words plural or past tense. ☐ Use words in sentences. ☐ Write sentences to show meaning. ☐ Word hunt: find words with the same patterns.
COMPREHENSION	**COMPREHENSION EXTENSION**

New Read: _____   Text Level: _____
 	
Before Reading
☐ Build background knowledge (if needed).
☐ Preview vocabulary.
☐ Set the purpose for reading.
 	
During Reading
☐ Stopping points/text-dependent questions
  •
  •
  •
  •
 	
After Reading
☐ Revisit vocabulary.
☐ Revisit purpose for reading.
☐ Comprehension conversation.
☐ Discuss writing extension.
	Writing Checklist:
	  ☐ Main ideas/details
	  ☐ Character traits
	  ☐ Problem/solution
	  ☐ Compare/contrast
	  ☐ Cause/effect
	  ☐ Sequencing
	  ☐ Other: _____

Fluent Assessment (Stage 5A)

1. paint

2. mall

3. drawn

4. cry

5. be

6. straw

7. bright

8. blind

9. thirst

10. flight

11. grind

12. told

13. tooth

14. noise

15. grow

16. blew

17. sound

18. joy

19. heat

20. thread

Fluent Assessment (Stage 5B)
Common Word Features

The teacher will use each word in a sentence to show meaning.
The students will write only the word.

1. everyone: Everyone went to the party.

2. preschool: My little sister goes to preschool.

3. unable: He was sick and unable to take the test.

4. nighttime: My room is dark at nighttime.

5. they've: They've already gone home.

6. haven't: I haven't seen your shoes.

7. classes: I am taking some classes with my friend.

8. ponies: My sister has two ponies.

9. overnight: I stayed overnight with my friend.

10. plane: I saw a plane in the sky.

11. eight: She is eight years old.

12. maid: The maid cleans my room.

13. anytime: I like to go to the movies anytime.

14. buy: We will buy groceries at the store.

15. she'd: She'd like to go outside and play.

16. male: The male horse jumped the fence.

17. plain: We ate plain yogurt for breakfast.

18. unfair: It was unfair that John lost the race.

19. shouldn't: I shouldn't have to do my homework.

20. precook: My mom will precook the pizza.

APPENDIX F:
Independent Reader and Writer, Stages 6A/B/C

Independent Stage 6A: Common Standards

Fluency

• Reads with sufficient accuracy and fluency to support comprehension.
• By the end of the year, reads and comprehends literature, including stories, dramas, and poetry, at the high end of the grades 2–3 text complexity band independently and proficiently.

Word Study

• Knows and applies 3rd grade level phonics and word analysis skills in decoding words.
• Identifies and knows the meaning of the most common prefixes and derivational suffixes.
• Decodes words with common Latin suffixes.
• Decodes multisyllable words.
• Identifies and know the meaning of the most common prefixes and derivational suffixes.

Vocabulary

• Determines the meaning of words and phrases as they are used in a text, distinguishing literal from nonliteral language.

Comprehension

• Refers to parts or stories, dramas, and poems when writing or speaking about a text, using terms such as *chapter*, *scene*, and *stanza*; describes how each successive part builds on earlier sections.
• Asks and answers questions to demonstrate understanding of a text, referring explicitly to the text as the basis for the answers.
• Recounts stories, including fables, folktales, and myths from diverse cultures; determines the central message, lesson, or moral, and explains how it is conveyed through key details in the text.
• Describes characters in a story and explains how their actions contribute to the sequence of events.
• Distinguishes their own point of view from that of the narrator or those of the characters.
• Explains how specific aspects of a text's illustrations contribute to what is conveyed by the words in a story.
• Compares and contrasts the themes, setting, and plots of stories written by the same author about the same or similar characters.

Writing About Reading
- Writes opinion pieces on topics or texts, supporting a point of view with reasons.
- Writes informative/explanatory texts to examine a topic and convey ideas and information clearly.
- Writes narratives to develop real or imagined experiences or events using effective technique, descriptive details, and clear event sequences.
- Writes routinely over extended time frames (time for research, reflection, and revision) and shorter time frames (a single sitting or a day or two) for a range of discipline-specific tasks, purposes, and audiences.

Independent Stage 6B: Common Standards

Fluency
- By the end of the year, reads and comprehends literature, including stories, dramas, and poetry, in the grades 4–5 text complexity band proficiently, with scaffolding as needed at the high end of the range.
- By the end of year, reads and comprehends informational texts, including history/social studies, science, and technical texts, in the grades 4–5 text complexity band proficiently, with scaffolding as needed at the high end of the range.
- Writes narratives to develop real or imagined experiences or events using effective technique, descriptive details, and clear event sequences.

Word Study
- Knows and applies grade-level phonics and word analysis skills in decoding words.
- Uses combined knowledge of all letter-sound correspondences, syllabication patterns, and morphology (e.g., roots and affixes) to read accurately unfamiliar multisyllabic words in context and out of context.

Vocabulary
- Determines the meaning of words and phrases as they are used in a text, including those that allude to significant characters found in mythology.
- Determines the meaning of general academic and domain-specific words or phrases in a text relevant to a *grade 4 topic or subject area.*

Comprehension
- Compares and contrasts the treatment of similar themes and topics (e.g., opposition of good and evil) and patterns of events (e.g., the quest) in stories, myths, and traditional literature from different cultures.

- Compares and contrasts the point of view from which different stories are narrated, including the difference between first- and third-person narrations.
- Describes in depth a character, setting, or event in a story or drama, drawing on specific details in the text (e.g., a character's thoughts, words, or actions).
- Determines a theme of a story, drama, or poem from details in the text; summarizes the text.
- Refers to details and examples in a text when explaining what the text says explicitly and when drawing inferences from the text.
- Determines the main idea of a text and explains how it is supported by key details; summarizes the text.
- Explains events, procedures, ideas, or concepts in a historical, scientific, or technical text, including what happened and why, based on specific information in the text.
- Describes the overall structure (e.g., chronology, comparison, cause/effect, problem/solution) of events, ideas, concepts, or information in a text or part of a text.
- Compares and contrasts a firsthand and secondhand account of the same event or topic; describes the differences in focus and the information provided.
- Interprets information presented visually, orally, or quantitatively (e.g., in charts, graphs, diagrams, time lines, animations, or interactive elements on web pages), and explains how the information contributes to an understanding of the text in which it appears.
- Explains how an author uses reasons and evidence to support particular points in a text.
- Integrates information from two texts on the same topic in order to write or speak about the subject knowledgeably.

Writing About Reading
- Writes opinion pieces on topics or texts, supporting a point of view with reasons and information.
- Writes informative/explanatory texts to examine a topic and convey ideas and information clearly.
- Writes narratives to develop experiences or events using effective technique, descriptive details, and clear event sequences from text.

Independent Stage 6C: Common Standards

Fluency
- Reads 5th grade level text with sufficient accuracy and fluency to support comprehension.

- By the end of the year, reads and comprehends literature, including stories, dramas, and poetry, at the high end of the grades 4–5 text complexity band independently and proficiently.

Word Study

- Knows and applies grade-level phonics and word analysis skills in decoding words.
- Uses combined knowledge of all letter-sound correspondences, syllabication patterns, and morphology (e.g., roots and affixes) to read accurately unfamiliar multisyllabic words in context and out of context.

Vocabulary

- Determines the meaning of words and phrases as they are used in a text, including figurative language such as metaphors and similes.
- Determines the meaning of general academic and domain-specific words and phrases in a text relevant to a *grade 5 topic or subject area.*

Comprehension

- Quotes accurately from a text when explaining what the text says explicitly and when drawing inferences from the text.
- Determines a theme of a story, drama, or poem from details in the text, including how characters in a story or drama respond to challenges or how the speaker in a poem reflects upon a topic; summarizes the text.
- Compares and contrasts two or more characters, settings, or events in a story or drama, drawing on specific details in the text.
- Describes how a narrator's or speaker's point of view influences how events are described.
- Compares and contrasts stories in the same genre.
- Quotes accurately from a text when explaining what the text says explicitly and when drawing inferences from the text.
- Determines two or more main ideas of a text, and explains how they are supported by key details; summarizes the text.
- Explains the relationships or interactions between two or more individuals, events, ideas, or concepts in a historical, scientific, or technical text based on specific information in the text.
- Compares and contrasts the overall structure (e.g., chronology, comparison, cause/effect, problem/solution) of events, ideas, concepts, or information in two or more texts.
- Analyzes multiple accounts of the same event or topic, noting important similarities and differences in the points of view they represent.

- Draws on information from multiple print or digital sources, demonstrating the ability to locate an answer to a question quickly or to solve a problem efficiently.
- Explains how an author uses reasons and evidence to support particular points in a text, identifying which reasons and evidence support which point(s).

Writing About Reading

- Integrates information from several texts on the same topic in order to write about the subject knowledgeably.
- Writes opinion pieces on topics or texts, supporting a point of view with reasons and information.
- Writes informative/explanatory texts to examine a topic and convey ideas and information clearly.
- Writes narratives to develop real or imagined experiences or events using effective technique, descriptive details, and clear event sequences.

Word Study: Scope and Sequence (Stage 6A)

Cycle	Week	Feature
1	1	Suffixes: Plurals: *-es*, *-s*, *-y* to *i* + *es*
	2	Possessives: *s*, *'s*, *s'*
	3	Suffixes: *-ed* (doubling, *e*-drop, nothing)
	4	Suffixes: Sounds of *-ed*
	5	Contractions: *have*, *not*, *will*
	6	Prefixes: *dis-* (not), *mis-* (not), *un-* (not)
	7	Compound words: *down*, *over*, *under*, *up*
	8	Suffixes: *-ing* (doubling, *e*-drop, nothing)
2	1	Compound words: *any*, *every*, *grand*, *water*
	2	*R*-controlled vowel patterns (multisyllabic): *ur*, *ure*
	3	Ambiguous vowel patterns (multisyllabic): *oi*, *ou*, *ow*, *oy*
	4	Ambiguous vowel patterns (multisyllabic): *au*, *aw*
	5	Syllable patterns: V-C-C-V (first syllable stressed)
	6	Syllable patterns: V-C-C-V, V-C-V (open and closed syllables)
	7	Syllable patterns: V-C-V open, V-C-V closed
	8	Syllable patterns: V-C-C-V, V-C-V (second syllable stressed)
3	1	Prefixes: *in-* (not), *pre-* (before), *re-* (again)
	2	Ambiguous vowels: *ew*, *oo* (stressed syllable)
	3	All contractions (review)
	4	Homophones
	5	*R*-controlled vowel patterns (stressed syllable): *air*, *ar*, *are*
	6	*R*-controlled vowel patterns (stressed syllable): *ear*, *eer*, *er*, *ere*
	7	*R*-controlled vowel patterns (stressed syllable): *ir*, *ire*
	8	*R*-controlled vowel patterns (stressed syllable): *oar*, *or*, *ore*, *our*
4	1	Prefixes: *en-* (in), *in-* (not)
	2	Ambiguous vowel patterns: *au*, *aw*, *wa*
	3	Compound words: *back*, *foot*, *head*
	4	Suffixes: *-ful* (full of, having), *-ly* (like, in a like manner), *-y* (having)
	5	Suffixes: *-er*, *-est*
	6	Vowel alternations: *-ion* (long to schwa, with predictable spelling changes: (*admit/admission*, *predict/prediction*)
	7	Homophones
	8	Complex consonants: *C+ ch*, *ch*, *tch*

Word Study: Scope and Sequence (Stage 6B)

Cycle	Week	Feature
1	1	Complex consonants: C + *ge, dge, ge*
	2	Spelling patterns at the end of words: *ar, er, or*
	3	Syllable patterns: V-C-C-V (regular and doublet, first syllable stressed)
	4	Syllable patterns: V-C-C-V doublets (first or second syllable stressed)
	5	Homophones (single syllable)
	6	Complex consonants: *scr, shr, thr*
	7	Prefixes: *mid-* (middle), *non-* (not)
	8	Prefixes: *inter-* (between, among), *super-* (above)
2	1	Prefixes: *ant-/anti-* (opposite), *auto-* (self)
	2	Prefixes: *pro-* (for), *trans-* (across, beyond, through)
	3	Unstressed syllable vowel patterns: *al, il, ile*
	4	Suffixes: *-ity, -ty, -y*
	5	Syllable patterns: V-C-V closed (first syllable stressed)
	6	Syllable patterns: V-C-C-V doublet and regular (first and second syllable stressed)
	7	Syllable patterns: V-C-C-V, V-C-V, V-V
	8	Root words: *tele* (far off)
3	1	Root words: *dict* (to say), *scribe* (to write)
	2	Suffixes: *-est* (comparative), *-ful* (full of), *-less* (without)
	3	Suffixes: *-fy, -ify* (to make, to cause, to become)
	4	Spelling patterns at the end of words: *en, in, on*
	5	Prefixes: *multi-* (many, multiple), *semi-* (half, partial)
	6	Prefixes: *re-* (again), *in-* (not), *non-* (not), *un-* (not)
	7	Prefixes: *dis-* (not), *pre-* (before)
	8	Prefixes: *de-* (away, opposite), *fore-* (before)
4	1	Prefixes: *over-, under-*
	2	Homophones (two syllables)
	3	All contractions (review)
	4	Prefixes: *em-, en-* (into, put into)
	5	Suffixes: *-er, -est, -ful, -ly, -y*
	6	Prefixes: *bi-* (two), *mono-* (one)
	7	Prefixes: *quad-* (four), *tri-* (three)
	8	Vowel patterns in the unstressed syllable: *age, edge, idge*

Word Study: Scope and Sequence (Stage 6C)

Cycle	Week	Feature
1	1	Sensitizing to stress: first or second syllable (review)
	2	Two-syllable homographs
	3	Two-syllable homophones
	4	Suffixes: *-er, -est*
	5	Root words: *hyper* (too much, over, excessive), *hyp/hypo* (under, less)
	6	Number-related prefixes: *dec-/deca-, oct-/octa-/octo-, pent-*
	7	Syllable patterns: V-C-C-V, V-C-V, V-V
	8	Vowel patterns in the stressed syllable: *A*
2	1	Vowel patterns in the stressed syllable: *E*
	2	Vowel patterns in the stressed syllable: *I*
	3	Spelling patterns at the end of words: *al, il, ile*
	4	Spelling patterns at the end of words: *el, le*
	5	Spelling patterns at the end of words: *ar, er, or*
	6	Spelling patterns at the end of words: *en, in, on*
	7	Final *K* sound: *c, ck, k, que*
	8	Prefixes: *cat-* (down), *circum-* (around), *peri-* (around, near)
3	1	Two-syllable homophones
	2	Homophones with three or more syllables
	3	Latin suffixes: *-able, -ible*
	4	Latin suffixes: *-ant, -ent*
	5	Vowel patterns in the unstressed syllable: Unaccented vowel sound, schwa+*n*
	6	Vowel patterns in the unstressed syllable (unaccented vowel sound, schwa+*n*): *en* (adjective), *in* and *on* (nouns)
	7	Vowel patterns in the unstressed syllable: *al, el, le*
	8	Vowel patterns in the unstressed syllable: *cher, sher, ure*
4	1	Vowel patterns in the unstressed syllable: *cher, ure*
	2	Vowel patterns in the unstressed syllable: *et, it*
	3	Vowel patterns in the unstressed syllable: *ace, ice, is, ise, uce*
	4	Consonant alternations: Silent versus sounded: *sign/signal, soft/soften*
	5	Vowel alternations: Long to short: *cave/cavity, please/pleasure*
	6	Vowel alternations: Long to schwa: *compose/composition*
	7	Vowel alternations: Long to schwa with predictable spelling changes: *simplify/simplification, verify/verification*
	8	Vowel alternations: Short to schwa: *critic/criticize, excel/excellent*

Independent Lesson Plan

FLUENCY	FLUENCY EXTENSION
Poem: _____	☐ Reread poem. ☐ Utilize readers theater. ☐ Other: _____

WORD STUDY	WORD STUDY EXTENSION
Features: _____ Cycle: _____ Week: _____ Word Sort: ☐ Open ☐ Closed ☐ Writing Sort ☐ Sound Boxes ☐ Meaning Discussions ☐ Student-Created Sentences *(oral or written)*	☐ Do a spelling sort with partner. ☐ Play Word Study Detectives. ☐ Write sentences to show meaning. ☐ Conduct a word hunt. ☐ Research words (e.g., words with the same pattern, root, prefix, suffix). ☐ Other: _____

COMPREHENSION	COMPREHENSION EXTENSION

New Read: _____ Text Level: _____
Before Reading
☐ Build background knowledge (if needed).
☐ Preview vocabulary.
☐ Set the purpose for reading.
During Reading
☐ Stopping points/text-dependent questions
•
•
•
•
After Reading
☐ Revisit vocabulary.
☐ Revisit purpose for reading.
☐ Have a comprehension conversation.
☐ Discuss writing extension.
	☐ Write a sentence with each vocabulary word that tells something about the text.
	Writing Checklists:
	    ☐ Narrative: 6A, 6B, 6C
	    ☐ Informative/Explanatory: 6A, 6B, 6C
	    ☐ Opinion: 6A, 6B, 6C
	☐ Other: _____
	(Checklists available at www.beverlytyner.net)
	☐ Teacher-created writing checklist
	☐ Graphic organizer

Independent Assessment (Stage 6A)
Evolving Reader Word Study Cycle Assessments

Evolving: Year 1 Cycle 1	Evolving: Year 1 Cycle 2	Evolving: Year 1 Cycle 3	Evolving: Year 1 Cycle 4
1. trains	1. everywhere	1. reclaim	1. insecure
2. dishes	2. anybody	2. premature	2. enjoy
3. carries	3. grandmother	3. incomplete	3. incomplete
4. boys'	4. purchase	4. applaud	4. fault
5. walked	5. mature	5. daughter	5. drawn
6. baked	6. unsure	6. awning	6. swap
7. treated	7. comment	7. mistook	7. knight
8. shouldn't	8. hockey	8. florist	8. background
9. she'll	9. compose	9. jewel	9. headache
10. they've	10. enroll	10. you've	10. directly
11. mistake	11. drowsy	11. they'd	11. graceful
12. unpack	12. lawsuit	12. haven't	12. constantly
13. disable	13. destroy	13. suite	13. funniest
14. downsize	14. avoid	14. theme	14. cleanest
15. upturn	15. awkward	15. scent	15. loudest
16. shouting	16. blizzard	16. aware	16. conclude
17. sobbing	17. traffic	17. marble	17. conclusion
18. shaping	18. dentist	18. we've	18. act
19. unwrap	19. famous	19. career	19. action
20. misspell	20. tablet	20. fearful	20. aisle
21. tracked	21. migrate	21. certain	21. hoarse
22. ponies	22. sequel	22. thirsty	22. whose
23. puffing	23. cartoon	23. entire	23. sketch
24. babies	24. express	24. pouring	24. switch
25. kitten's	25. proceed	25. chorus	25. couch

Independent Assessment (Stage 6B)

Stage 6B Cycle 1	Stage 6B Cycle 2	Stage 6B Cycle 3	Stage 6B Cycle 4
1. ledge	1. automatic	1. dictionary	1. overcast
2. sponge	2. antibiotic	2. predict	2. underlying
3. wage	3. transport	3. prescription	3. ceiling
4. calendar	4. proceed	4. beautiful	4. allowed
5. visitor	5. transform	5. restless	5. kernel
6. officer	6. neutral	6. biggest	6. review
7. furnish	7. pencil	7. qualify	7. there's
8. errand	8. fertile	8. stuffy	8. would've
9. injure	9. purity	9. amplify	9. embellish
10. gossip	10. nutty	10. pardon	10. envision
11. canyon	11. beefy	11. treason	11. encase
12. emblem	12. spicy	12. sharpen	12. mouthful
13. passage	13. glider	13. kitten	13. boastful
14. pollute	14. migrate	14. semicircle	14. abruptly
15. they're	15. remain	15. multicultural	15. quicker
16. coarse	16. beyond	16. nonfiction	16. monorail
17. mane	17. prepare	17. unaccountable	17. binoculars
18. scramble	18. cactus	18. reproduce	18. biracial
19. threat	19. rotate	19. inactive	19. triplets
20. shrunk	20. wrapper	20. disability	20. triangular
21. nonsense	21. mammal	21. precaution	21. quadrant
22. midnight	22. telescope	22. prejudge	22. porridge
23. supernatural	23. telegram	23. dehydrate	23. sausage
24. international	24. microscope	24. forecast	24. voyage
25. through	25. television	25. decompose	25. carriage

Independent Assessment (Stage 6C)

Cycle 1	Cycle 2	Cycle 3	Cycle 4
1. ledge	1. automatic	1. dictionary	1. overcast
2. sponge	2. antibiotic	2. predict	2. underlying
3. wage	3. transport	3. prescription	3. ceiling
4. calendar	4. proceed	4. beautiful	4. allowed
5. visitor	5. transform	5. restless	5. kernel
6. officer	6. neutral	6. biggest	6. review
7. furnish	7. pencil	7. qualify	7. there's
8. errand	8. fertile	8. stuffy	8. would've
9. injure	9. purity	9. amplify	9. embellish
10. gossip	10. nutty	10. pardon	10. envision
11. canyon	11. beefy	11. treason	11. encase
12. emblem	12. spicy	12. sharpen	12. mouthful
13. passage	13. glider	13. kitten	13. boastful
14. pollute	14. migrate	14. semicircle	14. abruptly
15. they're	15. remain	15. multicultural	15. quicker
16. coarse	16. beyond	16. nonfiction	16. monorail
17. mane	17. prepare	17. unaccountable	17. binoculars
18. scramble	18. cactus	18. reproduce	18. biracial
19. threat	19. rotate	19. inactive	19. triplets
20. shrunk	20. wrapper	20. disability	20. triangular
21. nonsense	21. mammal	21. precaution	21. quadrant
22. midnight	22. telescope	22. prejudge	22. porridge
23. supernatural	23. telegram	23. dehydrate	23. sausage
24. international	24. microscope	24. forecast	24. voyage
25. through	25. television	25. decompose	25. carriage

References

Armbruster, B. B., Lehr, F., & Osborn, J. (2001). *Put reading first: The research building blocks for teaching children to read: Kindergarten through grade 3*. Rockville, MD: Partnership for Reading.

Bear, D. R., Invernizzi, M., & Johnston, F. (2007). *Words their way: Word study for phonics, vocabulary and spelling instruction* (3rd ed.). Upper Saddle River, NJ: Prentice Hall.

Blachowicz, C. L. Z., & Fisher, P. (2000). Vocabulary instruction. In M. L. Kamil, P. B. Mosenthal, P. D. Pearson, & R. Barr (Eds.), *Handbook of reading research* (Vol. 3, pp. 503–523). Mahwah, NJ: Erlbaum.

Chard, D. J., Vaughn, S., & Tyler, B.J. (2002). A synthesis of research on effective interventions for building reading fluency with elementary students with learning disabilities. *Journal of Learning Disabilities, 35*(5), 386–406.

Clay, M. M. (2000). *Running records for classroom teachers*. Auckland, New Zealand: Heinemann.

Duke, N. K., & Pearson, P. D. (2002). Effective practices for developing reading comprehension. In A. E. Farstrup & S. J. Samuels (Eds.), *What research has to say about reading comprehension*, 3rd ed. (pp. 205–242). Newark, DE: International Reading Association.

Duke, N. K., & Roberts, K. M. (2010). The genre-specific nature of reading comprehension. In D. Wyse, R. Andrews, & J. Hoffman (Eds.), *The Routledge international handbook of English, language and literacy teaching* (pp. 74–86). London: Routledge.

Ebbers, S. M., & Denton, C. A. (2008). A root awakening: Vocabulary instruction for older students with reading difficulties. *Learning Disability Research & Practice, 23*(2), 90–102.

Farstrup, A. E., & Samuels, S. J. (2002). *What research has to say about reading instruction* (3rd ed.). Newark, DE: International Reading Association.

Ganske, K. (2000). *Word journeys: Assessment-guided phonics, spelling, and vocabulary study*. New York: Guilford.

Glende, L. (2013). Vocabulary and word study to increase comprehension in content for struggling readers. *Education Masters*, Paper 247.

Grabe, W., & Stoller, F. (2013). *Teaching and researching reading* (2nd ed.). London: Taylor & Francis.

Graham, S., & Hebert, M. (2010). *Writing to read: Evidence of how writing can improve reading*. Washington, DC: Alliance for Excellent Education.

Hennings, D. G. (2000). Contextually relevant word study: Adolescent vocabulary development across the curriculum. *Journal of Adolescent & Adult Literacy 44*(3), 268–279.

Hernandez, D. J. (2011). *Double jeopardy: How third-grade reading skills and poverty influence high school graduation*. Albany, NY: Annie E. Casey Foundation.

Invernizzi, M., & Hayes, L. (2004). Developmental-spelling research: A systematic imperative. *Reading Research Quarterly, 39*(2), 216–228.

Kamil, M. L. (2004). Comprehension and summary and implications of national research findings. In R. McCardle & K. Chhabra (Eds.), *The voice of evidence in reading research*. Baltimore, MD: Paul H. Brooks.

Kuhn, M. R., & Stahl, S. A. (2003). Fluency: A review of developmental and remedial processes. *Journal of Educational Psychology, 95*(1), 3–21.

Kuhn, M., Rasinski, T., & Zimmerman, B. (2014). Integrated fluency instruction: Three approaches for working with struggling readers. *International Electronic Journal of Elementary Education, 7*(1), 71–82.

Morris, D., Tyner, B., & Perney, J. (2000). Early Steps: Replicating the effects of a first-grade reading intervention program. *Journal of Educational Psychology, 92*(4), 681–693.

Nagy, W. E., & Scott, J. A. (2000). Vocabulary processes. In M. L. Kamil, P. B. Mosenthal, P. D. Pearson, & R. Barr (Eds.), *Handbook of reading research, Volume III* (pp. 269–284). Mahwah, NJ: Erlbaum.

Narvaez, D., van den Broek, P., & Ruiz, A. B. (1999). The influence of reading purpose on inference generation and comprehension in reading. *Journal of Educational Psychology, 91*(3), 488–496.

National Institute of Child Health and Human Development (NICHD). (2000). *Report of the National Reading Panel. Teaching children to read: An evidence-based assessment of the scientific research literature on reading and its implications for reading instruction* (NIH Publication No. 00-4769). Washington, DC: U.S. Government Printing Office.

Rasinski, T. V. (2010). Speed does matter in reading. *The Reading Teacher, 54*(2), 146–151.

Santa, C. M., & Høien, T. (1999). An assessment of Early Steps: A program for early intervention of reading problems. *Reading Research Quarterly, 34*(1), 54–79.

Shanahan, T. (2015). Relationships between reading and writing development. In C. A. MacArthur, S. Graham, and J. Fitzpatrick (Eds.), *Handbook on writing research* (2nd ed., pp. 171–210). New York: Guilford.

Stiggins, R. (2005). From formative assessment to assessment for learning: A path to success in standards-based schools. *Phi Delta Kappan*, 87(4), 324–328.

Sulzby, E. (2000, March). *Oral and written language relationships in early literacy development*. Conference on Literacy: Cross-Disciplinary Linkages Between Research and Practices to be sponsored by the American Speech/Language and Hearing Association (ASHA) and NICHD.

Tyner, B. (2004). *Small-group reading instruction: A differentiated teaching model for beginning and struggling readers*. Newark, DE: International Reading Association.

Tyner, B. (2009). *Small-group reading instruction: A differentiated teaching model for beginning and struggling readers* (2nd ed.). Newark, DE: International Reading Association.

Tyner, B., & Green, S. E. (2009). *Small-group reading instruction: A differentiated teaching model for intermediate readers, grades 3–8*. Newark, DE: International Reading Association.

Vygotsky, L. S. (1978). *Mind in society: The development of higher psychological processes*. Cambridge, MA: Harvard University Press.

Zhang, S., & Duke, N. K. (2008). Strategies for internet reading with different reading purposes: A descriptive study of twelve good internet readers. *Journal of Literacy Research*, 40(1), 128–162.

Index

The letter *f* following a page number denotes a figure.

About the Author

Beverly Tyner has been an educator for more than 30 years, serving as a classroom teacher, a school administrator, a college professor, and an international literacy consultant. Tyner is best known for taking literacy research and transforming it into easy-to-implement classroom strategies. She has published five prior books that focus on small-group differentiated reading instruction and produced several sets of video training materials. Her great passion is her work with teachers and students in long-term professional development that promotes literacy growth for all students. This book houses her continued focus on differentiated reading instruction and developmental writing. Appropriate for teachers of prekindergarten through 5th grade, it is intended to encompass a wide range of readers and writers, including special education and English language learners. Tyner lives in Signal Mountain, Tennessee, with her husband Paul and their dog Skyler. As the mother of four grown children, she enjoys travel and sharing her knowledge of literacy with other teachers.

Related ASCD Resources: Literacy

At the time of publication, the following resources were available (ASCD stock numbers in parentheses). For up-to-date information about ASCD resources, go to www.ascd.org. You can search the complete archives of *Educational Leadership* at www.ascd.org/el.

Print Products

A Close Look at Close Reading: Teaching Students to Analyze Complex Texts, Grades K–5 by Diane Lapp, Barbara Moss, Maria Grant, and Kelly Johnson (#114008)

Literacy Strategies for Grades 4–12: Reinforcing the Threads of Reading by Karen Tankersley (#104428)

Literacy Strong All Year Long: Powerful Lessons for Grades 3–5 by Valerie Ellery, Lori Oczkus, and Timothy Rasinski (#118013)

The Multiple Intelligences of Reading and Writing: Making the Words Come Alive by Thomas Armstrong (#102280)

The New Art and Science of Teaching Writing by Kathy T. Glass and Robert J. Marzano (#318145)

Reading, Writing, and Rigor: Helping Students Achieve Greater Depth of Knowledge in Literacy by Nancy Boyles (#118026)

Research-Based Methods of Reading Instruction for English Language Learners, Grades K–4 by Sylvia Linan-Thompson and Sharon Vaughn (#108002)

Research-Based Methods of Reading Instruction, Grades K–3 by Sharon Vaughn and Sylvia Linan-Thompson (#104134)

Vocab Rehab: How do I teach vocabulary effectively with limited time? (ASCD Arias) by Marilee Sprenger (#SF114047)

ASCD myTeachSource®

Download resources from a professional learning platform with hundreds of research-based best practices and tools for your classroom at http://myteachsource.ascd.org/.

For more information, send an e-mail to member@ascd.org; call 1-800-933-2723 or 703-578-9600; send a fax to 703-575-5400; or write to Information Services, ASCD, 1703 N. Beauregard St., Alexandria, VA 22311-1714 USA.

THE WHOLE CHILD

The ASCD Whole Child approach is an effort to transition from a focus on narrowly defined academic achievement to one that promotes the long-term development and success of all children. Through this approach, ASCD supports educators, families, community members, and policymakers as they move from a vision about educating the whole child to sustainable, collaborative actions.

Climbing the Literacy Ladder relates to the **supported** and **engaged** tenets. *For more about the ASCD Whole Child approach, visit* **www.ascd.org/wholechild.**

WHOLE CHILD
TENETS

1 HEALTHY
Each student enters school healthy and learns about and practices a healthy lifestyle.

2 SAFE
Each student learns in an environment that is physically and emotionally safe for students and adults.

3 ENGAGED
Each student is actively engaged in learning and is connected to the school and broader community.

4 SUPPORTED
Each student has access to personalized learning and is supported by qualified, caring adults.

5 CHALLENGED
Each student is challenged academically and prepared for success in college or further study and for employment and participation in a global environment.